ND
FOREIGN CAPITAL IN DEVELOPING ECONOMIES

Foreign Capital in Developing Economies

Perspectives from the Theory of Economic Growth

Stefano Manzocchi
Associate Professor of Economics
University of Perugia
Italy

Foreword by Enzo R. Grilli

First published in Great Britain 1999 by
MACMILLAN PRESS LTD
Houndmills, Basingstoke, Hampshire RG21 6XS and London
Companies and representatives throughout the world

A catalogue record for this book is available from the British Library.

ISBN 0–333–74703–8

 First published in the United States of America 1999 by
ST. MARTIN'S PRESS, INC.,
Scholarly and Reference Division,
175 Fifth Avenue, New York, N.Y. 10010

ISBN 0–312–22238–6

Library of Congress Cataloging-in-Publication Data
Manzocchi, Stefano.
Foreign capital in developing economies : perspectives from the
theory of economic growth / Stefano Manzocchi.
p.   cm.
Includes bibliographical references and index.
ISBN 0–312–22238–6 (cloth)
1. Investments, Foreign—Developing countries—Econometric models.
2. Capital movements—Developing countries—Econometric models.
I. Title.
HG5993.M355   1999
332.67'3'091724—dc21   99–18736
                                                                          CIP

© Stefano Manzocchi 1999
Foreword © Enzo R. Grilli 1999

All rights reserved. No reproduction, copy or transmission of this publication may be made without written permission.

No paragraph of this publication may be reproduced, copied or transmitted save with written permission or in accordance with the provisions of the Copyright, Designs and Patents Act 1988, or under the terms of any licence permitting limited copying issued by the Copyright Licensing Agency, 90 Tottenham Court Road, London W1P 0LP.

Any person who does any unauthorised act in relation to this publication may be liable to criminal prosecution and civil claims for damages.

The author has asserted his right to be identified as the author of this work in accordance with the Copyright, Designs and Patents Act 1988.

This book is printed on paper suitable for recycling and made from fully managed and sustained forest sources.

10 9   8   7   6   5   4   3   2   1
08 07 06 05 04 03 02 01 00 99

Printed and bound in Great Britain by
Antony Rowe Ltd, Chippenham, Wiltshire

For
Cristiana and Simone
and the coming one

Contents

List of Tables	x
Foreword by Enzo R.Grilli	xii
Acknowledgements	xvii
List of Abbreviations	xviii

PART I HISTORICAL PERSPECTIVE

1 Introduction: A Growth-theory Approach to Capital Flows in Developing Countries — 3

   1.1 The object of the volume — 3
   1.2 Economic development and capital flows — 5

2 Recovery, Insolvency and Stagnation: The Flow of Foreign Capital to Developing Economies in Historical Perspective — 10

   2.1 The cycles of capital inflows in developing economies — 11
   2.2 Historical patterns of capital movements in developing economies — 15
   2.3 Liberalisation and instability: the debate of the 1990s — 21

PART II THEORETICAL MODELS

3 Growth Theory and the Determinants of Capital Flows — 33

   3.1 Human capital and the neoclassical growth model: implications for capital movements — 34
   3.2 International capital flows in models of endogenous growth — 40
   3.3 Capital flows in a neoclassical model with restricted capital mobility — 44

	3.4	Demography and international capital movements	48
	3.5	Which implications for empirical analysis?	51

4 Growth Theory and the Effects of Capital Flows — 54

	4.1	Growth and convergence in neoclassical models with capital mobility	55
	4.2	An overlapping-generations model with restricted capital mobility	60
	4.3	A coordination-failure model of sectoral change and foreign borrowing	62
		Appendix: linearisation and the speed of convergence	74

PART III EMPIRICAL STUDIES

5 Measuring Capital Mobility in Developing Economies — 79

	5.1	The concept of capital mobility	79
	5.2	The measures of capital mobility	84
	5.3	Capital mobility in developing countries, 1960–88	94
		Appendix 1: integration and cointegration	101
		Appendix 2: definitions and sources of the empirical variables	103

6 Determinants of Net Capital Flows in Developing Countries — 105

	6.1	Discriminating among growth-theoretical approaches to capital movements	106
	6.2	An empirical assessment of the neoclassical model, with partial capital mobility, 1960–88	119
		Appendix: country sample – definitions and sources of the empirical variables	128

7 Capital Movements, Economic Growth and Investment in Developing Countries — 133

	7.1	Foreign capital and economic growth in a cross-section of developing countries, 1960–82	135
	7.2	Capital inflows, investment and consumption	147
		Appendix: definitions and sources of the empirical variables	152

8	**External Finance and Foreign Debt: A Study of the Transition Economies of Central and Eastern Europe**	**153**
	8.1 The role of external finance in the transition process: an overview	154
	8.2 Foreign financial flows in Central and Eastern Europe: a panel-data analysis	161
	8.3 The sustainability of foreign debt in Central and Eastern Europe	171
	Appendix: definitions and sources of the empirical variables	177

Notes and References	179
Bibliography	186
Index	197

List of Tables

2.1	Gross value of foreign capital stock in developing countries, 1870–1995	16
2.2	Net total capital flows including grants: all developing countries, 1970–94	22
2.3	Net long-term capital flows to developing countries, by region of destination, 1970–94	23
3.1	Predicted sign of the partial correlation with the marginal product of physical capital	44
4.1	Agent i's payoff matrix, financial autarky	68
4.2	Agent i's payoff matrix, financial integration	71
5.1	Main findings of the empirical literature on capital mobility in 33 developing countries	91
5.2	Results of the unit-root tests on ca_t^*	98
6.1	Regression of *per capita* net inflows, 1960–88, on the determinants of the MPK in 1960	112
6.2	Sensitivity analysis regressions of *per capita* net inflows, 1960–88	114
6.3	Sensitivity analysis regressions of *per capita* net inflows, 1960–88: regional dummies	115
6.4	Regression of *per capita* net inflows, 1960–72, on the determinants of the MPK in 1960	116
6.5	Sensitivity analysis regressions of *per capita* net inflows, 1960–72	117
6.6	Sensitivity analysis regressions of *per capita* net inflows in 1960–72: regional dummies	118
6.7	An econometric evaluation of the augmented neoclassical model over 1960–88	122
6.8	An econometric evaluation of the augmented neoclassical model over 1960–72	124
6.9	An econometric evaluation of the augmented neoclassical model over 1960–82	126
A6.1	Net capital inflows and relative *per capita* income in 33 developing economies, 1960–88	130
7.1	Descriptive statistics on economic growth in 33 developing countries over 1960–88	138

List of Tables

7.2	Cross-country correlation coefficients between average growth rates and average *per capita* net capital inflows, 1960–88	139
7.3	An econometric evaluation of the growth effect of net capital inflows over 1960–82	143
7.4	An econometric evaluation of the growth effect of net capital inflows over 1960–72	145
7.5	An econometric evaluation of the growth effect of net capital inflows over 1973–82	146
7.6	Cross-country correlation coefficients between average consumption and investment rates and net capital inflows, 1960–88	148
7.7	Change in average investment and consumption rates, 1960–5 to 1972–7	149
7.8	Change in average investment and consumption rates, 1972–7 to 1983–8	150
7.9	Cross-country correlation coefficients between the change in average consumption and investment rates and cumulated *per capita* inflows	151
8.1	Estimated correlation matrix of the explanatory variables	165
8.2	Determinants of net foreign borrowing in CEECs	167
8.3	Determinants of net foreign borrowing in CEECs	170
8.4	A comparison of gross vs. net debt–exports ratios in CEECs, 1990 and 1995	173
8.5	Alternative measures of the burden of the debt adjusted for economic growth	174
8.6	The composition of gross external debt in Central and Eastern Europe, end-1990 and 1995	176

Foreword

Economists have always considered capital central to the process of economic growth and to its explanation. Since the early seventeenth century, at the very beginning of systematic economic thinking, Antonio Serra identified investments in manufacturing as the source of those riches that could accrue to 'kingdoms where there were no [gold and silver] mines'. It took Adam Smith, almost at the end of the next century, to develop fully the role of capital in economic growth. The division of labour, in his thinking, had to be preceded by capital accumulation, and was dependent on it. 'Labour', he wrote, 'can be more and more subdivided in proportion only as stock is previously more and more accumulated', and again 'wherever capital predominates, industry prevails'. Capital, in turn, was 'increased by parsimony and diminished by prodigality'. Hence the role of saving in the creation of the wealth of nations.

Since then, capital accumulation has kept a central role in the thinking about growth. And until recently what economists intended for capital was essentially physical capital, even though the effects of improvements in the other type of capital – human – were already clear in Adam Smith, witness his appreciation of the role of education and of the economic advantages that derived from it to society as a whole.

It is not casual, therefore, that it was W. Arthur Lewis, an economist steeped in the classical tradition, who systematically differentiated in his *Theory of Economic Growth* between physical and human capital, and underlined the importance of the second in the challenge of growth faced by developing countries in the 1950s. Since then, the complementarity of physical and human capital in growth never left the domain of development economics, even though the latter was long forgotten in growth theory, and was not resurrected to some status within it until the late 1980s.

Another theme has been quite central in development economics since the early 1950s – that of foreign capital – in terms of both its absence and its presence in the investment equation of developing countries. The straight forward assumption of development economists was that, if (physical) capital was essential to growth, its origin did not matter. Foreign and domestic capital could both be useful in fostering economic progress in poor countries. If in the latter, because of low incomes, inefficient ways of mobilising it, and various other impediments to its full emergence, private saving was limited, an alternative to exploit was foreign savings, in the form of private capital inflows.

Their absence after the Second World War was much deprecated, and with hindsight also excessively feared, almost as much, one is tempted to say, as its presence seems to be feared today. At that time reliance on public flows of capital was thus considered inevitable, and indeed advocated as beneficial. Foreign aid was thought to be a way, and a key one for the poorest countries, to integrate and augment domestic resources for investments and therefore as a powerful tool to increase capital accumulation and fasten their economic growth. Public international institutions were created *ex novo* to re-intermediate emerging countries' access to private capital markets, unwilling or unable to channel to the vast majority of them the needed flows of capital even when risk-adjusted marginal returns to it appeared to be higher than in more mature economies.

The fundamental assumption, however, was that foreign capital could be added to domestic capital and augment in such a way the growth possibilities of the recipient countries. Its effects on growth were taken to be positive, and its additionality insurable, perhaps through careful public planning. The choice of what to finance with foreign (and domestic) capital could be guided by proper cost–benefit analysis, where social as well as private benefits were to be taken into account, especially in the case of public investments.

But, development economics, from Theodore Schultz onwards, also emphasised that investments in human capital – above all in education and health – were essential to economic growth in poor countries (and to the satisfaction of basic human needs in most of them). The importance and productivity of investments in education was consistently emphasised by an important component of the economic profession, and even more by practitioners of development. Successful efforts were made to show across countries and time that both private and social returns to education were positive and significant in size. Development of human capital was integrated into the practice of economic development much before theory came to the same conclusion.

The rediscovery of the role and relevance of capital in modern growth models came only recently, with the so-called 'endogenous growth theories'. Rather ironically, as recently observed by Robert Barro, an eminent exponent of the new neoclassical school of growth, the emphasis put by this generation of theorists on human capital to explain from within technological progress ended up mostly reinforcing the standard neoclassical model that they had found so wanting in completeness and explanatory power, and, I may add, also in improving the reputation of traditional development economists, who had continued to emphasise its role based on good economics and sound judgement.

Furthermore, neither the 'new and improved' neoclassical models that contained human capital among the arguments of the production function, nor the new growth models that emphasised the function of externalities, paid much attention to the role of foreign capital in economic growth, except perhaps from the angle of international capital mobility. In this area, only the possible explanations for capital's apparent difficulty in moving across countries, and in conforming to the patterns that growth theory would identify as warranted, attracted some attention. This was the strand of literature that mostly reflected on the Feldstein–Horioka puzzle.

A reconsideration of the causes of international capital flows, of the patterns that these flows take – in particular those going towards the capital-scarce countries, and of the various effects exerted by capital inflows in the countries that receive them in light of the improvements in knowledge brought about by developments in growth theory and related empirical evidence, was therefore due, perhaps even overdue.

Stefano Manzocchi's book has provided it. His is a contribution that not only fills an evident gap in the literature, but also pushes our knowledge of capital movements, their determinants and their growth consequence significantly forward.

This book deals with causes of foreign capital flows to developing countries and their effects on the growth of these countries, naturally taking a long-run view of them. This I found welcome, as a respite from the recent focus on the instability-creating effects of international capital flows. But, even more importantly, I found it refreshing for the balanced mix of theory, empirical evidence and plain good economic sense that the author brought to bear in dealing with such a difficult, and in many respect arid, subject.

Selecting a hypothesis of partial capital mobility for developing countries (a hypothesis that his own empirical analysis of capital flows from 1960 to 1988 confirms in the main), the author examines the implications that can be derived from several models of the 'most recent generation' on economic growth and convergence. Capital mobility, he finds, matters in a range of different situations, having to do with model structures and definitions of the constraints to capital mobility that are assumed to apply.

Foreign capital can enhance growth in the transitional period (up to the mythical 'steady state') and the speed of convergence, conditional as it may be, needs not become infinite, a conclusion that both empirical evidence and good sense would reject. The degree of restriction to the international flow of capital also matters in terms of income levels that can be achieved in the long term, at least if borrowing constraints are set at a fraction of current income instead of applying differentially to various types of capital assets.

The determinants of capital flows to developing countries, identified by the author's careful and lucid statistical work, are broadly coherent with the theoretical predictions of modern growth models. Capital productivity (however difficult to proxy) is shown to matter in shaping them, and so does the stock of human capital present in recipient countries. Trade openness has a positive effect on capital inflows, but, somewhat surprisingly, does not stand out in terms of statistical significance. Openness too is difficult to measure meaningfully. This may be part of the significance problem. Political instability, instead, hinders quite clearly capital inflows to developing countries. More generally, models that incorporate human capital perform better in predicting capital flows to developing countries than their standard and non-standard alternatives, such those incorporating scale effects.

The effects of foreign capital on actual growth in developing countries, as the present author still finds, are elusive to pinpoint, even with the help of modern growth structures. The results arrived at in this book on the subject parallel those of Peter Boone regarding aid, much debated, but recently confirmed by work done in the World Bank by David Dollar and his associates. Capital is indeed fungible, almost irrespective of its origin: public or private.

In the author's empirical work, the contribution of foreign capital to growth, positive in the developing countries he studied until 1972, evaporates in the 1970s. These were indeed years of heavy foreign borrowing, especially by middle-income developing countries, but capital so acquired went in the main to support public (and private) consumption, and not efficient investments. Available evidence, mostly regarding Latin America and North Africa, indicates that during the 1970s total factor productivity declined drastically in both areas. The same tendency is indicated by the behaviour over time of (*ex post*) incremental capital–output ratios. In the absence of appropriate policy regimes the positive effects of foreign capital (private and public alike) tend to wane, and only debt burdens remain. These are often the result of policy and governance failures, which no amount of subsequent debt forgiveness can cure or prevent from occurring again.

In summary, this is a cogent, interesting and significant book, which should be read and meditated by specialists and practitioners alike. Students of development will also find it extremely useful, as it marries good theory, ample evidence and very good judgement. One learns from it at almost every turn of page. I predict that it will be extensively read and used. I for one am very glad that Stefano Manzocchi wrote it.

ENZO R. GRILLI

Acknowledgements

My greatest intellectual debt in the preparation of this volume is with Hans Genberg and Pier Carlo Padoan who have been my teachers and have encouraged me to pursue the study of international financial relations, and in particular of the role of foreign capital in developing economies. Hans Genberg was especially helpful in supporting, and commenting on my work for the PhD dissertation at the Graduate Institute of International Studies of Geneva, a perfect environment for this kind of research. I am also greatly indebted with my fellow authors Alberto Bagnai and Philippe Martin, who share with me the interest in the theory and empirics of economic growth and capital mobility, and from whom I have greatly learned.

Many colleagues at the University of Ancona, where I was teaching at the time the book was prepared, have supported my work: among them, a special mention is due for Giuliano Conti. I would also like to thank the Research Department of the International Monetary Fund, and especially Donald Mathieson, for their hospitality in the Fall of 1996. During my stay there I also benefited from conversations with Enzo Grilli, whose work I already knew: I am grateful to him for that no less than for his Foreword to this book.

Many friends and colleagues, beyond those mentioned above, have at different stages provided useful comments on parts of the book: Leslie Armijo, David Bendor, Giuseppe Bertola, Paul Brenton, Luca Debenedictis, Thomas Helbling, Jack Lucchetti, Gian Maria Milesi-Ferretti, Gianmarco Ottaviano, Laura Sabani and Alessandro Vaglio. Helpful comments were also received from participants in seminars held at the Universities of Ancona, Bologna, Geneva, Pennsylvania, Roma 'La Sapienza', Roma Tor Vergata; and at the Italian National Research Council, the European Economic Association Meetings of Istanbul 1996 and Toulouse 1997, and the Research Department of the International Monetary Fund. I would also like to thank the Luigi Einaudi Foundation of Turin and the Italian National Research Council for their financial support. Last but not least, thanks to Sunder Katwala and Macmillan for helping this project become a book and to Keith Povey for excellent editorial assistance.

STEFANO MANZOCCHI

List of Abbreviations

ADB	Asian Development Bank
ADF	augmented Dickey–Fuller-test
CEECs	Central and Eastern European countries
CEFTA	Central European Free Trade Area
CIP	covered interest parity
CLI	Cumulative Liberalisation Index
CR	capital requirement
DC	developing country
DGP	data-generating process
EBRD	European Bank for Reconstruction and Development
ECM	error correction model
EPU	European Payments Union
EU	European Union
FDI	foreign direct investment
GDP	gross domestic product
GNP	gross national product
IBRD	International Bank for Reconstruction and Development
IMF	International Monetary Fund
MPK	marginal product of capital
NCI	net capital inflow
ODA	official development assistance
OECD	Organisation for Economic Cooperation and Development
OLG	overlapping-generations
PPP	purchasing power parity
R&D	research and development
RIP	real interest parity
TFP	total factor productivity
UIP	uncovered interest parity

Part I
Historical Perspective

1 Introduction: A Growth-theory Approach to Capital Flows in Developing Countries

1.1 THE OBJECT OF THE VOLUME

Foreign capital to developing economies is definitely one of the topics of the day. From the debt crisis of the early 1980s, which severely affected Latin America, Africa and some countries in Eastern Europe and Asia, throughout the years of debt negotiations and rescheduling until the new surge in capital flows to middle-income economies in the first half of the 1990s, academic and financial communities have extensively debated this issue, and some aspects have been publicised in the leading financial press. At the dusk of the millennium, as a new wave of currency and debt crises hits developing economies, shaking the apparently ordered pattern of renewed flows in East Asia (1997–8), Russia (1998) and maybe other regions, the debate has turned increasingly emotional.

Although it is routinely recognised that foreign capital is in principle beneficial for a developing economy whose capital requirement exceeds its saving capacity, several dangers connected with external capital have been stressed. Long-term gains are contrasted with short-term perils caused by macroeconomic mismanagement, financial liberalisation and debt overhang, and some esoteric trade-off between them is suggested.

Economic theory and applied economics offer some tools that can help approaching this issue in terms of social behaviours and material constraints. In general, there is no mechanical outcome of capital market integration that is valid for any economy either in the short or the long run. Sizeable amounts of foreign capital certainly require a careful macroeconomic management of the economy, especially if they materialise in a short period of time; the debt overhang can be an impediment for investment and growth in the medium run; and financial liberalisation can destabilise the credit sector of a developing economy. But there can be short-term *benefits* from capital inflows – for instance, foreign financial resources can help overcome the liquidity shortage in economies affected by sudden falls in the real value of monetary balances, as the recent experience of Eastern Europe shows. Moreover, capital inflows can provide foreign exchange reserves to finance the net import requirements of a transforming economy – especially those of machinery and other capital goods – and stimulate competition for external funds among domestic borrowers and credit institutions, enhancing the efficiency of the domestic financial system.

Conversely, there is no guarantee that capital inflows are conducive to higher income growth in the long-run. These sorts of benefits are by no means automatic; quite trivially, the long-run consequences of foreign capital depends on what use is made of the funds. From this point of view, it is more correct to say that *potential* long-term gains from capital inflows in developing economies should be compared with their likely short-term effects.

The short- and medium-run aspects of financial reform and macroeconomic management in developing economies in times of massive capital movements have been extensively analysed since the early 1980s, under the pressure of recurrent banking and currency distress. The international institutions mainly responsible for macroeconomic surveillance and development assistance (the International Monetary Fund, the World Bank, the American and Asian Development Banks, the European Bank for Reconstruction and Development) have been among the main promoters of a research effort aimed at understanding the consequences of capital inflows for financial stability, macroeconomic equilibrium and economic policy in developing countries.

The other side of the coin – namely the long-run aspects of capital movements in developing economies – has also motivated several of studies, but in a less consistent and systematic fashion. Typically the determinants or the effects of capital flows in the long run are either analysed separately, or treated as a secondary feature of a wider picture. There exist, of course, remarkable exceptions to this rule: few of them, though, consider both the *determinants* and the *consequences* of capital movements in the post-war experience of developing countries, and try to envisage a single theoretical framework to analyse them. This book is conceived as an attempt in this direction.

The object of the volume is to evaluate the pattern and the function of foreign capital in developing countries in a long-run perspective. The main conceptual instruments we employ for this purpose are the theory of economic growth, which has undergone a deep rethinking in

Introduction: A Growth-theory Approach to Capital Flows 5

the last fifteen years, and the techniques associated with recent advances in growth econometrics. The *structure* of the book is comprehensive: Chapter 2 on historical patterns, a theoretical Part II on the determinants and consequences of foreign capital in developing economies, requiring a basic knowledge of differential equations, and an empirical Part III with applications to the post-war period, which is more easily approached by readers with some notions of statistics and econometrics. However, the degree of formal complexity is not too high (apart perhaps in Chapters 4 and 5) and the analytical instruments and techniques employed are briefly illustrated, and all key references are noted. The volume is therefore targeted at both economists (either students or professionals) and at anybody who has an interest in the fields of economics, history and international relations. We now provide a brief summary of the main findings.

1.2 ECONOMIC DEVELOPMENT AND CAPITAL FLOWS

Growth theory establishes a relationship between the sources, and rate, of economic growth and international capital movements: in a sense, one can argue that a duality exists concerning, on the one hand, the growth rate, and on the other hand net (*per capita*) flows. Hence the determinants of international capital movements in representative-agent models can be viewed as the counterpart of variables affecting the distance between the steady-state position of an economy and its initial conditions. However, this is *not* equivalent to stating that a developing economy will necessarily attract net inflows: while this is true in one-capital-good setups, models featuring two types of capital assets and partial capital mobility suggest that a developing country will be a net capital importer only if its relative *human*-capital endowment is large enough. Moreover, the amount of net inflows is also related to the saving capacity of individual economies: overlapping-generations models show how demography affects net saving, although no general conclusion can be drawn regarding developing countries (Chapter 3).

The message of the neoclassical model is quite straightforward so far as the *consequences* of net capital flows in the long run are concerned: as foreign inflows are used to finance investment in physical capital, opening to capital mobility should make a developing country an attractive location for international investors (provided it is endowed with, and can accumulate, enough human capital, according to the augmented neoclassical model with partial mobility). Consequently, there are two main predictions of neoclassical theory. (1) the integration in international capital markets will foster the speed of convergence to the steady state and therefore raise the growth rate for those developing economies that become net capital importers. (2) the larger the (*per capita*) inflow of net foreign capital, the higher the *ex ante* marginal product of capital, and hence the more the underlying fundamentals of a developing country are conducive to economic growth. Similar predictions stem from an overlapping-generations model with restricted capital mobility. Less optimistic perspectives, however, may be derived from models in which residents in the developing country have the option of either investing net capital inflows or using them to raise current consumption standards at the expense of future ones. If the second option is selected, there is actually no contribution of capital movements to economic growth and investment in developing economies, and the conditions are set for the emergence of liquidity and solvency problems (Chapter 4). Of course, difficulties in the repayment of foreign debt and the possibility of capital account crises cannot be ruled out even if option (1) (investing foreign capital in productive activities) is picked: in this case it might happen that although external resources are used to finance investment projects in DCs, the *ex post* profitability of these ventures is low and the association between capital flows and economic growth is weak or even absent.

The empirical core of the volume is a study of different aspects of capital movements in 33 developing market economies over the period 1960–88 (Chapters 5–7). While the country sample is mainly selected according to the existence and reliability of macroeconomic and structural data, periodisation reflects the hypothesis of cyclical patterns in capital flows to developing countries and in particular of a cycle starting from the revival of the world financial system after the Second World War and ending with the debt crisis of 1982–3 (see Chapter 2). The empirical analysis is therefore extended to an entire sequence of recovery, crisis and stagnation in capital flows to developing economies.

In Chapter 5 we address the preliminary question of *capital mobility* in developing countries. First, although different approaches to the issue of measuring capital mobility exist, the 'quantity' approach – namely that of looking at saving–investment correlations – can be legitimately preferred to the 'price' approach – namely that of studying interest-parity conditions across countries. This is even more true in developing economies, as it is difficult to evaluate return equalisation across a wide range of comparable assets. Second, it does not seem that according to a net-flow criterion capital mobility has been low in developing economies over 1960–88: in fact, most developing countries look open to net capital movements if we track the dynamics of the current account. This does not mean that *perfect* mobility held, but possibly that a *partial* capital mobility assumption is supported by the empirical evidence.

Insofar as the determinants of (*per capita*) net inflows in developing economies are concerned, we find that growth models incorporating human capital as a production factor perform better than other models in accounting for the pattern of net capital flows over 1960–82 (Chapter 6). Notice, however, that cross-section econometric analysis can explain the relative distribution of net inflows across countries, not their absolute amount. After 1982, the outbreak of the debt crisis probably altered the pattern of international capital movements. Second, within that class of models, the augmented neoclassical setup (with partial capital mobility) is supported by the data while an alternative setup featuring scale effects is not. In particular, initial income appears to be negatively related to, and human capital proxies positively related to, *per capita* net inflows. Third, a measure of political instability turns out to be negatively (and significantly) associated with *per capita* inflows. Furthermore the coefficients of the regional dummies indicate that residents in Asian economies have comparatively received *less* capital from abroad than in the rest of the sample. Finally, demographic conditions that could have determined the peculiar behaviour of Asian economies *vis-à-vis* the rest of the countries, do not account for this feature and worsen the global fit of the empirical model. A few policy implications can be derived from this analysis – for instance that the promotion of human capital jointly favours growth and capital inflows, or that political instability significantly alters the pattern of relative investment opportunities.

Chapter 7 moves forward to the issue of the *consequences* of capital flows in developing countries. In general, even if the distribution of *per capita* inflows across countries is consistent with the neoclassical model, foreign capital is fungible, hence its effects in the recipient economies need not *ex post* conform to the predictions of this model. Chapter 7 yields mixed responses on the contribution of foreign capital to economic progress in developing economies: while there is evidence of a positive impact of external finance on growth over 1960–72, this effect vanishes over the following decade. Moreover, the Asian countries that received comparatively lower inflows fared better in terms of economic growth during the 1970s, and hence were better equipped to face the financial turmoil of the 1980s. This in turn appears to be associated with a weak correlation between foreign capital inflows and rising investment rates, and to a shift of resources towards government consumption, although we do not claim to have unveiled any causal links. Even if causation is uncertain, it is clear that a fading relation between net capital inflows, on the one side, and investment and growth, on the other, is a clue to forthcoming sustainability problems and possibly of financial instability: in this sense, the fading contribution of foreign capital to growth in developing countries after 1972 could have set the conditions for the debt crisis of 1982–3.

Therefore, at a time of strong recovery in capital flows to developing countries after 1972 (see Chapter 2), the conditions for sustainability were violated either because the funds were employed in non-productive activities (private or public consumption), or because over-borrowing led to an inflation of high-risk, low-return investment projects. Of course, we do not deny that negative external developments (the Volcker management of US monetary policy and the recession of the early 1980s) contributed to the outbreak of the debt crisis, but the roots of foreign debt unsustainability were partly set already.

Other transforming economies have (re)joined international financial relations in the 1990s: the so-called transition economies of Central and Eastern Europe and Asia. Chapter 8 deals with the determinants and sustainability of foreign financial inflows in a sub-set of these economies. In this case the time horizon is shorter, so we adopt a different theoretical approach based on the demand for funds and the incentive to lend in the medium run. The main findings are that the reorientation of external trade towards high-income and dynamic markets has been a driving element of creditworthiness during the transition, and that export growth favours the sustainability of foreign debt.

The experience of the whole 1960–88 foreign capital cycle in developing countries suggests that the distribution of *per capita* inflows was consistent with the augmented neoclassical model over 1960–82, but that the contribution of foreign capital to growth was evident only until 1972. This is a particularly disappointing evidence as after 1972 we observe a substantial surge in capital inflows towards developing countries. The enhanced availability of foreign resources was probably associated with excessive (government) consumption: alternatively, external borrowing led to an over-financing of high-risk, low-return investment projects. We have stressed the perverse effects this had on sustainability, and on the gestation of the 1982–3 crisis. Our empirical work notes that there is no mechanical trade-off between the short-term dangers and the long-run gains from capital market integration, but the growth benefits of foreign capital in transforming economies are conditional on an effective destination of the resources. Over-borrowing and excessive consumption are the main pitfalls in the short as well as in the long run. Nevertheless, foreign capital can be conducive to faster growth and possibly higher welfare: the responsibility of developing countries' governments therefore involves not only the *use* but also the *materialisation* of foreign capital inflows in the long run. Policies aimed at promoting the human-capital accumulation are among the major candidates in this perspective.

2 Recovery, Insolvency and Stagnation: The Flow of Foreign Capital to Developing Economies in Historical Perspective

The last two decades of the twentieth century have witnessed several episodes of balance of payments crisis in developing countries (DCs), starting from a Polish moratorium on foreign debt in 1981 up to financial distress and currency devaluations in Eastern Asia and Russia in 1997–8; in between, Latin American and African economies have also heavily suffered from external crises. Nonetheless, an unprecedented amount of capital inflows reached developing countries (including the transition countries in Europe and Asia) in the 1990s, exposing the recipient economies to old problems and new challenges. As stated in Chapter 1, this volume does not deal with various short- and medium-term concerns associated with capital movements in developing economies, focusing rather on the relationship with long-run growth; however, it would be difficult not to mention some of the themes related to the financial strains of the end of the century in a work on capital movements in DCs. In this chapter we confine ourselves to only a few topics that are functional to some of the arguments of Parts II and III: in particular, this chapter provides a stylised description of the cyclical pattern of capital inflows to developing countries (Section 2.1), an account of historical trends especially centred on the twentieth century (Section 2.2) and finally a brief review of some academic and policy-oriented debates triggered by the surge in capital flows of the 1990s (Section 2.3). Readers interested in a more complete treatment of these topics can find extensive reference to the recent contributions in these fields.

2.1 THE CYCLES OF CAPITAL INFLOWS IN DEVELOPING ECONOMIES

The international financial system has proved intrinsically prone to long-run swings in the degree of capital mobility (for an overview, see Obstfeld and Taylor, 1997), and this has significantly affected the relationship between developed (mainly creditor) economies and developing (mainly debtor) ones. Moreover, this cyclical behaviour has not only involved the amount of financial transfers but to some extent also the forms and instruments used to implement the transfers. This is not to deny that deep changes have occurred in the 1990s (for instance, the shift from public to private entities among the recipients of the funds, or the development of financial derivatives), but to recall that apparently new phenomena have to be put into historical perspective. We will come back to the issue of what kind of financial instruments are preferable from the standpoint of the recipient economy, and of financial stability altogether, in Section 2.3. In this section we sketch some basic mechanics of international capital transfers to DCs.

The existence of lending cycles in international finance is recognised by many authors (recent statements can be found in Eichengreen, 1990; International Monetary Fund, 1997, Annex VI); these cycles primarily concern the *amount* of capital transfer from high-income to developing economies. The issue of the nature and cause of this cyclical behaviour is more controversial. Here we do not take part in this controversy, as the main object of the volume is to study the relationship between foreign capital and growth within an individual 'capital-transfer cycle' and not to provide an ontological argument about these cycles, although some of our findings in the following chapters may shed light on their dynamics.

We would simply provide a very stylised description of a typical cycle, a description many scholars would broadly accept. Let us start from the recovery phase, when capital flows move again into DCs after a period of scarcity. This phase is commonly associated with a combination of 'push' and 'pull' factors, with the former being related to global or systemic factors and the latter to country- or region-specific determinants. Among global factors, Eichengreen (1990) stresses the role of financial innovation in stimulating the supply of foreign funds, while falling transaction costs due to information technologies are mentioned by the International Monetary Fund (1997, p. 243). The prevailing political attitude towards liberalisation and capital-account restrictions is another factor affecting both the 'push' side (the supply of funds from industrial countries) and the 'pull' side (the demand for foreign funds in DCs) (see Obstfeld and Taylor, 1997). Finally, the conditions of financial and economic activity in the Western (core) economies are frequently suggested as major determinants of a recovery in foreign lending to DCs. For instance, it has been argued that a large fraction of the 1990s' surge in capital flows is explained by a decline in international interest rates (linked to the interest rates prevailing in the USA and other industrial countries) after 1989, as the opportunity cost of investing in DCs had consequently declined (Dooley, Fernandez-Arias and Kletzer, 1996). The perspectives of the business cycle and the gap between actual and potential output in industrial economies is also likely to affect the demand for investment and credit there, and hence the availability of external funds for DCs (see Calvo, Leiderman and Reinhart, 1993; Fernandez-Arias, 1996; for a more critical assessment, see Fernandez-Arias and Montiel, 1996; and International Monetary Fund, 1997, p. 245).

Among 'pull', or country-specific, factors one can list all the features that make an individual economy more attractive to foreign capital than others. In principle, this has more to do with the *distribution* of external capital *across* DCs than with the global quantity of foreign resources transferred to developing economies. However, it is clear that a general improvement in fiscal sustainability, price stability, export dynamics and so on in the most important DCs can pull more capital towards them as a whole. The same can be true of other variables, such as the level or volatility of the terms of trade, or some indicators of banking-sector fragility. Even if it is difficult to disentangle the specific contributions of push and pull factors, what matters here is that a combination of them can start a recovery in capital inflows to DCs (Chuhan, Claessens and Mamingi, 1993; Taylor and Sarno, 1997).

The possibility that this recovery will turn into a boom is quite likely, according to a strand of theorising on capital markets. The foreign financial resources accruing to a DC are (partly) fungible – they can be used for alternative purposes (*see* Feyzioglu, Swaroop and Zhu, 1998, on the fungibility of foreign aid). While it is perfectly rational and economically sound to use foreign resources to finance excess consumption in the expectation of a rising income path, in order for external debt to be honoured a share of those resources must be devoted to investment in the recipient country. Moreover, investment must *ex post* contribute to the actual growth of GDP: provided real interest rates on foreign debt are positive, dynamic sustainability requires a positive impact of borrowing on GDP and export growth (see Section 8.3). This means that investment, either public or private, in physical or 'human'-capital assets, must yield sufficiently high (private or social) returns in the medium and long run.

However, it has been argued that the more foreign resources flow into DCs, the higher is the likelihood that foreign investors do not carefully assess the expected profitability of investment projects and the state of macroeconomic fundamentals in the recipient countries. This can be due to pure speculative behaviour, that leads investors anticipating a rise in asset prices to buy those assets in order to secure capital gains, therefore contributing to the creation of an asset-price bubble (Minsky, 1982, Chapter 6). Another explanation, particularly suited for periods of financial liberalisation in DCs, is that an increase in the number of economies in which to invest lowers the marginal incentive to acquire information on the individual borrowers. This can be rationalised in a theoretical context in which *risk-averse* global investors maximise expected profits according to a mean-variance model of optimal portfolio allocation: the reason is that a growing number of destination countries provides more opportunities for diversification hence reduces the risk associated with the global portfolio (Calvo and Mendoza, 1996, pp. 251–3). However, the same model predicts that the investor's reaction to the impact of adverse news or 'rumours' concerning an individual country is magnified by a large set of diversification opportunities.

Although an asset-price bubble can be sustained for quite a long time, it has to be corrected at some point with the ensuing capital losses: why do investors (whether international or domestic) therefore persist in this kind of dangerous conduct? The Calvo–Mendoza (1996) model provides an explanation. There can, however, be other interpretations: first, it is possible that nobody knows what the 'right' fundamentals are – namely, what worldwide or domestic variables one has to monitor and what their proper levels are. Second, everybody might believe that someone else will eventually pay the bill, that is he or she will get out of the market before the correction occurs: note that this option is by definition forbidden to the totality of investors. Third, 'moral-hazard' behaviour may prevail, because of the expectation of future bailouts operated by governments, central banks or international financial institutions. Note that moral-hazard behaviour can occur at both the national and the international level, and it may concern a number of interlinked markets (for instance, if a stock market bubble has a counterpart in commercial banks' assets, the consequences of a crash might shake the stability of the banking sector where a bailout is more likely to take place).

What are the key elements of a DCs' debt crisis? This partly depends on the *type* of assets at stake: in the case of bank lending, the 1982–3 crisis showed that insolvency, moratoria and a lengthy process of negotiation and rescheduling are part of the picture. Although it might seem that insolvent debtors carried much of the responsibility for the outbreak of the crisis, external factors mattered anyway as shown by the relation between the Volcker restriction in US monetary policy of the late 1970s and the rapidly rising costs of debt service in Latin America before 1982. In the case of portfolio flows, a jump in international interest rates can have an immediate impact on bond and equity markets: illiquidity as opposed to insolvency problems may arise and currency devaluations can soon follow. Real estate and land markets seem to be especially prone to periodic cycles of boom and deflation (Renaud, 1997), which sometimes are reinforced by sudden and unprecedented inflows of foreign funds and can eventually trigger external crises (see Edison, Luangaram and Miller, 1998).

Despite the fact that specific elements of the crises may differ, an underlying feature is likely to be similar: partly due to imperfect information and moral hazard, there is an *excess* of foreign funds flowing into a transforming economy that on average are not (or cannot be) employed in sufficiently high-yielding projects (whether they are partially consumed or invested in low-return activities is not really relevant). McKinnon and Pill (1997) argue that external over-borrowing is a recurrent phenomenon associated with liberalisation programmes in DCs.

After a correction has occurred, a prolonged drought of net foreign financial resources is part of the historical experience (see, for instance, Edwards, 1998b, on Latin America in the 1980s). The scope and length of this scarcity depends on the economic structures of the countries and regions involved (how much, for instance, they rely on the same export markets) and the extent of 'herd' behaviour on the part of international investors (to what extent agents that have been affected by euphoria abate their activities in DCs without making any distinction among individual economies). Usually, during the phase of stagnation growth and welfare deteriorate significantly in DCs for several reasons (see Astorga and Fitzgerald, 1997, on the deterioration of living standards in Latin America in the 1980s). First, as argued many times in this volume, net foreign capital can play a relevant growth-enhancing role in transforming economies. Second, long-lasting investment projects in the public or private sector may have to be abandoned as a result of external financial constraints, implying a net loss of resources. Third, expectations deteriorate as a result of the crisis itself and often of the severe policies adopted in response to it. Finally, the larger the number of countries involved, the more likely it is that economic policy measures undertaken without a coordination mechanism turn out to be inconsistent and counterproductive (for example, competitive devaluations or drastic fiscal contractions).

Because of the progressive exhaustion of the consequences of a crisis and of institutional management (Brady Plan, IMF intervention as an international lender), a new potential for foreign capital inflows in DCs eventually emerges – which, however, must be supported by favourable 'push and pull' conditions in order to materialise: at this point the stage is set for a new recovery phase. Section 2.2 claims that this sort of cyclical pattern can be detected in DCs' twentieth-century experience.

2.2 HISTORICAL PATTERNS OF CAPITAL MOVEMENTS IN DEVELOPING ECONOMIES

Although the history of foreign capital transfers to developing countries is part of the wider picture of international lending and borrowing, a few specific features are worth mentioning. First, DCs (including colonies) have usually been net borrowers from the rest of the world. Second, as discussed in Section 2.1 the record of external finance in DCs can be depicted as a sequence of sustained borrowing phases, debt crises leading to an interruption or even reversal of net flows and eventually new surges in capital inflows. Third, there are complex causal links between the conditions of financial activity in Western centres and the solvency and liquidity position of DCs: not only are 'external variables' among the main determinants of swings in capital movements to DCs, but debt crises in DCs may have a strong impact on Western financial markets, as shown by historical episodes (see the description of the 1890 Baring crisis in De Cecco, 1974) and more recent examples of financial distress in US institutions originating from 'bad loans' to Latin American borrowers (see United Nations, 1991).

The cyclical performance of capital flows to DCs is evident in the data (Table 2.1); what is more controversial is the interpretation of these cycles. A combination of favourable external conditions and improvements in the borrowing economies may trigger a lending boom: it is clear that domestic fundamentals and policies matter, as even during

Table 2.1 Gross value of foreign capital stock in developing countries, 1870–1995 (billion dollars at year-end)

	1870	1900	1914	1938	1950	1973	1985	1995*
Total in current prices	5.3	11.4	22.7	24.7	13.6	172	1118	2355
Total in 1980 prices	33.2	108.3	179.2	143.4	46.6	319.1	944	..
Total as a percentage of world GDP (1980 prices)	..	10.4	12.5	..	1.6	3.7	7.0	..
Total as a percentage of Asian and Latin American countries' GDP (in 1980 prices)	..	32.4	45	..	7.9	16.5	22.6	..

Notes:
·· Not available.
* Includes gross debt outstanding at end-1995, and net cumulated direct investment plus other equity flows.
Sources: OECD, *External Debt Statistics* (Paris, 1996); IMF, *World Economic Outlook* (Washington, DC, various issues, for the data on gross value of foreign capital); Maddison (1989), for the data on world GDP in 1980 prices.

a lending phase different countries or regions do not receive the same amount of resources, and can even be cut off from the flows (in Chapter 6 we study the cross-country determinants of *per capita* net inflows within a whole foreign capital cycle). The net inflow of foreign resources is compatible with a range of alternative performances in DCs both with respect to the *use* of foreign resources and the *impact* on growth and macroeconomic management. Not all indebted DCs in the past have run into insolvency and have eventually defaulted as external conditions have changed and a debt crisis has occurred. Foreign finance may or may not be associated with growth in different periods or regions (see Chapter 7), while domestic policies can contribute in many respects to the creation, or removal, of the circumstances leading to an external crisis (Sachs, Tornell and Velasco, 1996).

Capital flows to DCs during the nineteenth century were mainly associated with the functioning of London as the world financial centre. Latin American government issues covered the largest share of foreign government securities sold on the London Stock Exchange between 1822 and 1825, that is at the time of Latin American independence (Marichal, 1989, pp. 27–8).[1] Peru suspended payments on external debt in 1826, followed by Chile, Argentina, Mexico and others. A new surge in capital flows to Latin America occurred in the 1850s and 1860s, but ended at the dawn of the so-called 'First Great Depression' (1873–96) when a number of DCs defaulted again. The securities floated on the London market were mainly issued by the railway and public utility sectors, although part of them were used for rolling-over old debts or for speculative purposes (Marichal, 1989, pp. 243–55). The final stage of the international gold standard before the First World War witnessed a new upturn in capital inflows, in both absolute and relative terms, which led to the highest ever ratio of gross foreign capital to GDP in developing economies, colonial territories included (Table 2.1). During this period, total net capital outflows from Britain represented about 9 per cent of GDP, while comparable figures for France, Germany and the Netherlands were almost as high (International Monetary Fund, 1997, p. 113).

A geographical breakdown of the new foreign issues on the London Stock Exchange shows that African and Asian countries became important destinations of foreign capital after 1890, while the debt crisis in Argentina in 1890 had negative effects on Latin America (De Cecco, 1974, p. 36). The 1914 financial crisis in London and the outbreak of the First World War reshaped the pattern of world capital movements: net foreign lending to DCs shrank, and some major developing economies became net capital exporters during the war years (for instance, Argentina: see Taylor, 1997, p. 25). While inflows of foreign capital vanished during the First World War and capital flight mounted in DCs, the terms of trade of several commodity exporters improved, years leading to improvements in their net external positions (Veganzones and Winograd, 1997, p. 208). In the aftermath of the First World War, the world financial community was engaged in the resolution of the joint problems of German reparations and of inter-Allied loans; meanwhile New York gradually established its predominance over London as the leading international financial centre (De Cecco, 1985). Foreign lending stagnated until the Dawes Plan of September 1924 established a schedule for the compensation due by Germany to the Western allies, and generated the illusion that post-war problems were solved. In the second half of the 1920s there was a recovery in capital transfers to DCs, with loans to Asia and Africa mainly issued in London and New York mainly engaged in lending to Europe and Latin America (Kindleberger, 1973, p. 56).

Although the debt crisis of the 1930s is commonly associated with the 1929 crash of the New York Stock Exchange, financial conditions were already deteriorating in some debtor countries in the years before 1929 as a consequence of the decline in some commodity prices (sugar, rubber, coffee among others)[2] and of bad harvests in Argentina and Australia (see Kindleberger, 1973). The collapse of the New York Stock Exchange and the restrictive stance of monetary policy in several industrial and developing countries made access to financial markets difficult and expensive for many debtors and unleashed a wave of defaults and debt negotiations in the 1930s (Fernandez-Ansola and Laursen, 1995). Evaluated at 1980 dollar prices, the decline in the stock of gross foreign capital in DCs with respect to the peak of 1914 was remarkable in 1938 and almost dramatic in 1950 (Table 2.1).

The working of international financial markets during the nineteenth and the first three decades of the twentieth century partly explains the mechanics of foreign debt crises in DCs before the Second World War. International capital transfers were mainly accomplished through bond finance, particularly bonds issued by foreign entities that were negotiated by banking houses in Western financial centres: the role of banking houses was to lend to foreign borrowers at a discount and then sell the obligations to individual investors. A country's stock of debt was therefore eventually held by a large number of financial institutions and households: whenever a situation of illiquidity occurred, whether it involved a private investment project or a sovereign government, it was by no means automatic that an adequate provision of new funds could be extended to the debtor in distress before default had to be declared. In this context, free-riding among a very large number of creditors represented a formidable obstacle to the concession of new credit lines (Eichengreen, 1991).

The dispersion of a developing country's liabilities among a large set of investors could guarantee that the insolvency of a sovereign debtor did not threaten the stability of Western financial markets; however, there were cases when key Western financial institutions were shaken by the insolvency of DCs (the 1890 Baring crisis is an example). Moreover, a debt crisis rarely involved just one country. Even if default by some DCs did not necessarily imply bankruptcy in Western credit institutions, it is difficult to argue that no consequences were ever felt in industrial countries.

The defaults of the 1930s, the protracted negotiations (some lingering into the 1950s) and above all the collapse of the world trade and financial system, prevented substantial capital inflows into the DCs for almost three decades. It was only in 1958, when the convertibility of national currencies was reintroduced in Western Europe, that a seed of new international financial relations was set up (Obstfeld and Taylor, 1997, pp. 31–8).[3] At the end of the 1950s, American financial institutions had gained an extraordinary advantage over their overseas competitors. First, the reconstruction of the international payment system around the dollar had been completed, as clearly shown by the experience of the European Payments Union of 1950–8 when balance of payments imbalances among European countries were regulated in dollars (Solomon, 1982, Chapter 2). Second, the USA were the only industrial country with a large and persistent current account surplus, and hence the only one that could afford prolonged capital transfers to the rest of the world. Immediately after the war, the main channels of capital transfers had been grants (the Marshall Plan provides an example) and export credits. In the 1950s American direct investment abroad recovered, though it was mainly directed to DCs and especially to Europe. Restrictions on financial capital flows were widespread, and regulations and controls increased until the mid-1960s. The attitude in the USA with respect to foreign capital transactions had been very prudent after the Second World War, and under the Kennedy and Johnson administrations a restrictive stance was adopted leading to the approval of measures intended to discourage international short-term flows (Tew, 1982, Chapter 9).

Capital transfers to the DCs were slowly revived in the 1960s: official development assistance (ODA), foreign direct investment (FDI) and export credits were the main components of the flows at the beginning of the decade, but by 1970 bank lending had almost reached the amount of FDI (Maddison, 1989, p. 76; United Nations, 1991).

A lending boom oriented towards the DCs occurred in the 1970s and lasted for a decade until Mexico and Brazil suspended the service of external debt in 1982 and 1983, respectively. In this case, syndicated bank loans were the bulk of private capital flows to DCs, and the boom was focused on Latin America and to a lesser extent Asia. It is commonly argued that a combination of rising oil prices during 1973–4, which generated a huge current account surplus in oil-exporting countries, and the weak business cycle in major industrial economies in the mid-1970s was at the heart of the lending boom to DCs. Oil revenues were invested in highly liquid assets such as Western bank deposits, so the international banking network redirected an increasing supply of credit towards non-oil DCs. Banking regulations and capital controls were overcome through the basically unregulated Eurocurrency market (Obstfeld and Taylor, 1997, pp. 40–2).

The mechanism of syndicated loans was centred on large transnational banks which, after having negotiated the amount and conditions of the loan with the borrower, provided the resources and at the same time tried to gather a group of other banks willing to underwrite the loan. Both the DCs, who could obtain access to foreign credit rapidly and at low cost (world real interest rates remained quite low until 1979), and the organising banks, who were in search of profitable opportunities in a period of low demand for credit in industrial countries and could raise fees and commission income, had good reason to find this mechanism very convenient. Moreover, economic perspectives in DCs looked promising in the mid-1970s as exports were rising, the growth rate was high and the stock of outstanding foreign liabilities was rather low by historical standards in many countries. Unfortunately, this lending mania left little room for careful monitoring of the countries or projects of destination, as fierce competition among banks to gain new market shares prevailed over prudency considerations. In 1978–81 the burden of the debt was already heavy for DCs, but no clear signals of distress had emerged (apart from an incipient debt crisis in Poland in 1981): the international banking system was still lending to DCs, although partly as a consequence of the typical Ponzi game of rolling-over interest and repayments.

The roots and the development of 1982–3 crisis have been extensively analysed (see, among others, Diaz-Alejandro, 1983; Cohen, 1991a). A perverse association of external developments (a new stance of US monetary policy in 1979; a fall in the unit price of exports in some heavily indebted countries) and of misguided domestic investment and macroeconomic policies was at the heart of the distress. The scope of the 1980s' crisis has been extremely wide: almost every debtor country in Latin America and Africa has been involved, as well as several low-income Asian countries and a few in Eastern Europe. The ensuing negotiations reflected the nature of the lending boom: as commercial banks and official agencies instead of scattered households were the ultimate creditors of the insolvent countries, an alternative to explicit default was actively pursued by private and official creditors as well as by the IMF and the World Bank. Part of the debt due to official creditors was rescheduled under the terms agreed on by the Paris Club (IMF, 1995). A number of operations including rescheduling, principal and debt-service reduction, debt–equity swaps and others, were designed to deal with the liabilities owed to commercial banks;

the contribution of international financial organisations and creditor governments was particularly substantial after the announcement of the Brady Plan in 1989 (see Dooley, Fernandez-Arias and Kletzer, 1996). Nonetheless the real amount of net capital accruing to DCs severely contracted after 1982 (see Table 2.2) and Latin America became a net exporter of financial resources (Edwards, 1998b, p. 4). Moreover, a large portion of the new loans were not due to voluntary lending by Western creditors, but to 'defensive' behaviour aimed at preventing illiquidity and default in developing economies (Savvides, 1991).

2.3 LIBERALISATION AND INSTABILITY: THE DEBATE OF THE 1990s

The surge of capital flows to DCs in the early 1990s is commonly attributed to the implementation of the Brady Plan and a simultaneous downturn in the business cycle of industrial countries, with the associated fall in international interest rates. The net amount of external financial resources to the DCs grew by a factor of 1.5 in nominal terms from 1988 to 1994, and even more if we exclude the grant component (Table 2.2).

Briefly, the main statistical characters of the 1990s recovery are the following:

(1) Long-term debt-creating flows are a diminishing fraction of overall net flows. Official lending and grants peaked in 1990, the year after the Brady Plan was launched, and declined afterwards.
(2) Short-term debt-creating flows have been growing more or less in line with total net flows since 1987, with some fluctuations depending on the inclusion of interest arrears and IMF lending under this item.
(3) Portfolio flows replaced bank loans as the main instrument of private capital transfer to DCs from 1991 through 1994, although the evidence on 1995 and 1996 indicates that bank lending revived in the aftermath of the Mexican crisis (IMF, 1997, p. 75).
(4) Non-debt-creating inflows were the most dynamic components of capital movements to DCs. The contribution of FDI has been relevant since 1987, although not exceptional in historical viewpoint.
(5) The rapid increase of non-debt-creating components mainly reflects the dynamics of equity-related inflows to DCs, which

Table 2.2 Net total capital flows including grants: all developing countries, 1970–94

	1970	1980	1985	1989	1991	1994*	1970	1980	1985	1989	1991	1994*
	(billion US dollars)						(%) percentage					
Net capital inflows *plus* grants	11.4[a]	89.5[a]	60.8	105.2	147.7	255.3	100[a]	100[a]	100	100	100	100
Grants (excluding technical cooperation)	1.9	13.2	13.2	19.1	32.5	30.4	16.7	14.7	21.7	18.2	22.0	11.9
Net total capital inflows	9.5[a]	76.3[a]	47.6	86.1	115.2	224.9	83.3[a]	85.3[a]	78.3	81.8	78.0	88.1
Long-term debt of which:	6.8	71.7	36.4	36.1	47.8	79.5	59.6	79.8	59.9	34.4	32.4	31.1
Official creditors	3.4	21.9	20.9	23.3	29.2	23.9	29.8	24.5	34.4	22.0	19.8	9.4
Private creditors[b] of which:	3.4	49.7	15.5	12.8	18.6	55.6	29.8	55.3	25.5	12.3	12.6	21.7
Bonds	0[c]	2.6[c]	4.9[c]	5.3	12.5	..	0[c]	2.8[c]	8.1[c]	5.0	8.5	..
Commercial banks	0.6[c]	24.2[c]	6.6[c]	0.9	4.0	..	4.8[c]	27.0[c]	10.9[c]	0.9	2.7	..
Short-term debt[d]	..	..	0.6	20.9	23.1	28.1	..	..	1.0	19.9	15.6	11.0
Portfolio equity flows	0	0	0	3.4	7.5	39.4	0	0	0	3.2	5.1	15.4
Net FDI	2.3	5.3	10.6	25.7	36.8	77.9	23.7	5.9	17.4	24.4	24.9	30.5

Notes:
a Short-term debt is not recorded separately.
b Guaranteed and non-guaranteed debt generating flows from private creditors, including bonds, lending by commercial banks and other items (mainly export credits).
c Private nonguaranteed flows are excluded.
d IMF lending and interest arrears on long-term debt are included.
.. Not available
* 1994 World Bank estimates.
Source: World Bank, *World Debt Tables.*

moved from scratch to 40 billion dollars over 1986–94. Equity and FDI together accounted for almost half of the global net capital transfer to the DCs in 1994 (grants excluded), that is about 120 billion dollars (Table 2.2).

Net inflows mainly targeted three areas (Table 2.3): East Asia, where their rate of growth reached 50 per cent in 1992; Europe and Central Asia, where the rapid increase since 1989 was associated with the start of the transition process in formerly planned economies; and Latin America where the turning point was 1990 and net long-term inflows grew by 50 per cent in 1993. Net long-term inflows actually stagnated in Sub-Saharan Africa, where they amounted in 1993 to one-third of the value of 1980 *in nominal terms*; in South Asia, where the World Bank forecasts are more optimistic for the future; and in the Middle East and North Africa, despite the reconstruction process following the Gulf War. In other words, with the exception of some very large low-income countries such as China, and to a less extent India, *middle-income* developing or transition economies have mainly gained from the recovery in capital inflows.

Official and private long-term lending followed rather opposite paths in the first half of the 1990s: whereas official lending, which was distributed quite homogeneously among different regions including Africa and South Asia, declined after 1991, private lending more than doubled in 1992 but was heavily concentrated in East Asia, Eastern

Table 2.3 Net long-term capital flows to developing countries, by region of destination[a] in 1970–94 (billion US dollars)

	1970	1980	1985	1989	1991	1994*
All DCs	9.0	76.0	47.1	64.5	91.7	197.3
East Asia and the Pacific	1.5	11.9	14.3	23	31.9	89.5
Europe and Central Asia	0.5	16.6	3.5	11.7	16.8	33.4
Latin America and the Caribbean	3.9	29.5	12	5.5	25.5	40.7
Middle East and North Africa	0.8	3.8	8.3	7.9	4.5	9.2
South Asia	1.1	4	4.2	8.2	8.3	15.2
Sub-Saharan Africa	1.2	10.2	4.8	8.2	4.7	9.3

Notes:
a Excluding grants.
* Based on 1994 World Bank estimates.
Source: author's estimates based on World Bank, *World Debt Tables*.

Europe and Latin America. If we look at the *composition* of long-term private lending in the early 1990s, however, it emerges that banking involvement was proportionally larger in East and South Asia, while new loans were less relevant in Latin America and even negative in post-socialist Europe – that is, the two regions where commercial banks were more severely hit by the 1980s' debt crisis. Symmetrically, the contribution of international bond market was more effective for Latin American and European DCs.

The bulk of the equity boom of the early 1990s was located in only two regions, Latin America and East Asia, while Asian and Pacific countries were the destination of almost half of the net FDI accruing to DCs. Direct investment from abroad has also been sustained in Latin America, and in the transition countries of Europe and Central Asia, despite the uncertainty caused by the establishment and enforcing of property rights in formerly planned economies (see IMF, 1997).

This upturn in capital inflows in DCs has motivated a great deal of academic and policy-oriented debate. The main themes can be outlined as follows:

(1) What factors have generated the new surge (Calvo, Leiderman and Reinhart, 1993; Dooley, Fernandez-Arias and Kletzer, 1996)?
(2) What are the main short- and medium-term implications for the recipient economies, and the suitable policy responses (Corbo and Hernandez, 1996)?
(3) What are the foreseeable long-term consequences, particularly in relation with the experience of the 1970s and 1980s (Kaminsky and Pereira, 1996)?
(4) To what extent is the ongoing process of domestic and external liberalisation beneficial for DCs?
(5) Should we care about the financial instruments used to implement capital transfers to developing economies, and why?

Following the turmoil in Eastern Asian and Russian markets in 1997–8, the debate has move forward to the issue of finding warning indicators of impending fragilities in DCs, and to the question of how to manage the crises once they blow up. On point (1), we listed on pp. 11–12 the main determinants of the recovery stage within a capital-transfer cycle: although interlinked with 'push' factors, 'pull' or systemic aspects are more likely to affect the overall *volume* of capital inflows in DCs. Systemic elements include items that are largely out of the control of individual developing economies such as the conditions of the business cycle and the monetary policy stance in industrial countries, the soundness of the balance sheet of large international financial institutions and the dimension of their total outstanding assets in DCs. The *distribution* of net capital inflows across DCs, however, is more likely to depend on country-specific factors. We will come back to this in chapters 6 and 8, with empirical inquiries on the distribution of capital inflows in, respectively, developing and transition economies.

Point (2) is outside the scope of this volume, but it occupies a great deal of the most recent discussions about balance of payments crisis management. Chapter 7 deals with the (yet meagre) evidence on the long-run impact of capital inflows on growth in DCs, with special reference to the lessons of the past capital-transfer cycle (1960–88).

The remainder of this section focuses on some topics related to points (4) and (5) above. On point (4), it is clear that the global trend towards liberalisation of the current and capital accounts in DCs that has occurred in the last decade or so has a role in the renewal of capital inflows (Mathieson and Rojas-Suarez, 1993). Whenever the rise in capital inflows is due to the impulse given to financial liberalisation, we are likely to observe a *stock-adjustment* phenomenon on world capital markets: international investors are willing to diversify their portfolios in order to equalise expected returns and to protect themselves against country-specific risk, hence the opening of previously unavailable investment opportunities diverts some capital from existing placements and redirects it to the liberalising countries. This is, however, a one-shot reallocation that may take some time to be completed but is unlikely to be a permanent feature of a recipient country's balance of payments.

Other economic reforms may have a less transitory impact on a country's capital account, if they are able to affect the *ex ante* rate of return in a persistent way. These country-specific measures, including liberalisation of external trade, promotion of national export and fiscal reform, can persistently alter the relative convenience of investing in a given location rather than in other countries (or regions). If high rates of output and export growth as well as large returns on investment are forecast, a sustained inflow of financial resources need not be episodic. Reforms concerning the *real* economy (trade liberalisation; investment and export promotion; measures intended to enhance human-capital accumulation through direct government intervention or favourable detaxation; fiscal restructuring) are deemed to convey, with a few exceptions, a positive effect on long-term capital movements (Rodrik, 1996a; Fry, 1997).

The immediate effect of *financial* – as opposed to real-sector – liberalisation is a sort of portfolio-adjustment process leading major international investors to shift part of their funds into emerging markets (IFC, 1996, p. 7). Nevertheless financial liberalisation has, relative to other kinds of reforms, more controversial medium- and long-run consequences for developing economies. First, financial liberalisation can raise the degree of short-termism inherent in an economy: this is caused by the increase in the volatility and speculativeness of financial markets which can stress their 'bandwagon' or 'herd' features at the expense of long-term investment and growth. The increase in volatility is likely to be even larger if domestic and external liberalisation move on together, as this 'leads to close links between two inherently unstable markets... the stock and currency markets' (Singh, 1997, p. 779). However, it should be mentioned also that a tightly controlled market is prone to several dangers, for instance abuse of political and bureaucratic influence or a rise in rent-seeking activities.

A second concern with financial liberalisation is that it generates an 'excess demand' for prudential regulation and supervision by monetary and financial market authorities: this problem is more likely to be felt in the commercial banking sector which still accounts for a very large share of financial intermediation in DCs (Fry, 1997). Most domestic and external funds are likely to be channelled through commercial banks in developing economies. Whenever a surge in capital inflows or an increase in domestic saving raises the resources available for the banks, a deterioration of the quality of the balance sheet can occur if the financial enterprises are not able to appraise the riskiness of their potential investments but at the same time are under pressure to allocate their funds. Note that this problem is even more serious in a situation of rising interest rates, commonly associated with the early phases of financial liberalisation: high real interest rates tend to crowd-out less risky potential borrowers at the advantage of the risky ones (Rojas-Suarez and Weisbrod, 1995). The case for effective regulation and surveillance is therefore especially relevant in situations of ongoing domestic and external capital market reform, but the governments in DCs often lack the financial resources and the expertise required to supply them.

Finally, the medium- and long-term consequences on growth and welfare of opening an economy's capital account (external financial liberalisation) are crucially related to the *credibility* and *consistency* of the overall economic (and possibly political) reform package. The reason is simply that if domestic and foreign agents believe that the measures intended to liberalise the capital account and stabilise macroeconomic policy are not permanent and will be reversed in the future, their behaviour – although perfectly rational – will be led by the 'wrong' incentives from the point of view of aggregate domestic welfare (for instance, present consumption will be preferred to capital accumulation if a reversal in exchange rate stabilisation is predicted; or highly speculative instead of longer-term investment will be favoured).[4]

Turning to the question of what financial instruments, and institutions have intermediated the new surge in capital inflows to DCs and how they can affect outcomes, one has to recall that portfolio finance was the most popular medium of international capital transfer during the Gold Standard and in the 1920s, while FDI was the first to revive after the Second World War (see Section 2.2). Hence one needs to be cautious in stressing the absolute novelty of recent evolutions.

We can view different financial contracts as alternative systems of reaching a balance between the penalties imposed on the debtor for bad outcomes and the support extended to them in bad situations: for instance, we can think of bank lending as stressing the monitoring role of creditors over the debtor's activities, while portfolio finance underlines the sanctioning role of the markets. Ranking financial instruments according to their inherent 'quality' must take this balance into account. Bond issues are sometimes project-specific, hence one may argue that the refinancing of an investment project can be evaluated more carefully by the lender on the basis of the results obtained, and of future prospects. Moreover, the unwillingness to finance an individual project need not jeopardise the aggregate volume of capital transfers to a DC. However, these conclusions are often unwarranted. First, small investors tend to delegate monitoring of a debtor's activity to a financial institution even if this is a mutual funds investing in bonds. Second, commercial banks are often thought to perform a better monitoring of their debtors than other kind of financial institutions, precisely because their involvement with an individual borrower or project is likely to be larger, lasting and more direct. It is true that this involvement is a double-edged circumstance, as it may avoid the danger of crises merely due to liquidity (as opposed to solvency) problems in debtor countries, but it may also trigger Ponzi games of rolling over the debt service eventually leading to deeper and wider financial crises: this is an inevitable side effect of the difficulty of achieving the appropriate balance between penalty and support. Third, the project-specific nature of bond finance is likely to be an illusion if the lender has not constant and complete supervision of the borrower's accounts – and, more important, if the outcome of one project crucially depends on other complementary investments or on the global economic performance of the developing economy. In general major creditors have a stake in the debtor's economic survival, so syndicated bank lending can supplement bond finance in periods of distress, as the aftermath of the 1994 Mexican crisis suggests.

Equity is, in quantitative terms, the truly new instrument of capital transfers to DCs. In principle, its case is different from bond finance because the burden of the risk associated with the investment is *explicitly* transferred onto the shareholder. However, as mentioned in Section 2.2 default, the suspension of interest payments and the reduction in the nominal value of the assets have been historical features of the mechanism of international (sovereign) debt; one can thus argue that in principle this burden had always been carried to some extent by the creditors. From the recipient's viewpoint, equity markets are even more subject to booms, panics and crashes than bond markets, as the volatility of stock market investment is likely to be higher. Nevertheless, even in this case large investors such as mutual or pension funds have an interest in stabilising a market whenever they are exposed to huge capital losses. It has been argued that the existence of a stock market enhances the allocative efficiency of an economy. Recent econometric studies have shown that the relative dimension and the liquidity of the stock market is positively associated with growth in developed and developing countries (Levine, 1996), but the causal links underlying this relationship are very controversial and appear to be influenced by the characteristics of each individual country or region (Arestis and Demetriades, 1997).

Foreign direct investment (FDI) is, with some qualifications, a source of external capital whose positive contribution to economic growth in DCs has been empirically proved (Borensztein, De Gregorio and Lee, 1998; Balasubramanyam, Salisu and Sapsford, 1996). On the one hand, both human and physical capital transfers are in principle associated with FDI, so the constraint of labour skills in DCs can be more easily overcome; at the same time, as far as FDI is concentrated in the public utility sector or in infrastructures it can produce beneficial external effects for the whole recipient economy. On the other hand, *individual* FDI initiatives should be less volatile than portfolio investment. Note however, that this is not necessarily true at the *aggregate* level: Claessens, Dooley and Warner (1995) find that the distinction between 'hot' and 'cold' flows is largely conventional as the components of a country's capital account look high substitutable over time. It has also been argued that FDI in DCs can be 'incentive-compatible', as it may lower the incentive to default on external debt on the debtor's part and the incentive to free-ride on the part of the creditors (the general motivation being that FDI increases the openness of the developing economy to international trade and production, and therefore raises the penalties associated with insulation in case of insolvency and default, see Aizenman, 1991). It would be wrong to treat *every kind* of FDI as welfare-improving for the host economy; in fact, a chief determinant of FDI in the 'traditional' labour-intensive sectors is the search for lower labour costs even if this means a frequent relocation of productive capacity (so-called 'footloose' FDI). Foreign investment in low value-added sectors can lead to excessive specialisation of DCs in labour-intensive production that may prevent a future upgrading of the domestic industry (a 'lock-in' phenomenon). Moreover, the competition among countries to provide favourable locations for FDI can yield welfare-reducing side effects, such as a deterioration of environmental conditions, a reduction of civil and political rights, or a taxation regime that unduly favours capital over labour income.

Economics textbooks suggest that the integration in world capital markets favours economic growth and welfare for several reasons: the decoupling of domestic investment from national saving; the possibility of smoothing consumption in the face of country-specific shocks; the availability of a worldwide pool of financial instruments that allows a more efficient insurance against risk and lower borrowing costs (the advantages of capital market integration for DCs are more systematically highlighted in Chapter 5). However, the long-run benefits of capital market integration in terms of growth and welfare crucially depend on the *destination* of external financing to productive investment (rather than consumption or speculation), on the *allocation* of investment resources to highly profitable projects, on a domestic and international environment conducive to economic growth and also on favourable unexpected events (such as improvements in the terms of trade). Many conditions must therefore be fulfilled if capital inflows are to favour economic growth and welfare in DCs.

Moreover, only when external financing is associated with economic growth is the dynamic *sustainability* of the accumulation of foreign liabilities conceivable. The counterpart of the foreign capital contribution to growth is the building of an external debt (or, in general, of a negative net foreign asset position) that is viable only if domestic output and exports are growing as well (see Chapter 8 for an application to transition economies). These are benchmarks against which the outcome of the 1990s' recovery in capital flows to the DCs will eventually be evaluated. The kind of financial tools used to implement the capital transfer is not immaterial to these problems, because speculative short-term flows can be inconsistent with the accomplishment of productive investment projects, but it probably influences more the *type* and *timing* of the investors' reaction to news concerning unprofitable economic ventures and bad macroeconomic or financial management (Section 2.1).

Sound and credible policies are required to assure that the impact of foreign finance on long-term growth in DCs is positive: together with liberalisation (with all the caveats mentioned above), policies effectively promoting and supporting the accumulation of infrastructures and human capital (education, healthcare, on-the-job training, and so on) are likely to be advantageous for DCs (see Chapter 6). In this case, public external borrowing can also raise the private rate of return of an economy and therefore be sustainable in the long run. Quite trivially, the lesson of the historical experience is that, provided external factors matter, the sustainability of external debt as well as the impact of foreign capital on growth in the receiving countries are closely linked to an economically sound employment of the funds. However, finding sound investment opportunities can get difficult when a developing economy incurs overborrowing as is often the case during a liberalisation phase (see McKinnon and Pill, 1997). The danger of inflating high-risk projects starts to materialise at that stage, with the related negative consequences for the recipient economy in the medium and long run.

Part II
Theoretical Models

# 3 Growth Theory and the Determinants of Capital Flows

This chapter provides a theoretical investigation of the factors affecting the flows of net foreign capital in the long run, with special attention to the case of a developing economy. Our interest in long-run phenomena naturally leads us to adopt the theory of economic growth as the main reference in the study of the determinants of the net foreign asset position of a developing country (DC). Moreover, in the last ten years growth theory has undergone a radical process of renewal and has remarkably enlarged its scope, and this makes it an extremely promising tool for approaching the issue of capital movements. However, some old models are still very powerful and stand as starting points for more recent refinements: this is the case of the Solow (1956) model, for instance.

Sections 3.1 and 3.2 inspect a few prototype growth models, including the standard neoclassical model without or with human capital (Mankiw, Romer and Weil, 1992), and the endogenous growth model. This review makes no claim to exhaustiveness: special attention is devoted to the analytical treatment of 'human capital' and to the predictions concerning the direction and amount of capital movements, under different assumptions concerning capital mobility. As we will show in Chapter 5, assumptions of perfect capital mobility and of capital immobility are extreme ones; we therefore adopt an intermediate hypothesis of limited or restricted mobility whenever this is possible. Alternatively, full capital mobility can be assumed as a heuristic device. The exposition of Sections 3.1 and 3.2 is organised as follows: first a general growth model is developed, from which different prototype models can be derived under special assumptions; second, the basic features of these models as well as their implications for capital movements are discussed (Durlauf and Quah, 1998, follow the same expositional strategy in a different context). Given its heuristic aim, the general framework is extremely simple and the 'behavioural' approach of constant saving shares due to Solow (1956) is preferred to the 'optimising' approach with variable shares. The two approaches are often equivalent (see Durlauf and Quah, 1998) and in particular they yield similar predictions about the variables affecting net capital flows.

Section 3.3 elaborates a fully-fledged neoclassical model with 'partial' capital mobility – that is mobility restricted to one type of capital assets (physical as opposed to human). The purpose of this section is to show how the model yields accurate indications regarding the long-run amount of net capital flowing into a developing economy for a given configuration of fundamentals (initial income, human-capital levels, rate of growth of population, and so on).

Section 3.4 considers the influence of demographic variables on capital flows in the context of simple overlapping-generations (OLG) models which explicitly describe the dynamics of population cohorts in an individual economy. Although the evolution of population structures is a primary concern in the case of DCs because of the recurrent phenomenon of demographic transitions, it is difficult to reach *general* conclusions on the pattern of capital movements in OLG models as these rest on particular assumptions about the number and features of the cohorts.

It is important to note that in these models capital mobility is generally viewed as an instrument for the allocation of resources to the most productive investment opportunities: as we focus on the long run, the use of external capital as a mean of consumption-smoothing is neglected, while the possibility that a country mortgages a future stream of constant (*per capita*) incomes to anticipate consumption is often ruled out. However, as capital flows are usually fungible, there is no guarantee that foreign capital is *ex post* employed in investment projects. Section 3.5 argues that the theoretical suggestions derived from this chapter can form the background for an empirical screening of the determinants of net capital inflows in DCs over 1960–88, which is the topic of Chapter 6.

3.1 HUMAN CAPITAL AND THE NEOCLASSICAL GROWTH MODEL: IMPLICATIONS FOR CAPITAL MOVEMENTS

This and the following section apply a basic framework to uncover the main predictions on capital movements offered by growth models. We present here the building blocks of the framework as well as the special assumptions consistent with the neoclassical model; Section 3.2 deals with the parametrisations consistent with a class of endogenous growth models. Such a 'nested' approach allows a straightforward connection between the special hypotheses typical of some branch of the theory, and the ensuing predictions; there is however a cost, since only some theoretical configurations are well suited for this expositional strategy. Moreover, some endogenous growth models have to be modified to display the potential newness of their approach with respect to the neoclassical theory. Durlauf and Quah (1998) adopt a similar technique for assessing the empirical predictions on income growth and 'convergence'. The key idea is that:

> In so far as many models differs substantively only through alternative specifications of the production technology, formulating them within a general equilibrium framework might have only limited payoff empirically. (Durlauf and Quah, 1998, p. 11)

Translated into our context, this means that limiting the attention to the central features of the production technology permits an adequate analytical treatment of the empirical predictions concerning capital movements, while the dismissal of some general equilibrium aspects such as the maximising procedure for determining saving rates comes at very limited cost in terms of empirical indications.

Let us consider a homogeneous production function:

$$Y_t = AK_t^\alpha H_t^\gamma L_t^\beta \qquad (3.1)$$

where Y is the output of a homogeneous good that can be consumed or invested, K is physical capital, H is human capital, L is the labour force (assumed equal to the size of the population), A is a technical coefficient and t a time index. Labour is inelastically supplied. We further simplify the framework assuming that A is constant while L grows at a given exogenous exponential rate n:

$$A = A_0 \qquad (3.2)$$

$$L_t = L_0 e^{nt} \qquad (3.3)$$

The assumption of a stationary technology coefficient, equal across countries, is indeed a very restrictive one: as a matter of fact, one of the main limitations of the neoclassical model is that it provides no insights on the cross-section and time variation of A, while the improvement provided by endogenous growth models is often a better specification of the dynamics of A. We offer here two reasons for keeping A constant: first, DCs are commonly regarded as 'imitators' rather than 'innovators', meaning that improvements in the field of technological capacity in these countries are related to the transfer and adaptation of new production techniques from abroad. The technology transfer process is partially accomplished through the transfer of foreign capital so it is to some extent determined by the *same variables* (initial income, human-capital standards, the policy regime, and so on) which affect capital inflows. The cross-country and time variation of technology standards in DCs could therefore be at least partially captured by those variables. Second, even if there are some institutional arrangements and economic policy indicators that specifically influence the rate of technological upgrading in a developing economy (see, for instance, Romer, 1993), available data on a large enough set of DCs would not permit an *empirical* treatment of these aspects in Chapter 6. In conclusion, we stick to a position that can be blamed for 'capital fundamentalism' (King and Levine, 1994) but reflects the key role of capital accumulation in developing economies (see Temple and Voth, 1998, for a recent statement).

The dynamics of K and H are given by (3.4) and (3.5), respectively:

$$\dot{K}_t = s_k Y_t - \delta K_t \tag{3.4}$$

$$\dot{H}_t = s_h Y_t - \delta H_t \tag{3.5}$$

where s_k and s_h are the constant shares of investment in physical and human capital, δ is the depreciation rate (assumed equal for simplicity), and a dot over a variables indicates a time derivative. Let us define y, k and h as output, physical capital and human capital per worker (recall that 'per worker' is equivalent to '*per capita*' under our assumptions). Equation (3.1) can be restated as:

$$Y_t = A k_t^\alpha h_t^\gamma L_t^{(\alpha+\beta+\gamma)} \quad \text{or} \quad y_t = A k_t^\alpha h_t^\gamma L_t^{(\alpha+\beta+\gamma-1)} \tag{3.6}$$

The evolution of k and h over time can be approximated by:

$$\dot{k} = \dot{K}L^{-1} - k\dot{L}L^{-1} = \dot{K}L^{-1} - nk \tag{3.7}$$

$$\dot{h} = \dot{H}L^{-1} - h\dot{L}L^{-1} = \dot{H}L^{-1} - nh \tag{3.8}$$

where the time subscript has been omitted and the time derivatives of H and K are given by (3.4) and (3.5), respectively. The steady-state values k^* and h^* can be derived as solutions of (3.7) and (3.8) once the left-hand side is set equal to zero:

$$k^* = A^{\frac{1}{1-\alpha-\gamma}} \left(s_k^{1-\gamma} s_h^{\gamma}(n+\delta)^{-1} L^{\alpha+\beta+\gamma-1}\right)^{\frac{1}{1-\alpha-\gamma}} \quad (3.9)$$

$$h^* = A^{\frac{1}{1-\alpha-\gamma}} \left(s_k^{\alpha} s_h^{1-\alpha}(n+\delta)^{-1} L^{\alpha+\beta+\gamma-1}\right)^{\frac{1}{1-\alpha-\gamma}} \quad (3.10)$$

This elementary setup can be used to describe the main features of the neoclassical and endogenous growth models: we first consider a simplified version of the Solow (1956) model of constant returns to scale and diminishing returns to physical capital accumulation. The restrictions we impose on the general model are the following:

$$\gamma = 0; \quad \alpha + \beta = 1; \quad \alpha, \beta > 0 \quad (3.11)$$

From (3.6) we obtain:

$$y_t = A k_t^{\alpha} \quad (3.12)$$

The rate of growth of *per capita* income is an *increasing* function of the growth rate of k:

$$\frac{\dot{y}}{y} = (d \log y)/dt = \alpha[(d \log k)/dt] \quad 0 < \alpha < 1 \quad (3.13)$$

We know from (3.9) that k approaches a *finite* steady-state value once the set of restrictions (3.11) has been imposed, hence the rates of growth of k and y asymptotically approach zero in the steady state.[1] The main result of the Solow model is that there exists an *exogenous steady-state growth rate* (equal to zero in this simplified version) which does not depend on tastes (e.g. on the propensity to save) nor is affected by policy variables.

Let us study the implications of the Solow model for international capital movements. The assumption of *perfect* capital mobility is reflected in the arbitrage condition (3.14):

$$r^* = r_d \quad (3.14)$$

where r^* and r_d are the international and the domestic interest rate, respectively (we neglect any sort of risk premia). If at any point in time the domestic interest rate is above (below) the international rate, the domestic economy will experience a net inflow (outflow) of capital. Whenever the interest-parity condition is fulfilled, net capital flows do not occur.

In the Solow model we only have one type of capital asset – namely, physical capital. r_d therefore equals in equilibrium the marginal product of k *minus* the depreciation rate:

$$r_d = \alpha A k^{\alpha-1} - \delta \quad \text{or} \quad r_d = \alpha A^{\frac{1}{\alpha}} y^{\frac{\alpha-1}{\alpha}} - \delta \tag{3.15}$$

where the second expression in (3.15) takes into account equation (3.12).

Provided A, δ and α are constant across countries r_d is a decreasing function of the *per capita* stock of physical capital, hence if we assume full mobility of physical capital countries with a low k will experience net capital inflows and countries with a large k will experience net outflows. Moreover, as shown by (3.15) the Solow model predicts that the *amount* of capital inflows is inversely related to k – namely, capital should move from rich to poor countries.

Let us now consider the *augmented* neoclassical model suggested by Mankiw, Romer and Weil (1992). The authors explicitly refer to Solow (1956) and their model is indeed an extension of the neoclassical growth setup that includes human capital as a production factor. The dissatisfaction with the simple two-factor neoclassical model can be attributed to several reasons: first, invoking an exogenous rate of technical progress, independent of basic economic forces, to explain long-run growth is unsatisfactory. Second, the historical acceleration of long-run growth comes with an increase in *per capita* physical capital, which contradicts the law of diminishing returns (Romer, 1986). Third, convergence among countries to the same long-run income level is not a general phenomenon (Barro, 1991). Fourth, capital flows do not move according to the predictions of the Solow model, and arbitrage conditions based on this model are not fulfilled (Lucas, 1990). Finally, growth-accounting exercises show that output growth is only partially accounted for by the increase in employment and physical capital (the so-called 'Solow-residual' or 'total factor productivity' (TFP) puzzle: see Maddison, 1987). The augmented growth model deals with some of these problems.

The restrictions imposed on the general model are the following:

$$\alpha + \beta + \gamma = 1; \quad \alpha, \beta, \gamma > 0 \tag{3.16}$$

Per capita income is given by:

$$y_t = A k_t^\alpha h^\gamma \tag{3.17}$$

and the rate of growth of y is:

$$\frac{\dot{y}}{y} = (d\log y)/dt \qquad (3.18)$$
$$= \alpha[(d\log k)/dt] + \gamma[(d\log h)/dt] \quad 0 < \alpha,\ \gamma < 1$$

One can check from (3.9) and (3.10) that both k and h reach a finite steady state under this parameter configuration, hence the rate of growth of y approaches zero in the steady state. However, y does not only depend on physical capital but on human capital as well. This has three relevant implications: first, while the model still predicts convergence to a unique *growth rate* starting from different initial conditions, convergence in *per capita income levels* depends on both s_k and s_h which may differ across countries ('conditional convergence', see Mankiw, Romer and Weil, 1992). Second, growth-accounting exercises are misspecified if they admit only two factors of production, neglecting the role of human capital. Last but not least, the predictions concerning capital movements must be reconsidered (see Lucas, 1990).

The question of international capital mobility can be restated to allow for the existence of two types of capital assets. For instance, Barro, Mankiw and Sala-i-Martin (1995) analyse the issue of capital mobility in an 'augmented' optimal growth model: the first question they address is: 'What kind of asset are traded internationally?'; the second one is 'What are the consequences of human capital on the arbitrage conditions?' Barro, Mankiw and Sala-i-Martin assume that human capital and raw labour are *immobile* factors of production (no migration), while physical capital accumulation can be financed through foreign borrowing; this 'partial' mobility assumption is intended to capture the idea that capital mobility does not extend to any type of asset.[2] The interest-rate parity condition therefore holds across *physical, but not human*, capital assets: it is in any case straightforward to show that the marginal product of capital (hereafter MPK) *depends on h*:

$$r_d = \alpha A k^{\alpha-1} h^{\gamma} - \delta \quad \text{or} \quad r_d = \alpha A^{\frac{1}{\alpha}} y^{\frac{\alpha-1}{\alpha}} h^{\frac{\gamma}{\alpha}} - \delta \qquad (3.19)$$

where the second expression in (3.19) can be obtained from (3.17) solving for k.

The MPK is a decreasing function of k and an increasing one of h: as argued by Lucas (1990) the association between *poor* countries and high marginal product of capital can be misleading as human capital must be taken into account, and its relative endowment could be lower in poor countries than in rich ones.

The 'augmented' neoclassical model predicts that countries with low levels of physical capital *and* high levels of h will benefit from net capital inflows, and that capital movements will persist until condition (3.14) is fulfilled, once r_d is given by (3.19).

3.2 INTERNATIONAL CAPITAL FLOWS IN MODELS OF ENDOGENOUS GROWTH

Three seminal contributions to the theory of *endogenous* growth – namely, the Romer (1986), Lucas (1988) and Rebelo (1991, 1992) models – are briefly reviewed in this paragraph. The analytical structure of early models of endogenous growth is presented in detail in Romer (1989) and Barro and Sala-i-Martin (1995, Chapter 4): here we focus on one aspect of these aggregate models, namely the implications for international capital flows.

Why *endogenous* growth theory? The emphasis is on some of the limitations of the neoclassical theory that 'augmented' models do not overcome: first, the existence of an exogenous steady-state rate of growth, which does not depend on preferences or policy variables; second, the conditional convergence prediction which implies that, *ceteris paribus*, countries with high levels of (broad) capital per worker will eventually grow slower than countries with low levels of k and h. These growth models have been labelled 'endogenous' because they yield unbounded growth of *per capita* income without relying on a *given* rate of technical progress.

In his path-breaking work, Romer (1986) considers a wide class of mathematical representations of a deterministic process of unbounded growth driven by increasing returns to the accumulation of knowledge. For our limited purposes we may refer to the general growth model of the previous paragraph and modify one of Romer's specifications with the following restrictions on the aggregate production function:[3]

$$\alpha = 1; \quad 0 < \beta < 1; \quad \gamma = 0 \tag{3.20}$$

This set of restrictions yields the following expression for y:

$$y_t = A k_t L_t^{\beta} \tag{3.21}$$

The rate of change of *per capita* income is given by:

$$\frac{\dot{y}}{y} = (d\log y)/dt = [(d\log k)/dt] + \beta n \qquad (3.22)$$

Two results must be stressed: first, the rate of growth of *y* is a positive function of the rate of growth of population (*n*). This depends on the assumption of *increasing returns to scale* (or positive *aggregate* scale effects), an assumption that has often been questioned in the empirical literature (Backus, Kehoe and Kehoe, 1992; Jones, 1995a; see also Young, 1995). The second result is that the rate of growth of *per capita* income is fully endogenous – namely, it depends on the rate of change of *k* at any point in time. Indeed, one can check that *k does not approach a finite steady-state value* in this case (see 3.9). Note that the endogenous-growth result is *not* due to the presence of increasing returns to scale but to *constant returns to the reproducible input* (*k*), captured by the parameter α.[4] In this 'modified' Romer (1986) model, an increase in the rate of investment s_k raises the rate of output growth: any policy measure that permanently affects s_k has an impact on the growth rate.

Let us turn to the implications of the Romer model for international capital movements. The domestic interest rate in the Romer model is given by the following expression:

$$r_d = \alpha A k^{\alpha-1} L^{\alpha+\beta-1} - \delta = AL^\beta - \delta \qquad (3.23)$$

and from condition (3.14) we conclude that *larger* economies will benefit from net capital inflows, regardless of their relative capital endowment.[5]

Human capital does not feature in the Romer model; conversely, it plays a relevant role in the Lucas (1988) model. Lucas assumes that the average endowment of *per capita* human capital enters the aggregate production function with a positive coefficient and that there exists a linear technology for the accumulation of human capital (1988, pp. 17–27). As the predictions of the Lucas model concerning the determinants of capital flows are not qualitatively different from that of Mankiw, Romer and Weil (1992), we will modify the Lucas model in order to include scale effects in the picture and distinguish between the two models. The modified Lucas (1988) model implies the subsequent restrictions on the aggregate production function:

$$0 < \alpha, \beta < 1; \quad \alpha + \beta + \hat{\gamma} > 1; \quad \hat{\gamma} = \gamma_P + \gamma_E > \gamma \qquad (3.24)$$

where γ_p is the *private* rate of returns to human capital and γ_E captures the *external* effect generated by the accumulation of h, and their sum is larger than γ (the human-capital coefficient in the 'augmented' neoclassical model).

The rate of growth of *per capita* income is given by:[6]

$$\frac{\dot{y}}{y} = (d \log y)/dt$$
$$= \alpha[(d \log k)/dt] + \hat{\gamma}[(d \log h)/dt] + (\alpha + \beta + \hat{\gamma} - 1)n \quad (3.25)$$

The evolution of the stock of *physical* capital can be approximated by (3.7), while the rate of change of *per capita human* capital in the Lucas model is given by (3.26):

$$\dot{h}_t = h_t \lambda (1 - u_t) \quad \text{or} \quad d \ln h_t = \lambda(1 - u_t) \quad (3.26)$$

where $(1 - u_t)$ is the share of time devoted to education and λ is a positive constant. The rate of growth of h is always positive provided the initial stock of h is non-zero and u_t is less than one, hence there is no finite steady-state value of h and we obtain endogenous growth *driven by human capital accumulation* (see 3.27).

As far as capital movements are concerned, the Lucas model yields a prediction that recalls the 'augmented' neoclassical model. Provided *physical* capital is the only internationally mobile input (partial capital mobility), the domestic interest rate is given by:

$$r_d = \alpha A^{\frac{1}{\alpha}} y^{\frac{\alpha-1}{\alpha}} h^{\frac{\hat{\gamma}}{\alpha}} L^{\frac{\alpha+\beta+\hat{\gamma}-1}{\alpha}} - \delta \quad (3.27)$$

where the expression on the right-hand side of (3.27) is obtained in the same way as in (3.19).

In contrast to the 'augmented' model we have here: first, an external effect associated with human capital accumulation such that h has a larger impact on the MPK; and second, a term related to the dimension of the economy (because of the presence of increasing returns to scale) that does not appear in the augmented neoclassical model. A common feature of the two models is that of diminishing returns to physical capital (that is, the mobile factor) which implies a *negative* association between r_d and k.

The last model we analyse is due to Rebelo (1991, 1992). On the one hand, Rebelo assumes that a single type of capital good Z (a composite of physical and human capital) is used in the production process (1992, p. 8); on the other hand, unskilled labour does not enter the production function. This linear growth model is derived from the general setup with the following restrictions:

$$\beta = 0; \quad \alpha + \gamma = 1; \quad h \equiv k \equiv z \qquad (3.28)$$

In this case it is straightforward to check that the rate of growth of *per capita* output is equal to:

$$\frac{\dot{y}}{y} = (d \log y)/dt = [(d \log z)/dt \qquad (3.29)$$

the rate of growth therefore depends on the endogenous rate of factor accumulation. The dynamics of z are subject to constant returns, and the rate of change of z does not approach zero over time. Insofar as capital movements are concerned Rebelo (1992) provides a peculiar prediction – namely, that there exist *no incentives* for capital movements under the standard assumptions on technology, transaction costs and saving behaviour (1992, pp. 22–7). The domestic interest rate in the Rebelo model is given by:

$$r_d = A - \delta \qquad (3.30)$$

As a result, the interest rate is constant across different economies provided A and δ are the same. However, Rebelo (1992) argues that if the marginal tax rate on capital is larger in DCs than in industrial countries, or the average tax rate is expected to be larger in the future, capital could well flow *from* developing to developed economies, even in the presence of capital controls (the so-called 'capital flight' phenomenon).

In Table 3.1 we report the predicted signs of the partial correlations between the marginal product of k and the economic fundamentals analysed by the five models we have just reviewed. Clearly, a positive partial correlation implies that a larger (smaller) value of the explanatory variable raises (lowers) the MPK hence leads, *ceteris paribus*, to a tendency towards net capital inflows (outflows), while the opposite holds in case of a negative partial correlation. Section 3.3 draws on these insights, building a complete neoclassical setup with partial capital mobility.

Table 3.1 Predicted sign of the partial correlation with the marginal product of physical capital

Model (author and year)	Stock of physical capital (or per capita income)	Stock of human capital	Size of the economy (scale effect)
Solow (1956)	Negative	(Not included)	None
Mankiw, Romer and Weil (1992)	Negative	Positive	None
'Modified' Romer (1986)	None (or positive)	(Not included)	Positive
'Modified' Lucas (1988)	Negative	Positive	Positive
Rebelo (1992)	None	None	None

3.3 CAPITAL FLOWS IN A NEOCLASSICAL MODEL WITH RESTRICTED CAPITAL MOBILITY

The basic aggregate neoclassical model (Section 3.1) suggests that, if capital is mobile, one should observe net capital inflows in countries where the (closed-economy) marginal product of capital is higher; under the law of diminishing returns, this should lead to interest rate equalisation, provided one considers risk-adjusted interest rates which approximate the marginal product of capital in different countries. In a two-factor setup, this amounts to saying that capital should move from rich to poor countries.

As shown in Sections 3.1 and 3.2, if we abandon the two-factor neoclassical model we reach different conclusions on the pattern of capital flows. Indeed, several authors have argued that 'capital does not flow from rich to poor countries' because the neoclassical proposition of the two-factor model – namely, that *per capita* income is a good proxy for the inverse of the marginal product of capital – is not supported by the data. Moreover, they have shown that under alternative assumptions returns on capital need not be larger in poor countries (see, among others, Lucas, 1990; Gundlach, 1994).

In a theoretical setup with two capital goods (physical and human capital) one can make alternative assumptions on the extent of capital mobility – that is, one can specify which goods are internationally traded or which goods can be accumulated by borrowing abroad. In a theoretical model of growth and international lending, Cohen and Sachs (1986) assume that only a fraction of the domestic capital stock can be financed with foreign borrowing; Barro, Mankiw and Sala-i-Martin (1995) suppose that all physical capital can be used as collateral for external credit, while human capital cannot (*partial* capital mobility). Obstfeld and Rogoff (1996, pp. 469–73) follow an alternative route and suggest that a constant share of current output can be used as collateral. Chapter 4 provides summaries of the models by Barro, Mankiw and Sala-i-Martin (1995) and Obstfeld and Rogoff (1996), which are focused on the *consequences* of capital mobility for growth and convergence. Here, we will adopt the hypothesis of Barro, Mankiw and Sala-i-Martin (1995).

An implication of partial capital mobility in the neoclassical model is that external borrowing should be consistent with the determinants of the long-run growth rate of an economy, as well as with the hypothesis of 'conditional' convergence (see Section 4.1). Manzocchi and Martin (1997) elaborate an open-economy version of the augmented Solow model featuring partial capital mobility; this section draws on the Manzocchi–Martin (1997) model to provide some refinements of the neoclassical framework. We show how a simple equation for foreign capital inflows can be derived from the augmented Solow model assuming an exogenous dynamics for human capital.[7]

Consider an economy where output (Y) consists of a homogeneous good produced with raw labour, physical capital and human capital (L, K, H, respectively) according to a Cobb Douglas function (we drop the time subscript):

$$Y = AK^\alpha H^\beta L^{1-\alpha-\beta} \quad (3.31)$$

where α and β are positive parameters. Y can be either consumed or invested in the accumulation of H or K. Exogenous technical change is ruled out. We can rewrite this equation in intensive form as:

$$y = f(k; h) = Ak^\alpha h^\beta \quad (3.32)$$

where y, k and h are output, physical and human capital per worker, respectively. For simplicity, we assume that employment is equal to population: setting the initial employment level equal to unity, L grows according to a positive rate of growth of population (n):

$$L = e^{nt} \quad (3.33)$$

The law of motion of human capital is given by:

$$\dot{H} = s_h Y - \delta H \quad \text{or} \quad \dot{h} = s_h y - (n+\delta)h \quad (3.34)$$

where a dot over a variable indicates a time derivative; s_h is the constant fraction of output invested in human capital accumulation and δ is a positive depreciation rate (common to human and physical capital). As far as k is concerned, we assume its accumulation can be fully financed by external borrowing; so we have not the usual dynamic equation linking the evolution of the capital stock to the rate of saving s_k (see 3.4), but instead an arbitrage condition that relates the equilibrium stock of domestic physical capital to the international interest rate and the relevant domestic fundamentals. If individual countries are 'price-takers' on world financial markets, the interest-parity condition requires that the steady-state rate of return on physical capital in the domestic economy be equal to an exogenously *fixed* world interest rate (r, which is assumed to be positive):[8]

$$f_k(k^*; h^*) - \delta = \alpha A(k^*)^{\alpha-1}(h^*)^\alpha - \delta = r \tag{3.35}$$

The steady-state level of k can be expressed as a function of r and h^*:

$$k^* = \left\{ \frac{\alpha A}{r+\delta}(h^*)^\beta \right\}^{\frac{1}{1-\alpha}} \tag{3.36}$$

while h^* can be obtained from (3.34):

$$h^* = \left\{ \frac{s_h A}{n+\delta}(k^*)^\alpha \right\}^{\frac{1}{1-\beta}} \tag{3.37}$$

We can use (3.37) in order to substitute for h^* into equation (3.36) and obtain a reduced form for k^*

$$k^* = \left\{ \frac{\alpha A}{r+\delta} \left(\frac{s_h A}{n+\delta} \right)^{\frac{\beta}{1-\beta}} \right\}^{\frac{1-\beta}{1-\alpha-\beta}} \tag{3.38}$$

We can therefore define the *capital requirement* (or CR) of a developing economy as the distance between the steady-state value of k, which is dictated by the interest-parity condition (3.35), and the initial stock of physical capital per worker (the initial condition $k(0)$):

$$CR = k^* - k(0) \tag{3.39}$$

The assumption of *partial* capital mobility implies that *per capita* net capital inflows are equal to the capital requirement *less* the amount of domestic resources which are neither consumed nor used in the accumulation of human capital. Let us define *per capita* net foreign debt b_t as:

$$b_t = \left(\frac{B}{L}\right)_t \tag{3.40}$$

where B is net cumulated capital inflows (the negative of the cumulated current account balance):

$$B_t = -\int_0^t (\text{current account})_t \tag{3.41}$$

The difference between the steady-state value of *per capita* external debt b^* and its initial value $b(0)$, that is *per capita* net foreign borrowing during the transition is then equal to the capital requirement *minus* the cumulated amount of domestic saving *not* used for human capital accumulation:

$$b^* - b(0) = k^* - k(0) - \int_0^T s(y - rb)_t \tag{3.42}$$

where s is the saving rate related to the resources that are neither consumed nor devoted to human-capital accumulation, the term into parenthesis is *per capita* GNP and T is the period when a steady state is reached.[9] By substitution into (3.42), one gets:

$$b^* - b(0) = \left\{\frac{\alpha A}{r+\delta}\left(\frac{s_h A}{n+\delta}\right)^{\frac{\beta}{1-\beta}}\right\}^{\frac{1-\beta}{1-\alpha-\beta}} - \left\{\frac{y(0)}{A(h(0))^\beta}\right\}^{\frac{1}{\alpha}}$$
$$- \int_0^T s(y - rb)_t \tag{3.43}$$

where the second expression on the right-hand side corresponds to $k(0)$. From (3.43) one can easily check that net capital inflows throughout the transition to the steady state, namely $[b^* - b(0)]$, are a positive function of $h(0)$ and s_h, and a negative function of $y(0)$, n and s, which is consistent with the neoclassical model under the assumption of partial capital mobility (see Mankiw, Romer and Weil, 1992; Barro, Mankiw and Sala-i-Martin, 1995).[10] Notice that under our assumptions on capital mobility, the saving rate s *does not* determine k^* as in the closed-economy augmented Solow model; however, it *affects* the long-run net foreign position of a country as it determines the national resources that enter the worldwide saving pool, and that must therefore be deducted from the domestic capital requirement in order to establish the amount of net *per capita* inflows in the long run. Section 3.4 deals with the demographic determinants of the saving rate.

The model described in this section links capital flows to the initial level of income accounting at the same time for the variables which affect the steady-state *per capita* income of an economy: in other words, it predicts that international capital flows favour conditional (rather than 'absolute') convergence. In the steady state, *per capita* gross output (GDP) and national income (GNP) are given by (3.44) and (3.45), respectively:

$$GDP^* = f(k^*; h^*) \tag{3.44}$$

$$GNP^* = f(k^*; h^*) rb^* \tag{3.45}$$

We will come back to the implications of capital flows for convergence of *per capita* income in Chapter 4.

3.4 DEMOGRAPHY AND INTERNATIONAL CAPITAL MOVEMENTS

In this section we consider the impact of demographic variables on net international capital flows; an overlapping-generations (OLG) setup is outlined which allows a neat description of the age structure of population. We will confine the analysis to a simple model without human capital, and with a unique asset that can be saved and invested either in physical capital or in foreign assets. Nonetheless, under the hypothesis of capital mobility limited to physical assets, and with a fixed share of *per capita* output invested in human capital, one can envisage the qualitative predictions of a more complete model concerning net capital inflows. In general, the implications of OLG models for capital flows chiefly depend on the inherent cohort structure of the population: in the following two-generation framework an increase in n, the growth rate of population, leads to an increase in *per capita* investment *and* saving, while in more complex generational setups it can lead to a fall in the saving rate.

Consider some basic accounting identities for an open economy inhabited by individuals who live two periods; for simplicity, each generation consists of only one individual and a new generation is born each period.[11] If only young individuals work and save, while the old generation does not work and dissaves, aggregate saving (of the young) is given by:

$$S_t = K_{t+1} - B_{t+1} \tag{3.46}$$

where S, K and B are, respectively, aggregate saving, the capital stock and net foreign debt. If in the steady state the capital–labour ratio is fixed at the international level by an arbitrage condition analogous to (3.15) and individual saving is constant (this is due to the assumption of perfect capital mobility in a two-factor setup, see Obstfeld and Rogoff, 1996, p. 158), then aggregate saving of the young must satisfy:

$$s_t^Y = (1+n)(k_{t+1} - b_{t+1}) \tag{3.47}$$

where lowercase variables denote aggregate variables divided by the size of the labour force L at time t. Notice, however, that in this case L_t is the size of the cohort which is born at time t (the young) and not overall population as in Section 3.1. As s^Y and k are constant in a steady state at s^{Y*} and k^*, b^* is also constant:

$$b^* = k^* - \frac{s^{Y*}}{1+n} \tag{3.48}$$

One can check that, if b^* is positive, the amount of net foreign debt due by each member of the young generation at the end of the working period is an increasing function of the growth rate of population: if generations grow at a faster pace, the savings of each generation at time t cover a lower portion of the aggregate capital requirement at time $(t+1)$ hence more foreign borrowing is required in the steady state. However, as foreign debt (or assets) grow at the same rate as the labour force and output solvency is assured (Obstfeld and Rogoff, 1996, p. 159).

We can now address the question of the effects of population growth on the saving rate of this economy; provided s^O is the (negative) saving rate of the old generation, the aggregate *per capita saving rate* in the steady state is given by:

$$\frac{S_t^Y + S_t^O}{L_t + L_{t-1}} = \frac{(1+n)}{(2+n)} s^Y + \frac{1}{(2+n)} s^O \tag{3.49}$$

(recall that $L_t = L_{t-1}(1+n)$) hence higher population growth raises the overall *per capita* saving rate as it shifts the composition of population towards young savers instead of old dissavers.

The steady-state rate of *per capita investment*, in the absence of depreciation, is that required to keep k at its stationary value of k^* in the presence of a rising labour force:

$$\frac{K_{t+1} - K_t}{L_t + L_{t-1}} = \frac{(1+n)n}{(2+n)}(k^*) \qquad (3.50)$$

A rise in n will therefore lead to an increase in *both per capita* saving and investment in the steady state even if the capital–labour ratio and the young's saving rate are constant. The impact on net capital flows is ambiguous: if the saving effect prevails, a rise in n tends to improve the current account, hence to reduce *per capita* net foreign borrowing; if the converse is true, *per capita* net foreign borrowing is fostered. A comparison of these results with (3.13) reveals that an increase in n affects both the capital requirement and the overall saving rate in an economy with overlapping generations. The higher s^Y with respect to s^O, the more an increase in n has a positive impact on *per capita* saving; the larger the distance between the initial and steady-state capital–labour ratio, the more population growth raises the capital requirement of a developing economy. We can speculate on how extending this model to human capital could affect the results: if the saving rate referred to human capital is *fixed* as in Section 3.3, and capital mobility is limited to physical assets, a larger growth rate is likely to negatively affect the MPK (see the first term on the right-hand side of (3.13)) hence to reduce the capital requirement of a developing economy. However, this speculation is largely imperfect as it is based on a two-generation model where investment in human capital of the young necessarily has to be financed by the saving of the old generation: the insights could be partly different in a model that explicitly allows for a dependent young generation.

This leads us to the main limitations of the former theoretical setup: first its predictions are valid only in a two-generation context, where the young are *necessarily* net savers (no bequests); second it is based on the comparative analysis of alternative steady states and neglects transitional 'out-of-steady-state' features.

The behaviour of saving and investment rates in response to changes in population growth depends in OLG models on the number and characteristics of the cohorts: if instead of a two-generation setup with no bequests, we build a model with three generations including dependent youth, the conclusions are radically altered. Higgins and Williamson (1996, pp. 13–14) show that in this case a rise in n still leads to an increase in the investment rate while the impact on aggregate saving consists of two elements: on the one hand, faster population growth lowers saving by boosting the young dependent cohort; on the other hand, it promotes saving by reducing the burden of the dissaving elderly. The net effect on *per capita* saving is likely to depend on initial conditions such as the shares of the individual cohorts over total population and the initial rate of growth of L; however the investment channel is likely to dominate so that a fall in the current account (an increase in net borrowing) occurs in response to a rise in n.

Yet another case is when the old cohort does not fully dissave its wealth but partially transfers it to the dependent youth or to the working-age generation. In this case a reduction in n could actually raise the saving rate through a downsizing of the 'true' dissaving cohort, the dependent youth.

Higgins and Williamson (1996) emphasise another drawback of the basic OLG model and of its refinements – namely, that they restrict the analysis to steady-state positions, dismissing transitional behaviour that might however be rather persistent in the case of demographic dynamics. Kuznets (1966, pp. 437–44) provides an early statistical account of the so-called 'demographic transition' in DCs, which has been historically triggered first by a fall in death rates, especially infant mortality, which raises the rate of population growth and afterwards by a gradual decline in fertility rates which temporarily inflates the relative share of working-age adults but over time causes an expansion of the old generation. This pattern has emerged, with various peculiarities, from demographic developments in Europe, North America and more recently Latin America and East Asia: the study of demographic patterns should therefore not exclusively focus on steady-state phenomena (a permanent rise in n) but also on this kind of transitional but long-lasting evolution.

3.5 WHICH IMPLICATIONS FOR EMPIRICAL ANALYSIS?

The models reviewed in Sections 3.1 and 3.2 enable us to establish a link between the marginal product of physical capital (MPK) and other fundamental variables of a developing economy. As shown in Table 3.1, the basic neoclassical model predicts that the MPK is negatively linked with *per capita* income, hence 'poorer' countries should, *ceteris paribus*, look more attractive for investment on an international basis. Several reasons can be advanced to argue why this need not be the case, as pointed out by Lucas (1990), but the more interesting ones from our perspective dwell on the recent refinements of growth theory itself. The 'augmented' Solow model, suggested by Mankiw, Romer and Weil (1992) to deal with some drawbacks of the original model, predicts that the MPK is negatively correlated with *per capita* income only if the stock of human capital per worker is constant across countries (or periods): otherwise, the MPK depends on both *per capita* income (negative partial correlation) and *per capita* human capital (positive partial correlation). In a model with many capital assets, an additional assumption on the different degree of capital mobility concerning these assets can be made: we adopted the notion of 'partial' capital mobility which implies full (no) mobility for physical (human) capital, and the predictions of the augmented model stem from this assumption as well. (The implications of the augmented model for capital flows in a developing economy are spelled out fully in Section 3.3).

The original Romer (1986) endogenous growth setup is open to various parameter configurations, and one can slightly modify it to show that it is possible to break the negative connection between *per capita* income and the MPK: all that is needed is a model where physical capital does not display decreasing returns. Moreover, scale effects can be easily introduced, leading to a positive partial correlation between the return on capital and the size of the economy (measured by population or GDP). The case of the Lucas (1988) one-good model is even more intriguing: although the model yields endogenous growth caused by the absence of decreasing returns in the accumulation of human capital (recall 3.25 and 3.26),[12] the predictions on the MPK do not qualitatively differ from those of the augmented neoclassical model. This is true if we make the assumption of partial capital mobility, therefore preventing an external financing of human capital accumulation, and if there are no 'scale effects' (as in the original Lucas paper): if one allows for economywide scale economies, the positive correlation between the MPK and size re-appears. However, both the augmented and the original Lucas model predict a negative partial correlation between the MPK and *per capita* income if one controls for human capital endowments.

Two main lessons for empirical research on capital inflows in DCs arise from Section 3.4: first, the predictions of OLG models in terms of saving, investment and net capital flows are sensitive to changes in the

Growth Theory and the Determinants of Capital Flows 53

cohort design incorporated in the model; second, the actual outcomes of demographic dynamics are better captured in an empirical model if the growth rate of population is supplemented by some indicator of the age structure, such as dependency rates.

Three general conclusions can be drawn that will prove useful in the econometric investigations of Chapter 6. First, as capital mobility is neither absent nor perfect in actual economies, and in DCs in particular (see Chapter 5), a concept of 'restricted' mobility can be adequate to approximate reality. Capital mobility can be restricted to a portion of the capital stock (as in Cohen and Sachs, 1986), to some specific capital assets (Barro, Mankiw and Sala-i-Martin, 1995) or to a portion of output (Obstfeld and Rogoff, 1996, Chapter 7). In a growth-theory context, 'partial' capital mobility (limited to physical capital) turns out to be an interesting hypothesis as it allows us to discriminate among different prototype models. Second, growth models offer downright predictions about the relation between the MPK and some structural variables: these predictions constitute the background for the empirics of Chapter 6. However, it is not always possible to discriminate across alternative models on the basis of this set of variables: obviously, much has to be done in order to further distinguish among different theories, and to corroborate or falsify them. Third, while the fully fledged neoclassical model of Section 3.3 links the *per capita* amount of foreign inflows to domestic fundamentals, one can check that (3.43) is not a 'true' reduced-form equation as the integral of domestic saving on the right-hand side includes *per capita* income that is a function of previous (and current) capital inflows. This points to one of the most serious problems in growth econometrics – namely, endogeneity: instead of addressing this problem with complex but controversial techniques, we will seek a way of by-passing it in Chapter 6.

The models exposed in this chapter were adapted with an emphasis on the *determinants* of capital movements, especially in DCs; Chapter 4 looks at growth models with a focus on the *consequences* of capital flows.

4 Growth Theory and the Effects of Capital Flows

This chapter deals with the long-run effects of international capital flows from the perspective of growth theory. Our main concern is with the impact of capital flows on growth and 'convergence', a concept which is variously defined according to the underlying theoretical framework; as in Chapter 3 we outline different models that are of general relevance, but we then apply them to the case of developing economies. As we focus on the long run, the use of external capital as an instrument for consumption-smoothing is neglected. However, while in Sections 4.1 and 4.2 we rule out the possibility that a country mortgages a constant stream of future (*per capita*) income to increase current consumption, this possibility is allowed for in the model of Section 4.3. This enriches the range of feasible outcomes stemming from integration in world capital markets.

We illustrate three approaches to the long-run consequences of capital movements derived from recent refinements in the theory of economic growth. Two models share an assumption of restricted, or limited, capital mobility, while a third postulates either null or complete mobility. The first is a neoclassical model based on Mankiw, Romer and Weil (1992) and Barro Mankiw and Sala-i-Martin (1995): it offers a basically optimistic view of the effects of capital mobility in developing economies. Foreign capital leads to a faster rate of 'conditional' convergence to the steady state, even if the model does not yield instantaneous convergence as in the open-economy extension of the Solow model (Section 4.1). We then outline the main findings of an overlapping-generations (OLG) model by Obstfeld and Rogoff (1996) which embodies a different constraint on capital mobility, based on current income rather than capital endowments: the authors argue that this assumption provides a more realistic picture of international credit relations (Section 4.2). Their results on growth and convergence in developing economies are at first glance less favourable than those of the neoclassical model with partial mobility: as the ability to borrow hinges on current income rather than on the stock of human capital, 'impatient' countries may not reach under restricted mobility the same steady state they would approach with full mobility. A restriction on capital mobility does not only affect the speed of convergence but can therefore also lead to a lower level of *per capita* output in the steady state. A coordination-failure model is then introduced in Section 4.3: it shows that capital mobility is ineffective to raise average labour productivity in a backward economy unless a sufficient degree of coordination among atomistic agents is achieved. In this model, foreign borrowing can alternatively be used to discount a constant stream of future income or to lift *per capita* output, depending on the ability to coordinate decentralised decisions. Hence the latter model allows for a more pessimistic scenario of the consequences of capital flows in developing economies.

The theoretical findings of this chapter set the stage for an empirical analysis about the impact of capital flows on growth in DCs, as well as on the related comovements in consumption and investment (Chapter 7).

4.1 GROWTH AND CONVERGENCE IN NEOCLASSICAL MODELS WITH CAPITAL MOBILITY

We mentioned in Section 3.3 that the issue of long-term capital flows has an obvious relation with the debate on the sources of economic growth and 'convergence'. According to Mankiw, Romer and Weil (1992), one ought to distinguish between 'absolute' and 'conditional' convergence: the former refers to the narrowing of *income differentials* among economies that are all moving towards a unique steady state; 'conditional convergence' means that the *rate of growth* of an economy is proportional to the distance from the steady state, but different countries may end up in different steady states and their income levels may *not* converge.[1] Under this definition, convergence in the closed economy is conditional on the evolution of physical and human capital, as well as other variables (see Levine and Renelt, 1992). As far as physical capital is concerned, Barro (1991) and Mankiw, Romer and Weil (1992) following Solow (1956) stressed the relevance of investment rates, while De Long and Summers (1991, 1993) and Lee (1994) found that equipment investment was positively related to income growth over 1960–85, and Knight, Loayza and Villanueva (1993) that public investment promotes growth. The empirical relation between human capital and growth is analysed in Romer (1990), Barro (1991), Mankiw, Romer and Weil (1992), Barro and Lee (1994) and Benhabib and

Spiegel (1994), while Barro and Lee (1993) and OECD (1998) provide international comparisons of educational attainment.

The open-economy version of the neoclassical growth model (with one capital good) predicts that convergence will occur *instantaneously* if full capital mobility holds and there are no adjustment costs; however, the empirically estimated coefficient of international or interregional convergence is clearly finite, with estimates ranging from 2 per cent per year (Barro and Sala-i-Martin, 1992) to 6–15 per cent in more recent studies (Islam, 1995; Evans, 1997). A rather popular argument is that a low speed of convergence among countries is due to the absence of international capital mobility, particularly in developing countries (DCs), but recent empirical studies tend to reject the hypothesis that capital mobility is absent in DCs (see Section 5.3).

The picture changes if capital mobility is present but limited in neoclassical models. Barro, Mankiw and Sala-i-Martin (1995) explore this perspective on the links between capital mobility and convergence, showing that the speed of convergence is substantially lower in the open economy if capital mobility applies to only a sub-set of capital assets – for instance, to physical but not human capital (*partial* capital mobility). They argue that human capital cannot be used as collateral for external borrowing because property rights on human capital are hardly enforceable at the international level. Another reason why human capital accumulation might not be financed through foreign borrowing is that even in the closed economy the incompleteness of financial markets hinders trade in human capital assets (De Gregorio, 1993; Goldstein and Mussa, 1993; Ljungqvist, 1993). The assumption of partial mobility is interesting because it provides a simple approximation of an empirical evidence – namely, that international capital mobility is neither null nor perfect, but is present and bounded in the real world and especially in DCs (we shall have more to say on this point in Chapter 5).

The conclusions obtained by Barro, Mankiw and Sala-i-Martin (1995) can be replicated in models such as those of Chapter 3, in which consumption does not follow an optimising rule but is a constant fraction of current *per capita* income. Let us start from the one-capital good Solow model in a closed-economy context. In order to find a measure of the speed of convergence to the steady state, we combine (3.7) and (3.4) to get:

$$\dot{k} = s_k y - (\delta + n)k \qquad (4.1)$$

where lowercase letters indicate *per capita* variables (recall that the labour force is set equal to population). Now, if we adopt the parameter restrictions of the Solow model on the aggregate production function (see 3.1), we obtain:

$$\dot{k} = s_k A k^\alpha - (\delta + n)k \qquad (4.2)$$

while the rate of change of k is given by:

$$\frac{\dot{k}}{k} = s_k A k^{-(1-\alpha)} - (\delta + n) \qquad (4.3)$$

Taking a linear approximation of (4.3) in the neighbourhood of the steady state, we obtain (see the Appendix on p. 74):

$$\frac{\dot{k}}{k} = \frac{(d \log k)}{dt} \cong -\beta \left[\log \left(\frac{k}{k^*} \right) \right] \qquad (4.4)$$

where β is the speed of convergence to the steady state whose value is given by:

$$\beta = (1-\alpha)(\delta + n) \qquad (4.5)$$

The speed of convergence indicates how rapidly an economy approaches its stationary equilibrium in terms of *per capita* variables, hence for a developing economy starting below its steady-state position it is a measure of how fast it can grow and fill the gap with its long-run *per capita* income level.[2] One can check that is also the speed of convergence of *per capita* output; rewrite (3.13) as

$$\frac{\dot{y}}{y} = \alpha \frac{(d \log k)}{dt} \cong -\beta \left[\alpha \log \left(\frac{k}{k^*} \right) \right] = -\beta \left[\log \left(\frac{y}{y^*} \right) \right] \qquad (4.6)$$

hence β is the rate of convergence of y as well.

One can check that the speed of convergence is inversely related to the capital share α: the larger the capital share, the less effective are diminishing returns to capital accumulation, hence the longer the transition to the steady state. The case of a developing country can be represented by an initial condition $k(0) < k^*$: one can then verify that the logarithm into brackets on the right-hand side of (4.4) is negative, hence *per capita* growth is positive. When α equals unity we have endogenous growth: in this case there are no diminishing returns to capital accumulation hence there is neither a steady state nor a tendency toward convergence in this one-capital good framework (see Section 3.2).

What happens to the speed of convergence in the Solow model if we assume perfect capital mobility? Equations (3.14) and (3.15) in Section 3.1 imply that in equilibrium the marginal product of capital (MPK), and therefore k^*, are tied to their international levels by an arbitrage condition. This means that the accumulation of physical capital no longer depends on domestic saving and the speed to convergence to the steady state is infinite. In other words, the gap between $k(0)$ and k^* is covered instantaneously once existing barriers to capital mobility are removed: a crucial condition for this result is the absence of adjustment or time-to-build costs in the investment process. An *infinite* speed of convergence in the open-economy Solow model is a disturbing theoretical prediction as it clearly stands in contrast to actual experiences of international or inter-regional convergence, even in periods and areas of relatively high capital market integration. The estimates of the speed of convergence range from 2 per cent a year in early studies (Barro and Sala-i-Martin, 1992) to 6–15 per cent in more recent works (Islam, 1995; Evans and Karras, 1996; Evans, 1997; Caselli, Esquivel and Lefort, 1997).

The assumption of *partial* capital mobility in neoclassical growth models is a solution, not the unique one, to this theoretical impasse. It makes the neoclassical model consistent with a finite speed of convergence to the steady state both in the closed- and the open-economy setup; moreover it delivers the optimistic prediction that capital mobility, although restricted, enhances the transitional growth rate in developing economies (Barro, Mankiw and Sala-i-Martin, 1995). These theoretical findings can be replicated in a two-capital good framework such as the one of Sections 3.1 and 3.3. Consider first the closed-economy case and notice that, while the growth rate of physical capital is still ruled by (3.7) and (3.4), we can rewrite it in the following way:

$$\frac{\dot{k}}{k} = s_k A k^{-(1-\alpha)} h^\gamma - (\delta + n) \qquad (4.7)$$

under constant returns to scale (see 3.16). Analogously we can rewrite the equation for the growth rate of human capital:

$$\frac{\dot{h}}{h} = s_h A k^\alpha h^{-(1-\gamma)} - (\delta + n) \qquad (4.8)$$

Linearising around the steady state, and recalling that finite values for k^* and h^* are given in (3.9) and (3.10), one can show that the speed of convergence in the neoclassical model with two capital goods is:[3]

$$\beta^C = (1 - \alpha - \gamma)(\delta + n) \quad (4.9)$$

which is lower than in the closed-economy Solow model if the value of all parameters is invariant across models (see Mankiw, Romer and Weil, 1992, pp. 422–3). If we introduce partial capital mobility in this setup, the level of k is no longer dictated by domestic saving, but instead by an international arbitrage condition that equalises the domestic MPK (given by 3.19) to the world interest rate. From these relationships one obtains:

$$y = [\alpha A^{\frac{1}{\alpha}} h^{\frac{\gamma}{\alpha}}]^{\frac{\alpha}{1-\alpha}}(r + \delta)^{\frac{\alpha}{\alpha-1}} \quad (4.10)$$

An expression for the rate of growth of human capital – that is, the variable driving the transition of *per capita* output once the level of physical capital is permanently governed by international arbitrage – follows from (3.5) and (4.10):

$$\frac{\dot{h}}{h} = s_h[\alpha A^{\frac{1}{\alpha}}]^{\frac{\alpha}{1-\alpha}}(r + \delta)^{\frac{\alpha}{\alpha-1}} h^{-\frac{(1-\alpha-\gamma)}{(1-\alpha)}} - (\delta + n) \quad (4.11)$$

while the linearisation around the steady state yields the subsequent speed of convergence for the open economy with partial capital mobility (see the Appendix on p. 76):

$$\beta^O = \frac{(1 - \alpha - \gamma)}{(1 - \alpha)}(\delta + n) \quad (4.12)$$

One can easily check that the speed of convergence is larger in the open (β^O) than in the closed economy (β^C) as long as the physical capital share α is positive and less than one as postulated in the neoclassical model. This means that capital mobility, even if limited to physical assets, accelerates the transition to the steady state and raises the growth rate of a developing economy. The rationale for this result is that partial mobility removes one of the constraints which holds in the closed economy (namely, that imposed by s_k on the growth rate of k). However, convergence does not occur instantaneously in the open economy as in the Solow model, thus the speed of convergence β^O is finite.

In conclusion, the message of the neoclassical model with restricted capital mobility is rather optimistic as far as a developing economy is concerned: first, this economy presumably becomes open to capital flows when its *per capita* physical capital stock is below its steady-state level, hence a DC gains from international integration as the speed of convergence is enhanced.[4] Second, with partial capital mobility the transition is never instantaneous and the speed of convergence is always finite: this prediction is reassuring as it is more easily reconciled with a broad set of empirical evidence on conditional convergence. Nevertheless, a few substantial warnings are required that are also relevant for an empirical research on the impact of capital flows in DCs. The optimistic outcomes of the neoclassical model are warranted *if and only if* the initial levels and accumulation rates of human capital are sufficiently high in developing economies: from (3.19) it is clear that in any period the MPK depends on the *current* stock of human capital, hence it is not at all obvious that a DC will be a net recipient of international flows. Moreover, the steady-state level of h depends on the domestic accumulation rate s_h which imposes another constraint on the long-run inflows of net resources from abroad (see Section 3.3 for a more detailed exposition of this argument). There is yet another problem, related to the fungible nature of capital inflows: a common assumption in the previous analysis is that foreign resources are *effectively* employed in capital accumulation and not consumed, and that investment is always successful. However, there is no guarantee that this is the case: foreign capital inflows could be channelled to raising current consumption standards, or could be engaged in (*ex post*) weak investment projects. Chapter 7 will look at the empirical evidence on growth and foreign capital in DCs over a whole capital-flow cycle (that of 1960–88).

4.2 AN OVERLAPPING-GENERATIONS MODEL WITH RESTRICTED CAPITAL MOBILITY

Obstfeld and Rogoff (1996, pp. 469–73) model restricted capital mobility in a different way than Barro, Mankiw and Sala-i-Martin (1995), yet reach comparable results in a two-period overlapping-generations (OLG) model of growth and international lending. Instead of imposing a borrowing constraint based on the distinct nature of capital assets, Obstfeld and Rogoff require a country's net foreign debt not to exceed a fraction of current wage income: their rationale is that seizing physical capital assets is no easier than capturing future earnings from human capital in an international setting. Although their criticism can be justified by actual experiences of foreign debt default and bargaining, it misses a point: as argued in Section 4.1, debt leverage is more likely to be available for investment in physical capital than in education and training even within the boundaries of a national economy.

The implications for growth and convergence of this kind of restriction on capital mobility are more gloomy for a developing economy (an economy with a lower autarky stock of k) than in the neoclassical model with partial mobility: 'impatient' countries may not be able to reach under restricted mobility the same steady state they would approach under full mobility *with the same configuration of parameters*. Restricted mobility does not therefore affect only the speed of convergence but can also lead to lower *per capita* output in the steady state with respect to the full-mobility condition. To see why this result holds, consider the autarky interest rate which is given by:

$$r_d = \alpha k^{\alpha - 1} - \delta \tag{4.13}$$

as the model is simplified by ruling out human capital. The borrowing constraint is:

$$b_{t+1} \leq \eta w_t \tag{4.14}$$

where b is *per capita* net foreign debt, w is the wage earned by each young individual and η is a positive parameter less than unity. The most relevant case for a developing economy is when the autarky interest rate is above the world rate (see also Section 4.3); in this case individuals will always choose the highest level of borrowing – in other words, the constraint (4.14) is binding. Obstfeld and Rogoff (1996, p. 472) show that under these conditions the developing economy will reach a steady state where k is smaller than in the unconstrained steady state if (4.15) holds:

$$(s + \eta)\bar{w}_U < \bar{k}_U \tag{4.15}$$

where s is the young-generation saving rate while the values of the wage rate and the capital stock are those of the *unconstrained* equilibrium. The interpretation of condition (4.15) is straightforward: if in the steady state with unrestrained borrowing (or full capital mobility) the stock of k is larger than *per capita* saving *plus* the maximum amount of credit available under the borrowing constraint, then the unrestrained steady state is not feasible when the constraint is binding. To see why, one can check that the left-hand side of (4.15) represents all resources available for investment if a country starts from the unconstrained steady state but can borrow only a fraction η of the young's wage: hence *that* steady state is dynamically unsustainable and the economy will converge towards a lower level of k.

The message conveyed by this model looks thus less favourable concerning the impact of capital flows for DCs: while we saw in Section 4.1 that *partial* capital mobility leads to a slower speed of convergence compared with full mobility in the neoclassical model, here a limitation on the amount of resources that can be borrowed abroad may also lead to an inferior equilibrium. However, this contradiction is partly apparent: our focus on the speed of convergence in Section 4.1 was motivated by the need to contrast the finite speed predicted by the partial-mobility model with the infinite speed of the open-economy Solow model, but we were referring to *conditional* convergence. The neoclassical model with human capital and partial mobility predicts that the steady state *is the same* for a given configuration of preferences and technological parameters (see for instance Barro, Mankiw and Sala-i-Martin 1995, p. 106): preferences (namely, saving rates) enters the definition of k^* (see 3.9 and 3.38), thus individual economies will *not* converge to the same stationary equilibrium unless they share the same parameters. Obstfeld and Rogoff show that under some conditions unlimited capital mobility can be consistent with absolute convergence even if preferences differ across countries (1996, pp. 471–2): nonetheless, a ceiling to the amount that can be borrowed re-establishes the role of cross-country idiosyncrasies in the definition of long-run equilibrium.

Until now, we have emphasised that foreign capital contributes to the accumulation of the domestic capital stock; Section 4.3 illustrates a case in which external borrowing can be used either for raising *per capita* output or for discounting a *constant* flow of future output.

4.3 A COORDINATION-FAILURE MODEL OF SECTORAL CHANGE AND FOREIGN BORROWING

Cross-country econometric studies of growth and catching-up among national economies (see Feder, 1986; Cho, 1990b; Dowrick and Gemmel, 1991; Naqui, 1995), as well as comparative research on the industrialisation process (see the essays collected in Chenery, Robinson and

Syrquin 1986) stress two relevant features, among others, of the development process. First, absolute convergence in *per capita* income occurs only between those countries which have overcome some 'threshold' level of development, and the industrial countries, while poor countries lag behind.[5] Second, 'industrialisation' or the process of structural change defined as the shift of productive resources from 'traditional' to 'modern' sectors, comes along with a strong increase in average factor productivity, a true peak in the rate of change of output per worker that partly accounts for the 'Solow residual' of growth-accounting studies (the so-called total factor productivity or TFP).[6]

The revival of growth theory triggered by the works of Romer (1986) and Lucas (1988) has yielded a large number of theoretical models which try to reproduce some features of actual growth experiences, features that were not accounted for by old-style models.[7] Hence, there have been a few attempts within the tradition of equilibrium theory with efficient competitive markets to model the peak in productivity growth corresponding to the industrialisation process, and to account for the empirical results on 'convergence' and 'divergence' of *per capita* incomes (see Dowrick and Gemmel, 1991; Barro and Sala-i-Martin, 1992).

First, in the context of one-sector models, non-linearities have been introduced in the aggregate production function which generate bifurcations in correspondence with 'threshold' levels of development (as measured by levels of *per capita* income): once a country attains a given level of development, it enters a phase of large productivity gains so that convergence with more developed countries occurs.[8]

Second, a modelling strategy has been to postulate the existence of two different production techniques in a one-sector economy, and of a fixed cost to be incurred by each individual in order to move from the traditional (inferior) technique to the modern (superior) one. Individual agents are supposed to be heterogeneous in terms of their capital endowments, so that the probability of adopting the modern technique while fulfilling the constraints of intertemporal utility maximisation is different among agents. As a result, the change from the old to the new technique is a continuous process displaying the mentioned properties of the industrialisation process in terms of TFP and convergence.[9]

Finally, two-sector models where one ('traditional') sector is characterised by constant returns to scale and the other ('modern') one by increasing returns have been introduced by Krugman (1991) and Matsuyama (1991, 1992). In the Krugman model, agents are homogeneous and total adjustment costs are quadratic implying a limitation on the amount of resources reallocated in each period. In this setup, 'convergence' can be defined as the consequence of a process of sectoral shift from the traditional to the modern sector, and it may or may not occur depending on what are the determinants of the sectoral allocation of labour in the long run.

In this section we study the implications of capital mobility in a simple *two-sector* model of resource allocation and 'industrialisation'. Two issues are addressed. First, provided a DC has access to the world credit market, what are the effects of capital inflows for the development process? In other words: under what conditions can foreign borrowing contribute to the 'take-off' of a 'poor' economy? We will show that, in the presence of external economies of scale at the aggregate level, foreign borrowing may either play a purely financial role or affect the productive structure of the economy, depending on the persistence of 'coordination failures' among individual agents.[10] Second, under what conditions can the amount of foreign borrowing of a developing country be 'sub-optimal'? Lucas (1988, 1990) argues that a low amount of long-run inflows is a consequence of the poor endowment of human capital in DCs (see Section 3.2). An alternative explanation of the low amount of long-run capital inflows in DCs is provided in this section: it is shown that the amount of external borrowing of a 'poor' country can be bounded by the inability of individual agents to coordinate themselves in an environment where positive production externalities are at play.

Briefly, the argument is as follows: a process of sectoral change ('industrialisation') that moves productive resources towards a 'modern' sector allows for a rise in average factor productivity in an economy previously specialised in 'traditional' activities. However, such a process is costly in terms of forgone current utility: rational agents will compare current losses and future gains according to a domestic discount rate, in order to decide on the future allocation of their resources. The relevant point is that the outcome of their choices crucially depends on the decisions of other identical agents, as production is characterised by external economies of scale in the modern sector. Therefore, there is room for coordination failures in a decentralised economy.[11] Foreign borrowing *can* be a key factor in economic development whenever the domestic discount rate is too high for the process of sectoral change to start; in any case, the coordination problem just mentioned must be solved. Otherwise, foreign credit will merely be an instrument for the intertemporal redistribution of a given amount of output. The main conclusion is that, contrary to the neo-classical model, *even full capital mobility may not be a sufficient condition for 'convergence'* (which in this context is defined as a sectoral shift of labour from the traditional to the modern sector) whenever there exists a coordination deficit. The absence of convergence cannot in this case be attributed to the low degree of capital mobility, but rather to the structural features of the development process and to its coordination requirements.

The Model with no Capital Mobility

A sharp distinction has often been drawn in international economics between the theory of international trade and balance of payments theory: in the first case, it is often assumed that the current account is balanced; in the second case, usual one-commodity models prevent the analysis of patterns of specialisation and trade (at least in the common meaning of the exchange of different goods: they deal, of course, with intertemporal trade). This dichotomy does not necessarily apply in the present context: a country's productive specialisation and its net foreign asset position can be simultaneously determined as a consequence of its integration in the world capital market. Notice that the model is not meant to reproduce alternative growth patterns, but to analyse the conditions under which a process of structural change towards an increasing-returns-to scale technology may occur.

The setup is highly stylised: consider a two-period, two-sector small economy, where one industry (the traditional one) operates under constant returns to scale, while the modern industry operates under increasing returns due to *external* economies of scale. In the Ricardian tradition, there is just one homogeneous factor of production (labour). Aggregate production activities in the two sectors are described by (4.16) and (4.17), respectively:

$$Q_1 = l_1 \tag{4.16}$$

$$Q_2 = l_2^{(1+\alpha)} \tag{4.17}$$

where Q_i and l_i are, respectively, final output and the number of workers employed in the ith industry ($i = 1, 2$), and α is a positive parameter. All workers are self-employed, hence the number of firms equals that of workers.

Labour supply (assumed equal to population) is constant and equal to L over the two periods, and the full employment condition holds:

$$l_1 + l_2 = L \tag{4.18}$$

(where L, l_1 and l_2 are integers).

Labour is allowed to move from one industry to the other, but there is a cost involved in the process of sectoral change. For example, we can assume that in order to switch into the modern sector each worker must devote part of her current-period working time to self-made training which allows her to raise her future productivity.

Provided γ is the *individual* adjustment cost that must be paid (in period 1) by a worker in order to move from one sector into the other in period 2, the *aggregate* adjustment cost associated with the reallocation of labour is given by (4.19):

$$C = \frac{1}{2}\gamma \sum_i |dl_i| \quad i = 1, 2 \tag{4.19}$$

where C is the aggregate adjustment cost to be paid in period 1 to modify the composition of the productive activity in period 2, and $|dl_i|$ is the absolute value of the differential in the number of workers operating in the ith sector from period 1 to period 2.

Let us now define a 'developing' or 'Southern' economy as an economy that is *fully specialised* in the constant-returns-to-scale sector in period 1 (i.e. l_1 is equal to L in period 1); under the assumption of complete traditional specialisation, (4.19) can be re-stated as (4.19′):

$$C = \gamma l_2 \tag{4.19′}$$

as, by definition, l_2 is zero in period 1. Furthermore, let us assume that this economy is 'small' and integrated in international trade – namely, its residents can exchange goods at the world terms-of-trade (p), where p is the price of good 2 in terms of good 1. As far as capital mobility is concerned, we distinguish between two regimes: regime 1 (financial autarky) in which foreign borrowing or lending is prevented, and the current account is constantly equal to zero; and regime 2 (perfect financial integration), in which foreign borrowing and current account imbalances are allowed provided the solvency requirement is fulfilled.

Let us assume that individual discounted utility is a linearly separable function of personal consumption in periods 1 and 2. First, let us consider the case of *no foreign borrowing* (*financial autarky regime*). The discounted utility of a representative agent (a worker) in the developing economy, who remains in the traditional sector in period 2, is equal to:

$$v = 1 + \left(\frac{1}{1+\rho}\right) \tag{4.20a}$$

where ρ is the (positive) domestic rate of intertemporal discount.

If otherwise the individual enters the modern sector in the second period *together with other* $(l_2 - 1)$ *fellow-workers*, her discounted utility is given by:

$$v' = 1 - \gamma + \left(\frac{1}{1+\rho}\right) p(l_2)^\alpha \qquad (4.20b)$$

where $p(l_2)^\alpha$ is the value of *per capita* output in sector 2, expressed in terms of commodity 1. As mentioned before, the individual adjustment cost (γ) is incurred in period 1 in order to enter the modern sector in period 2. We make the following hypothesis on the content of the 'information set' of the representative agent: she knows exactly the 'structure' of the economy (namely, she knows the functional form of each equation of the model, and the correct value of each parameter, including L, ρ and p), but she can only *ex post* observe the behaviour of other agents in the economy (namely, she does not know in advance whether her fellow-workers will choose to move into the increasing-returns sector or will stay in the constant-returns one).

We have two relevant cases:[12]

Case 1

$$\frac{1}{1+\rho} < \frac{\gamma}{pL^\alpha - 1} \qquad (4.21)$$

Condition (4.21) states that the domestic discount factor is lower than the ratio of the unit cost of adjustment to the average productivity advantage of the modern industry when *all* the workers move away from the traditional sector ($pL^\alpha - 1$). Under the assumption of increasing returns to scale in the modern sector, the (*ex post*) average productivity advantage is a monotonic (increasing) function of l_2: if (4.21) holds, total labour supply is insufficient to yield a large enough gain in productivity from sectoral change even when every worker shifts into the modern sector.

As individuals are aware of the meaning of condition (4.21), nobody will enter the modern sector in period 2. Hence, the productive structure of a backward economy will not evolve from 'traditional' to 'modern', and no 'jump' in factor productivity will occur: we have an example of 'lock-in' traditional production.

Case 2

$$\frac{1}{1+\rho} = \frac{\gamma}{p(l_2^*)^\alpha - 1} \quad L > l_2^* > 1 \quad (4.22)$$

In this case, one can show that it is convenient for an individual worker to enter the modern sector if *at least* other l_2^* agents do the same: to check for this result, substitute the right-hand side of (4.22) for the discount factor into (4.20a) and (4.20b), set l_2 equal to $(l_2^* + 1)$ in (4.20b), and verify that v' is larger than v. However, an individual worker will suffer from a reduction in her discounted utility whenever she enters the modern sector in period 2 and less than other $(l_2^* - 1)$ workers decide to enter.[13]

The existence of a 'coordination failure' can be shown as follows: define each agent's strategy as $S \in \{T; M\}$ where T stands for the decision of remaining in the traditional sector, and M for the choice of moving into the modern industry in period 2. Thus, S is a binary variable. Consider the payoff matrix of agent $(i = 1, 2, \cdots, L)$ which depends on her strategy, and on the strategy of all other $(L - 1)$ agents j in the economy $(j \neq i)$, which are assumed to behave identically (see Table 4.1).

According to (4.22), agent i's payoffs can be ranked as follows (the first term in brackets refers to agent i's strategy; the second one to agent j's strategy):

$$P(M, M) > P(T, T) = P(T, M) > P(M, T)$$

An individual agent has clearly no incentive to deviate from strategy T if all other agents choose T, and similarly she has no incentive to deviate from M if the other agents choose strategy M.

Hence, both (T, T) and (M, M) are symmetric Nash equilibria.[14] Moreover, they can be Pareto-ranked as (M, M) Pareto-dominates (T, T). As both conditions are fulfilled (namely, the existence of multiple Nash symmetric equilibria and the possibility of a Pareto-ranking

Table 4.1 Agent i's payoff matrix, financial autarky

Agent i's strategy	Other agents choose T	Other agents choose M
T	$1 + (1/1 + \rho)$	$1 + (1/1 + \rho)$
M	$1 - \gamma + (1/1 + \rho)p$	$1 - \gamma + (1/1 + \rho)pL^\alpha$

of the equilibria), we have a 'coordination failure' as defined by Cooper and John (1988, p. 448).

The 'coordination failure' in this context amounts to this: if the whole economy is initially specialised in the traditional activity, *no individual agent has an incentive to enter the modern sector in the decentralised equilibrium* (in other words, to modify her strategy). Therefore, as Cooper and John (1988) point out, 'the economy can get stuck at an inefficient equilibrium with a low level of economic activity, even though a better equilibrium exists'.[15] The main result under the 'financial autarky' regime is that, while under case 1 the productive specialisation of the developing economy is necessarily static, in case 2 a process of structural change with the associated increase in average factor productivity is feasible, but can be prevented by the existence of a 'coordination failure' in the decentralised economy.

The Case of Perfect Financial Integration and Sub-optimal Borrowing

In the 'financial integration' regime the small economy is perfectly integrated in the international credit market – namely, its residents can lend or borrow at the prevailing world interest rate. We assume that the world interest rate is determined by the interplay of the demand and supply of credit among 'Northern' developed economies, and therefore it can be taken as exogenous by the residents of a developing economy (Chapter 2 of this volume suggests that indeed this is what the historical experience shows). The current account need not be constantly balanced: what is required is that the external balance is maintained over the two periods.

Let us define b as *per capita* net foreign borrowing ($b > 0$) or lending ($b < 0$) in period 1 (in terms of good 1) and as θ the world interest rate. We assume that the intertemporal budget constraint is fulfilled – namely, there is no default on foreign debt. As individuals can now anticipate or postpone consumption through external borrowing and lending, the representative agent's discounted utility is now equal to:

$$w = 1 + b + \left(\frac{1}{1+\rho}\right)(1 - b(1+\theta)) \qquad (4.23a)$$

if she stays in the traditional sector and:

$$w' = 1 - \gamma + b + \left(\frac{1}{1+\rho}\right)(pl_2^\alpha - b(1+\theta)) \qquad (4.23b)$$

if she enters the modern sector together with other $(l_2 - 1)$ individuals in period 2. Both (4.23a) and (4.23b) incorporate the external budget constraint (in terms of good 1).

Different solutions can be found depending on the values of ρ and θ: we are mainly interested in analysing the ones in which foreign borrowing *can* play a crucial role in promoting the industrialisation path and the growth of *per capita* output. The key role of international capital flows emerges neatly when the only feasible equilibrium in the 'financial autarky' regime is the one where the 'traditional' production structure is fully maintained (no industrialisation): this occurs under condition (4.21). Therefore, we assume that *condition (4.21) holds throughout cases 3 and 4*.

We have two different cases, as on pp. 67–8 above:

Case 3

$$\theta > \rho \tag{4.24}$$

Whenever the world interest rate is larger than the domestic discount rate, the developing country will lend in the first period to the rest of the world. The partial derivative of discounted utility with respect to b (both in (4.23a) and (4.23b)) is negative in this case (the individual increases her present-value utility if she lends in period 1):

$$\frac{\partial w}{\partial b} = 1 - \frac{1+\theta}{1+\rho} < 0 \tag{4.25}$$

Since her income amounts to unity in period 1, she will lend 1 in period 1 and receive $(1 + \theta)$ in period 2. One can check that discounted utility w in (4.23a) is larger than v in (4.23a) when $b = -1$.

Under case 3, the advantage of being part of the world credit market relies on the possibility of a profitable arbitrage for rational agents in the developing economy, when they lend in period 1 and receive back principal and interest in period 2. Obviously, capital mobility has no impact on production and *per capita* output 'convergence' in this case.

Case 4

$$\theta = \frac{p(l_2^*)^\alpha - 1}{\gamma} - 1 \quad L > l_2^* > 1 \tag{4.26}$$

Condition (4.26) combined with (4.21) implies that the world interest rate is lower than the domestic discount rate. Individuals in the developing economy now have an incentive to borrow in period 1:

$$\frac{\partial w}{\partial b} = 1 - \frac{1+\theta}{1+\rho} > 0 \qquad (4.27)$$

Provided each rational agent borrows from abroad, they are still left with two alternative strategies concerning future production – namely, strategies T and M, as defined above. The payoff matrix of a representative agent is reproduced in Table 4.2.

The payoffs can be Pareto-ranked as follows (under condition 4.26):

$$P(M,M) > P(T,T) = P(T,M) > P(M,T).$$

The same argument of pp. 68–9 applies here: even if the (M,M) equilibrium Pareto-dominates (T,T) no individual agent deviates from strategy T in a decentralised economy, hence the developing country may get stuck in the inferior equilibrium as a consequence of a coordination failure.

Foreign borrowing could in principle play a crucial role for industrialisation in case 4. Free access to foreign credit removes one type of 'bottleneck' along the path toward economic development – namely, the intertemporal constraint due to a high rate of discount (or a high level of domestic 'impatience' as in the OLG model of Section 4.2) which prevents the economy from undertaking a process of sectoral change.[16] However, *foreign borrowing cannot by itself remove the second type of 'bottleneck'* – namely, the coordination constraint arising in this decentralised context in the presence of external economies of scale.[17] Rational agents will always borrow from abroad when the world interest rate is lower than the domestic discount rate, but if they find themselves in the (T,T) Nash equilibrium they will just use foreign borrowing as an instrument for the intertemporal redistribution of a constant stream of output (financial arbitrage alone is behind the positive differential in discounted utility with respect to financial autarky).

Table 4.2 Agent i's payoff matrix, financial integration

Agent i's strategy	Other agents choose T	Other agents choose M
T	$1 + (1/1 + \theta)$	$1 + (1/1 + \theta)$
M	$1 - \gamma + (1/1 + \theta)p$	$1 - \gamma + (1/1 + \theta)pL^\alpha$

Both in the 'financial autarky' and the 'financial integration' regime, the presence of production externalities requires that a 'coordination failure' be overcome along the path towards a superior equilibrium.

Until now, we have shown that the impact of foreign borrowing (and especially its contribution to 'convergence', intended as the process of sectoral reallocation of labour towards a 'modern' production activity) crucially depends on the degree of coordination among individual agents in this model. Moving one step ahead, we can argue that even the *amount of capital inflows* hinges on that. We know from the sign of the partial derivative of the objective function (4.27) that each individual will borrow in case 4: more precisely, one can check that she will borrow the *maximum* amount consistent with the solvency requirement and will fully devote period-2 income to debt repayment in this linear setup. Hence, *per capita* foreign debt will be:

$$b = \frac{1}{(1+\theta)} \qquad (4.28)$$

or alternatively:

$$b' = \frac{pL^\alpha}{(1+\theta)} \qquad (4.29)$$

depending on whether the economy ends up in the (T,T) or (M,M) equilibrium. One can check that b' is larger than b under condition (4.26), therefore the amount of net capital inflows is larger in the Pareto-superior equilibrium or, in other words, the coordination failure is associated with a *sub-optimal level of foreign borrowing*.[18] Paraphrasing Lucas (1990), the reason why 'capital does not flow [enough] to the poor country' in this model of production externalities, is that agents in the developing economy do not coordinate their actions. However, while the inflow of foreign capital could be larger if agents could coordinate themselves in order to introduce modern technology, it must be underlined that all external finance is used to raise current at the expense of future consumption in the 'inferior' equilibrium. This kind of behaviour is potentially unsustainable, as argued in Chapters 7 and 8.[19]

The main purpose of this section is to investigate the relation between structural change, productivity 'convergence' and international capital flows in an economy where production externalities exist. Within a stylised two-period, two-sector model, a few results have been established which provide more insights on the role of foreign capital in economic development. First, a developing decentralised economy can be faced by a 'coordination problem' along the process of structural change from a 'traditional' constant-returns-to-scale sector to a 'modern' sector featuring external economies of scale. Second, foreign borrowing can either be a mere instrument of financial arbitrage, whenever there is a wedge between the domestic discount rate and the international interest rate, or it can play a crucial role for convergence by removing the intertemporal constraint on resource allocation (the high rate of discount). Finally, the economic effects as well as the amount of foreign borrowing depend on the degree of coordination among individual agents: if a sufficiently large number of agents (possibly all of them) manage to move together into the modern sector, the amount of net capital inflows will be larger, and the economy can benefit from a peak in productivity growth associated with the 'take-off' stage of economic development. In this case only, we can argue that foreign borrowing has actually promoted 'convergence' – that is, an increase in *per capita* output in our model. Otherwise, foreign capital promotes current at the expense of future consumption.

The parameters of the model play a sort of 'heuristic' function, and comparative dynamics exercises yield conventional results: an increase in p or α will make it more profitable to reallocate resources into modern industry, while the opposite is true for γ. One must be careful, though, not to misunderstand the meaning of those exercises. For instance, it is true that an increase in L will, *ceteris paribus*, raise the virtual average productivity of sector 2; at the same time, however, one can reasonably argue that achieving coordination among a larger number of agents is more difficult.

Indeed, the core of this section is to show some consequences of 'coordination failures' in an intertemporal context. Of course, a coordination problem can be solved in many alternative ways: we mention only some of them. The first and more trivial solution is to introduce a central planner who internalises the external effects. More interesting, perhaps, are some solutions suggested by two outstanding scholars of the mid-twentieth century. Paul Rosenstein Rodan, who was writing on the problems of economic transition in Eastern Europe, envisaged the creation of an Eastern European Industrial Trust that could centralise investment and production decisions in order to exploit external economies of scale.[20] In the basic game-theoretic language of this section, this amounts to saying that a sufficiently large coalition of at least $(l_2^* - 1)$ agents can overcome the 'coordination failure'. Any kind of market structure consistent with the coordinated action of a large enough number of individuals will do the job.[21] Tibor Scitovsky blamed the price system of a decentralised economy, based on private and not social returns, for the emergence of 'coordination failures'. He suggested an alternative solution – namely, the introduction of 'some additional communication system to supplement the pricing system as a signalling device'.[22]

APPENDIX: LINEARISATION AND THE SPEED OF CONVERGENCE

We often refer in this chapter to the 'speed of convergence' to the steady state in neoclassical models. The speed of convergence provides an approximation of how fast dynamic systems such as those of Section 4.1 reach their stationary equilibria – that is, conditions in which no further adjustment occurs until new perturbations displace the system from its equilibrium or modify the steady state. The speed of convergence can be derived from a linear approximation of the local behaviour of k, h and y, which move according to non-linear dynamics, around their steady-state values (see, for instance, Blanchard and Fischer, 1989, p. 47). Here we show how to proceed in the case of the three models outlined in Section 4.1.

Let us start from the closed-economy Solow model: consider (4.3) and recall that the time derivative of $\log(k)$ equals the rate of change of k. If we express all variables in logarithms we can rewrite:

$$\frac{(d \log k)}{dt} = s_k A \exp[-(1-\alpha) \log k] - (\delta + n) \tag{A4.1}$$

where $\exp(\cdot)$ denotes the exponential operator. In the steady state this expression equals zero, thus we get:

$$\exp[-(1-\alpha) \log k^*] = \frac{(\delta + n)}{s_k A} \tag{A4.2}$$

We can take a first-order linear approximation of (A4.1) around the steady state according to Taylor's theorem[23] and obtain (A4.3):

$$\frac{(d \log k)}{dt} \cong -(1-\alpha)(\delta + n)[\log k - \log k^*] \tag{A4.3}$$

It is straightforward to check that (A4.3) is identical to (4.4) namely, the expression from which the speed of convergence (β) in the Solow model is derived. β is the derivative of the right-hand side of (A4.1) with respect to $\log(k)$ evaluated at $\log(k^*)$, which enters the first-order Taylor's expansion of the rate of change of k. It is important to stress that this definition of the speed of convergence holds only in the neighbourhood of the steady state, while the global dynamics of β have to be analysed differently.

Let us now turn to the local behaviour of the augmented neoclassical model including both physical and human capital; as in Section 4.1, we retain the assumption of constant saving shares. In this case, we can study the speed of convergence of *per capita* income starting from (3.18) that we rewrite here as (A4.4) for ease:

$$\frac{(d\log y)}{dt} = \alpha \frac{(d\log k)}{dt} + \gamma \frac{(d\log h)}{dt} \qquad (A4.4)$$

The equivalent of (A4.2) for physical and human capital can be obtained drawing on (4.8) and (4.9); after a few analytical steps, one can show that:

$$\exp[-(1-\alpha)\log k^*] = \frac{(\delta+n)}{s_k A \exp[\gamma \log h^*]} \qquad (A4.5)$$

and

$$\exp[-(1-\gamma)\log h^*] = \frac{(\delta+n)}{s_h A \exp[\alpha \log k^*]} \qquad (A4.6)$$

The next step is to compute the first-order Taylor expansion of (A4.4) around the steady state; then we can then plug (A4.5) and (A4.6) into the linear approximation of the rate of change of y. After a few manipulations, this yields:

$$\frac{(d\log y)}{dt} \cong [-\alpha(1-\alpha) + \gamma\alpha](\delta+n)[\log k - \log k^*]$$
$$+ [\alpha\gamma - \gamma(1-\gamma)](\delta+n)[\log h - \log h^*] \qquad (A4.7)$$

One more step allows us to rewrite (A4.7) as (A4.8):

$$\frac{(d\log y)}{dt} \cong [-(1-\alpha-\gamma)](\delta+n)[\alpha(\log k - \log k^*)$$
$$+ \gamma(\log h - \log h^*)] \qquad (A4.8)$$

which is just another way of writing (A4.4). The reader can easily check that, in the neoclassical model with two capital goods, the speed of convergence to the steady state (defined as β^C) is exactly the same we presented in (4.9).

Finally, we turn to the open-economy version of the augmented neoclassical model with *partial* capital mobility (see Sections 3.3 and 4.1). In this case, it is straightforward to see by inspection of (4.11) that a linear approximation of the rate of change of h is provided by:

$$\frac{(d \log h)}{dt} \cong \left[-\frac{(1-\alpha-\gamma)}{(1-\alpha)} \right] (\delta + n)[\log h - \log h^*] \qquad (A4.9)$$

As the dynamics of the growth rate of *per capita* output is governed *only* by the rate of change of h in this model, the speed of convergence (β^O) is given by (4.12). Therefore, the main finding of Section 4.1 – namely, that the speed of convergence in the augmented model with partial mobility is finite and larger than β^C – holds, provided the neoclassical restrictions on the parameters are maintained.

Part III
Empirical Studies

5 Measuring Capital Mobility in Developing Economies

Part III of this volume – devoted to empirical studies of foreign capital in developing economies – starts with a chapter on capital mobility. The definition, and measurement, of the degree of integration in international capital markets is a widely debated issue with a number of related policy implications. Moreover, the evaluation of capital mobility in developing economies is a crucial prerequisite for the subsequent analyses of the determinants and consequences of capital flows in developing countries (DCs). If an individual economy is found to be insulated from world capital markets, it makes little sense to establish the role of foreign capital there. Conversely, if DCs are relatively well integrated in the international financial network, questions concerning the functions of capital flows become very relevant. The chapter is organised as follows: we first provide an introduction to the concept of capital mobility and highlight its major implications in terms of intertemporal allocation, financial diversification and economic policy (Section 5.1). We then review the debate on the measurement of capital mobility (Section 5.2). This is a 'hot' topic as many operational definitions and alternative empirical tests exist. A new methodology based on time-series econometrics is introduced in Section 5.3, and applied to the assessment of capital mobility in 33 DCs over 1960–88. In general, we cannot reject the hypothesis that several developing economies were integrated in international capital markets in this period. Some details on the statistical procedures adopted and the data sources can be found at the end of the chapter.

5.1 THE CONCEPT OF CAPITAL MOBILITY

The integration of world capital markets has become a popular subject. Large amounts of assets are traded by residents of different countries, either institutions or private citizens, regardless of the currency of denomination and the national origin of the assets. Quantitative assessments of the volume and range of these transactions, as well as an overview of the recent legislative measures on financial activities, suggest that international finance has been the most dynamic component of the world economic system in recent decades (Goldstein and Mussa, 1993, p. 5).

However, the nature and extent of world financial integration are still highly controversial topics. Different concepts of capital mobility coexist, as there are different tasks that can be carried out by capital markets; this in turn leads to different approaches to the issue of measuring international capital mobility. One can in principle define *perfect* capital mobility in a rather simple fashion:

> Capital is freely mobile within a multi-country region when its residents face no official obstacles to the negotiation and execution of financial trades anywhere and with anyone within the region, and face transaction costs that are no greater for parties residing in different countries than for parties residing in the same country. (Obstfeld, 1993, p. 2)

As we will see, it is almost impossible to establish whether or not this definition of free capital mobility holds for a sub-set of countries in the real world. Therefore, a *relative* concept of capital mobility is often adopted where the yardstick is not an ideal measure of perfect mobility but instead the result of tests effectively performed on different countries, or regions within one country, or even the same group of countries in another time span.

The above definition of free capital mobility obviously implies that one possible strategy for assessing the degree of financial integration is to look at official barriers to cross-border capital flows; the main drawback of this approach is that although information on these restrictions is extremely useful, their economic *impact* cannot easily be evaluated (Goldstein and Mussa, 1993, p. 14).

Another 'direct' approach to capital mobility is centred on the 'law of one price', which predicts that returns on comparable assets freely traded at different locations must be equalised after accounting for a variety of risk premia. In practice, defining and measuring capital mobility under this approach requires one to deal with a number of questions. First, what is the relevant range of financial transactions even *within* national borders – namely, how complete are asset markets and what kind of assets cannot be traded even in a domestic context? Second, to what extent is the composition of financial portfolios affected by transaction costs – as opposed to, for instance, a preference for domestic assets? Third, how do we measure different types of risk associated with capital assets? Fourth, does the time horizon matter – that is, do things change from the short to the long run? These and other questions deserve an answer before one looks at return differentials in order to assess the degree of financial integration.

Consider, for instance, the case of two countries where agents can accumulate wealth in only two alternative ways: one, by subscribing to risk-free, tax-free three-month Treasury bonds; and two, by investing in real estate. Suppose that portfolio preferences are different across nations – namely, that residents in one of the two countries, *ceteris paribus*, choose to have a larger share of real estate in their portfolios based on their expected-utility function. Now, let us analyse the case when returns on Treasury bonds are equalised across the two countries (after accounting for exchange rate risk, which is a nightmare by itself), while returns on comparable real-estate assets are not equalised. Can we infer something on capital mobility from that? Of course, it depends on *why* this has happened. It might be the case that restrictions are imposed on foreign investors in the real-estate market, but not in the Treasury bonds market: this would lead to international arbitrage in the bond but not in the real-estate market. The conclusion one draws is that *capital mobility is limited to one type of asset* (Treasury bonds).

Alternatively, let us assume that in the previous example no legal restrictions exist on investment in the real-estate market, but that residents in the two countries have a preference for investing in *nation-based* real estate (in other words, they are averse to 'external' risk, see Niehans, 1994, pp. 26–7). Once again, there would be (adjusted) interest parity in the bond market but not in the real-estate market. Notice that *capital mobility is not restrained in this case*: residents in different countries simply have different expected-utility functions and are oriented towards domestic real estate. However, as far as the international comparison of (expected) returns is concerned the two situations are observationally equivalent.

Hence, pursuing the 'law-of-one-price' approach to financial integration calls for a detailed evaluation of the features of a wide range of assets, as well as an inquiry into the portfolio preferences of residents in different countries. As this is rather difficult and costly to implement, empirical tests of the 'law of one price' have been usually confined to *short-term* debt assets (see, for instance, Frankel, 1989, Obstfeld,

1993). Furthermore, tests of arbitrage conditions are designed to evaluate the responsiveness of international investors to changes in the relative prices of assets. The response to such changes, however, requires adjustments only *at the margin* in international portfolios, hence it might be accomplished without any *net* international capital movements across countries (see Niehans, 1994).

In order to evaluate the scope of *net* capital mobility across countries, more 'indirect' approaches have been advocated that are focused 'on the implications of enhanced capital mobility for comovements of other economic variables across countries' (Leiderman and Razin, 1994, p. 2). The analysis of saving–investment correlations and international consumption comovements is among these 'indirect' methods. They suffer from another common drawback – namely, that they are more 'theory-dependent' than direct methods as they always consist of a *joint* test of the capital mobility hypothesis and of some other theoretical assumption. We will come back to this issue in Section 5.2; let us briefly look now at some of the economic implications of capital mobility.

The hypothesis of perfect capital market integration is crucial in a wide range of economic models. The open-economy version of the popular Keynesian macroeconomic setup, the so-called 'Mundell–Fleming' model, leads to different comparative-statics conclusions with respect to the relative effectiveness of fiscal and monetary policy, depending on whether or not capital mobility holds (see Blanchard and Fischer, 1989, p. 537). In the Dornbusch (1976) overshooting model, the results crucially depend on the assumption that capital markets are perfectly integrated (and adjust immediately to exogenous shocks, while goods markets adjust only slowly). The relevance of the capital mobility issue is by no means confined to either the Keynesian macromodel or the exchange rate literature. Among other domains where capital mobility is relevant, both on analytical and practical standpoints, one can mention the following.[1]

- The economics of intertemporal allocation, growth and development, where it is crucial to establish whether the process of accumulation, productivity improvement and growth may be financed by external resources or is bounded by the domestic 'closed-economy' budget constraint (see Chapter 4). Financial integration opens new opportunities for international trade – namely, for the exchange of financial assets and of income streams at different points in time; therefore, there is room both for new 'gains from trade' and new 'term-of-trade shocks' (world interest rate shocks). Let us consider some examples. International differences in the intertemporal rate of time preference are a sufficient condition for the emergence of credit relations between countries in simple overlapping-generations (OLG) models (Azariadis, 1993, pp. 180–1). Historical studies have argued that secular patterns of capital flows between Europe and the 'New World' may be accounted for by demographic factors (Taylor and Williamson, 1994). Alternatively, other structural features of the economy such as the potential for sectoral change may lead to international capital movements (see Section 4.3).

- The intertemporal analysis of the response to economic shocks. This is related to intertemporal allocation, but the focus is on short-term adjustment rather than long-run trends. The literature on this aspect has pointed out that if domestic residents are allowed to borrow or lend abroad, the performance of a national economy in the aftermath of a country-specific shock is very different from the response in the case of financial autarky (see Genberg and Swoboda, 1992, for a survey).
- The study of the effects of the taxation of capital income, which of course depends on what kind of restrictions are imposed on domestic and foreign residents with respect to their portfolio choices. In their seminal paper, Feldstein and Horioka (1980, p. 315) have argued that a large part of the burden of a capital income tax may be shifted on domestic labour 'if capital is free to leave the country'. They conclude that the evidence on capital mobility may call for a revision of standard theories of tax incidence.
- The analysis of the effectiveness of the 'inflation tax' – that is, of the seigniorage exerted by national governments through the mechanism of generating increases in the domestic price level and thereby reducing the real value of domestic monetary balances. The effectiveness of the inflation tax is severely reduced whenever domestic residents are allowed to hold liquid balances denominated in foreign currencies: in this case, the domestic monetary authority cannot affect the real value of such balances, and, more important, it cannot raise the proceeds of a devaluation of monetary balances;
- The issue of the viability of an interest rate regime 'managed' by the domestic monetary authority, which is not consistent with the joint assumption of perfect financial integration and 'small economy' (Haque and Montiel, 1991).

It is clear that some of these aspects are especially relevant for both theoretical considerations and policy advice concerning developing economies (think, for instance, of the role of the 'inflation tax' in countries where virtually no fiscal structures exist, apart from the system of custom duties). What is more controversial among economists is not the weight to be assigned to the capital mobility question, but rather the methodological issue of how to measure capital mobility in the real world (Goldstein and Mussa, 1993, pp. 13–15).

5.2 THE MEASURES OF CAPITAL MOBILITY

Many excellent surveys of the empirical literature on capital mobility are available, and each of them deals with the methodological problems involved in the econometric evaluation of the degree of capital market integration. Moreover, each author provides a personal perspective on the matter (see Frankel, 1989; 1992; Tesar, 1991; Montiel, 1993; Obstfeld, 1993).

It is not our intention to add one more general survey to the existing stock. Rather, we would like to introduce an econometric procedure employed in Section 5.3, and to do so we start from an article by Feldstein and Horioka (1980). As the logic of the empirical tests of Section 5.3 of this chapter is derived from Feldstein and Horioka (1980), this idiosyncratic review provides a closer look at the methodological debate on the *saving–investment approach* to capital mobility, while less attention is paid to other approaches (the direct ones based on the 'law of one price' as well as other indirect approaches).

The impact of Feldstein and Horioka (1980) was enormous. Their argument is that, if the hypothesis of perfect capital mobility holds, it may be possible to decouple domestic saving and investment through the functioning of a global capital market which offers either investment opportunities in the case of excess domestic saving or additional external resources in the case of excess domestic investment. In an integrated world capital market, it is the relative return to investment in different countries, and not domestic saving, which drives the amount of aggregate domestic investment: different national saving propensities, or a shock to domestic saving, should affect only the world global saving pool, and should have no immediate consequences on domestic investment. Moreover, if the country is not large enough for the shock to significantly affect the world saving rate, domestic investment should be uncorrelated with domestic saving.

Feldstein and Horioka (1980) proposed to estimate the following equation in a cross-section of OECD countries with annual data averaged over 1960–74, as well as over shorter sub-periods:

$$i_t = \alpha + \beta s_t + e_t \qquad (5.1)$$

where i_t is domestic investment, s_t is domestic saving (variables are expressed as shares of GDP) and e_t is a white noise – i.e. an identically and independently distributed stochastic process with zero mean and constant variance.

The system of hypotheses to be tested is the following:

$$\begin{cases} H_0: (\alpha, \beta) = (0, 1) \\ H_1: (\alpha, \beta) \neq (0, 1) \end{cases} \qquad (5.2)$$

where the null hypothesis implies perfect saving–investment correlation. The shocking result of Feldstein and Horioka (1980) is that the point estimate of the parameter β was about 0.9 and that the hypothesis H_0 could not be statistically rejected, while *a priori* we would expect β to be close to zero (and the hypothesis H_0 to be rejected) *if* the argument of Feldstein and Horioka (1980) is correct *and if* we expect high capital mobility in their sample of countries. Moreover, the findings of Feldstein and Horioka (1980) are robust with respect to changes in the years selected for the estimates (the early 1970s instead of the 1960s), in the econometric techniques adopted (ordinary least squares, instrumental variables, simultaneous equations) and in the set of additional right-hand-side variables included in the regression (such as the size of the country or the rate of growth).

The conclusions of Feldstein and Horioka (1980) are even more surprising because another type of tests of international capital mobility – namely, tests of the covered interest-rate parity condition – indicate that OECD financial markets are integrated. Interest-rate parity conditions are a simple but powerful way of implementing direct tests of the capital mobility hypothesis. *Covered* interest parity (CIP) holds whenever the returns on comparable assets in different countries are equal provided one accounts for the rate of change of the forward exchange rate. *Uncovered* parity (UIP) holds if no arbitrage opportunities exist between equivalent assets across countries, regardless of exposure to exchange risk. Finally, *real* interest parity (RIP) means that real interest rates on comparable assets are equalised across countries (see Frankel, 1992; the results for OECD countries are summarised in Frankel, 1989).

The debate on the methodology and results of Feldstein and Horioka (1980) has taken two main avenues. First, what measurement methodology is to be preferred, the one suggested by Feldstein and Horioka (1980), the approach of the 'law of one price', or others?[2] Second, what is the correct economic interpretation of the Feldstein–Horioka (1980) findings?

As far as the first issue is concerned, notice that direct tests based on the 'law of one price' can be implemented only on a limited range of assets, usually short-term non-equity financial assets. Nevertheless, the results of these tests can be usefully compared over time and across countries to obtain a relative measure of financial integration, especially for short-term financial assets (see Section 5.1). The apparent tension between the validity of CIP among OECD countries and the Feldstein–Horioka result can be explained, in this context, by arguing that saving and investment are driven by *real* interest rates, and that RIP does no hold even across OECD countries (see Frankel, 1992). Moreover, interest-rate parity conditions do not necessarily require *net* capital movements recorded in a country's balance of payments (Niehans, 1994).

The Feldstein–Horioka approach is based on the correlation between domestic saving and investment, and therefore on net capital flows (Feldstein and Horioka, 1980, p. 320). Notice that, contrary to the law-of-one-price approach, the Feldstein–Horioka method does not distinguish between different types of assets – that is, different means of filling the gap between domestic saving and investment (bank lending, issues of bonds or equity, foreign direct investment, and so on). However, this approach is *indirect* – it is based on one of the possible implications of capital mobility and not on capital market integration itself. Hence, it is not difficult to imagine hypothetical situations in which capital mobility holds but no net movements actually occur.

Some authors have criticised, on different grounds, the Feldstein–Horioka econometric framework. Wong (1990) and Tesar (1991) argue that the Feldstein–Horioka findings are severely affected by 'sample bias' – namely, they are not robust with respect to a change in the sample of countries included in the regressions. Sinn (1992) shows that if cross-section regressions are estimated year by year, instead of averaging annual data over some longer period, the hypothesis of capital mobility is more difficult to reject even for the countries considered by Feldstein and Horioka. Gundlach and Sinn (1992) argue that the Feldstein–Horioka time-series tests prevent many of the drawbacks of the cross-sections. Several scholars have questioned the reliability of national accounts data on saving and investment, especially in DCs (see Montiel, 1993). Finally, Leachman (1991), Gundlach and Sinn (1992) and De Haan and Siermann (1994) provide statistical tests of the saving–investment correlation based on the integration and cointegration properties of the time series.[3] The econometric procedures applied in Section 5.3 follow this strand of the literature.

The second aspect of the debate is centred on the economic interpretation of the Feldstein–Horioka result: as we are dealing with an indirect approach, we must recognise that we are testing one of the implications of capital mobility. Many scholars have indeed shown that the Feldstein–Horioka *result* does not necessarily lead to the Feldstein–Horioka *conclusions*: a strong correlation between domestic saving and investment may actually be consistent with capital mobility. The crucial assumption of these contributions is that the statistical series of s and i are both driven, at least partially, by some common underlying variable(s). Of course, the existence of such variable(s) would by itself generate a high β even under perfect capital mobility.

The distinction between cross-section and time-series regressions is crucial for identifying the source of the correlation: in the case of cross-sections, the correlation between s and i may be due to long-run phenomena such as the impact of demographic factors or the equilibrium rate of growth of the economy; in the case of time-series, short-run phenomena such as the behaviour of s and i over the business cycle are the natural candidates for an explanation of the high. Other attempts to identify the source of the correlation stress the role of non-tradables, or that of government policies (see Montiel, 1993, pp. 15–17).

Each of these methodological critiques of the Feldstein–Horioka approach must be taken very seriously, and cannot be neglected when one compares alternative measures of capital mobility. Nevertheless, further reflections suggest that the Feldstein–Horioka approach should not be fully dismissed.

First, while we have seen that a strong correlation between saving and investment cannot be taken as a proof of financial autarky, a loose correlation can be considered a clue of capital mobility. Second, by comparing the results of Feldstein and Horioka (1980) over time and across countries, one can at least obtain a *relative* measure of capital mobility (the benchmark being not the ideal value of the parameters as in (5.2), but instead the actual value obtained in other historical or geographic contexts).[4] Third, a new strand of the empirical literature has argued that the study of the statistical properties of the relevant *time series*, particularly those emphasised by the 'unit-root econometrics', can prevent many of the drawbacks of the original Feldstein–Horioka cross-sections without throwing the whole Feldstein and Horioka (1980) approach away. Section 5.3 on capital mobility in DCs draws on these new directions of research.

Quantifying capital mobility in DCs faces some additional obstacles in addition to the measurement problems already outlined. First of all, many developing countries maintain legal barriers to private international capital transactions, as mentioned by Goldstein and Mussa (1993, p. 31). Moreover, interest rates are sometimes under direct legal control of some government agency in these countries, and therefore standard 'law-of-one-price' tests are problematic (Haque and Montiel, 1991). Finally, macroeconomic data are usually less reliable in developing countries than in industrial ones and this poses some problems for 'indirect' tests based on such information. However, more and more evidence is currently being accumulated on these countries (among recent papers, see Dooley, Fernandez-Arias and Kletzer, 1996; Vamvakidis and Wacziarg, 1998).

Before turning to the evidence, we may assess whether economic theory offers some insights on the issue of capital mobility in DCs. We can identify several elements that suggest that capital mobility might be lower in developing countries, in addition to the ones mentioned above. First, legal frameworks of *property rights* as well as commercial, tax and bankruptcy legislation are often below (Western) standards in the DCs, especially in the poorest ones of Africa and Asia, and this may hinder international investors from lending to them (incidentally, this also applies to the economies in transition in Central and Eastern Europe: see Chapter 8). Second, export revenues are more uncertain in DCs than in OECD countries, owing to the volatility of export prices; this phenomenon is particularly relevant in countries whose exports are concentrated in primary products and fuel (see Ghosh and Ostry, 1994). Residents of these countries may therefore suddenly lack the resources required to honour foreign credit contracts. Finally, financial historians point out that widespread problems of insolvency and foreign debt default in developing countries have cyclically disrupted their credit relations with the world financial centres, reducing the degree of capital mobility either temporarily or permanently (see Chapter 2).

On the other hand, we must mention at least one factor that may trigger capital mobility in the DCs – namely, their *growth potential*: the standard neoclassical theory of growth (as well as others based on the catching-up hypothesis, such as the technology-gap model) suggests that these economies should grow faster than richer economies. Consequently, returns on capital accumulation and financial assets could be larger and capital mobility should increase their 'speed of convergence' (see Chapters 3 and 4). While this statement must not be taken at face value, the growth potential of developing economies may provide a rationale for speeding up the process of liberalisation of their capital accounts.

Until recently, empirical studies of capital mobility had mainly been confined to developed countries, apart from some work done on few DCs (Mexico, Argentina, Colombia, Singapore). This gap has been filled by some excellent pieces of research in recent years; this survey will briefly deal with 'law-of-one-price' exercises and with tests of consumption comovements in the DCs, while it will go into greater details about saving–investment correlations.

A few tests of interest-parity conditions in individual developing countries go back to the 1980s (see Montiel, 1993, pp. 20–2). In his broad survey of capital mobility in the 1980s, Frankel (1989) concludes that CIP is rejected for Mexico and Malaysia, but not for Hong Kong and Singapore, while RIP is rejected for Malaysia and Hong Kong but not in Mexico and Singapore. Except for Singapore, no clear-cut conclusion emerges.

However, the application of these techniques to a wide range of DCs was often prevented by the doubtful quality of interest rate data: as already mentioned, legal systems of financial 'repression' that keep official interest rates below the market-clearing levels are, or have been, in place in many DCs, while no reliable data are available about the 'informal' market rates.

Haque and Montiel (1991) have developed an econometric device that overcomes this obstacle. They suggest that a reduced form of a model consisting of both a money-demand function and an interest-parity condition be estimated: the advantage of this approach is that one does not need *domestic interest rate data* but rather data on national income, consumption prices, the real money supply and the US interest rate. The findings of Haque and Montiel (obtained with a non-linear instrumental variables technique) cover 15 DCs over 1969–87 and indicate that, with the exception of India, capital mobility is quite high.[5]

Insofar as the comovement between domestic and 'world' *per capita* consumption rates is concerned, this is a proxy for the degree of risk diversification that can be attained in an individual country: the more domestic residents can insure themselves in the global market against country-specific risks, the more domestic and world *per capita* consumption will move together. Obstfeld (1993) reports the values for the simple correlation coefficient between domestic and 'world' consumption for 24 DCs over 1951–72 and 1973–88. All coefficients are low in the first time span, but the correlation usually rises after 1972. The drawback of this approach in its more sophisticated format (Obstfeld, 1994) is that it relies on special theoretical assumptions (dynamic utility maximisation with identical parameters of the objective function in different countries). Tests based on dynamic utility maximisation in DCs have been made by Montiel (1993, pp. 17–19): his synthetic evaluations are reported in column (4) of Table 5.1.

Drawing on Feldstein and Horioka (1980), several scholars have estimated the correlation between domestic saving and investment with cross-section data on the DCs. Dooley, Frankel and Mathieson (1987) found that the correlation between the average saving and investment rates over 1960–73 and 1974–84 is lower in a sample of 48 DCs than in a sample of 14 developed countries. Their findings hold if instrumental variables rather than OLS are used, while a decomposition between market borrowers and official borrowers demonstrates that the latter show a looser correlation.

Vos (1988) obtains comparable results with a partially different set of countries and data from a different source. Wong (1990) confines his analysis to the period 1975–81, reporting no significant correlation between saving and investment in a sample of 45 DCs (β is not statistically different from zero). However, Wong's main concern is to show that his regression is extremely 'fragile' as the exclusion of five countries from his sample (Jordan, Saudi Arabia, United Emirates, Yemen, St Lucia) raises β up to 0.6, making it significantly different from zero. Hence, a relevant sample-bias problem arises which is shared also by the original Feldstein–Horioka (1980) regressions (Wong, 1990, p. 62). Notwithstanding, the conjecture that DCs display a lower saving–investment correlations than industrial economies has been recently confirmed by Vamvakidis and Wacziarg (1998) who use various techniques and country samples, and try to cope with measurement errors, business-cycle effects and so on.

All this requires some comment. No doubt the Feldstein–Horioka (1980) findings are plagued by a sample bias, not to mention the problems of economic interpretation just stressed. However, this should not automatically lead to a rejection of the whole Feldstein–Horioka (1980) approach. A better solution is to move from a cross-section to a

Table 5.1 Main findings of the empirical literature on capital mobility in 33 developing countries

Author(s)	Haque and Montiel (1991) (1)	Mamingi (1993) (2)	Mamingi (1993) (3)	Montiel (1993) (4)
Years	1969–87	1970–90	1970–91	Various intervals
Data	Time series – annual	Time series – annual	Time series – annual	Time series
Technique	Non-linear inst. variables	OLS	Fully modified OLS	Various techniques
Approach	Interest-rate parity condition	Saving–investment correlation	Saving–investment correlation	Interest-rate parity conditions; Saving–investment correlations; Euler's equations
Countries				
Kenya	Mobility	Mobility	..	Immobility
Malawi	..	Immobility	Immobility	Intermediate
Mali	..	Intermediate	Mobility	Inconclusive
Senegal	..	Intermediate	Intermediate	Mobility
Tanzania	..	..	..	Inconclusive
Tunisia	Mobility	Immobility	Immobility	Immobility
Zambia	Mobility	Mobility	Immobility	Inconclusive
Costa Rica	..	Mobility	Inconclusive	Intermediate
Dominican Rep.	..	Intermediate	Intermediate	Mobility
El Salvador	..	Intermediate	Intermediate	Immobility
Guatemala	Mobility	Immobility	Immobility	Intermediate
Honduras	..	Immobility	Immobility	Immobility
Jamaica	..	Intermediate	Mobility	Mobility
Mexico	..	Intermediate	..	Intermediate
Panama	..	..	..	Mobility
Argentina	..	..	..	Inconclusive

Table 5.1 (Continued)

Author(s)	Haque and Montiel (1991) (1)	Mamingi (1993) (2)	Mamingi (1993) (3)	Montiel (1993) (4)
Bolivia	..	..	..	Mobility
Brazil	Immobility	Intermediate	Intermediate	Inconclusive
Chile	..	Intermediate	Intermediate	Mobility
Colombia	..	Mobility	Mobility	Intermediate
Ecuador	..	Intermediate	Intermediate	Intermediate
Paraguay	..	Intermediate	Mobility	Immobility
Peru	..	Mobility	Mobility	Inconclusive
Uruguay	Mobility	..	..	Mobility
Venezuela	..	Mobility	Mobility	Immobility
India	Immobility	Intermediate	Intermediate	Immobility
Indonesia	Mobility	..	..	Inconclusive
Israel	..	Mobility	Mobility	Mobility
Korea	..	Intermediate	Mobility	Intermediate
Malaysia	Mobility	Mobility	Inconclusive	Intermediate
Philippines	Mobility	Immobility	Immobility	Immobility
Sri Lanka	Mobility	Mobility	Mobility	Immobility
Thailand	..	Immobility	Intermediate	Intermediate

Notes:
Intermediate means that both the perfect capital mobility and the capital immobility hypotheses were rejected.
Mobility means that only the hypothesis of perfect capital mobility was not rejected.
Immobility means that only the hypothesis of no capital mobility was not rejected.
Inconclusive means that the tests could not discriminate among these possible outcomes.
.. Not available.

time-series environment: the advantage of this strategy is two-fold. First, countries integrated in the world capital market are not 'merged' together with 'closed' countries in a single regression. Second, the modern theory of intertemporal economics shows that, even under financial integration, an individual country may in general experience periods of net capital inflows followed by periods of net outflows, or vice versa (Genberg and Swoboda, 1992). While the analysis of the time series would capture this phenomenon, the values computed in a cross-section context would average periods of net inflows and outflows, introducing a bias *against* the capital mobility hypothesis (Gundlach and Sinn, 1992).

Of course, the possibility of an *endogeneity* bias is not avoided within a time-series framework, especially if s_t and i_t move together along the business cycle. However, drawing on a recent strand of the literature (Leachman, 1991; De Haan and Siermann, 1994) one can evaluate the *long-run* correlation between s_t and i_t and test the hypothesis of co-integration. The statistical theory of cointegration developed by Engle and Granger (1987) allows one to deal at the same time with the issue of endogeneity and with the problem of spurious regressions (see Granger and Newbold, 1974), therefore limiting the distortions due to the business cycle. Moreover, it is the length of the time interval and not the number of observations that is relevant in this case, hence this methodology can be applied also to DCs for which annual data on s_t and i_t are often available only since the 1960s.[6] Gundlach and Sinn (1992) use the simple national accounting identity ($ca_t = s_t - i_t$), where ca_t is the ratio of the current account to GDP, to rewrite (5.21) as:

$$ca_t = -\alpha + (1 - \beta)s_t - e_t \qquad (5.3)$$

They show that the information on the order of integration of the series ca_t is equivalent to the information on the cointegrating relation between s_t and i_t. Moreover, the methodology of Gundlach and Sinn (1992) avoids the pre-testing problems involved in the preliminary estimation of the order of integration of s_t and i_t. Leachman (1991) considers only OECD countries, while De Haan and Siermann (1994) study India, Korea and Taiwan among others. Gundlach and Sinn (1992) argue that their technique is not suitable for DCs because of the role played by foreign aid in these countries: in Section 5.3 we show how this problem can be partially accounted for and their technique applied to the DCs.

94   *Empirical Studies*

Montiel (1993) and Mamingi (1993) do not directly test the hypothesis of cointegration between domestic saving and investment, but estimate an Error Correction Model (ECM) whose econometric properties are consistent with an indirect test of cointegration (see Engle and Granger, 1987).[7] Mamingi's findings for the countries analysed in Section 5.3 are reproduced in Table 5.1 (columns (2) and (3)): the evaluation in column (2) is based on simple OLS regressions, while that of column (3) on OLS regressions adjusted for endogeneity and serial correlation (Mamingi, 1993, pp. 7–9).

Montiel (1993, pp. 29–36) provides results for both static and dynamic empirical models of the relation between s_t and i_t, including an ECM, and tries to cope with the problem of international aid transfers to the DCs. His synthetic classification, based not only on the Feldstein–Horioka (1980) tests but on other methods as well, is replicated in Table 5.1 (column (4)).

5.3 CAPITAL MOBILITY IN DEVELOPING COUNTRIES, 1960–88

The purpose of this section is to discuss a statistical procedure designed to identify the order of integration of the current account balance, net of aid flows, in the DCs. This strategy for the measuring of capital mobility in DCs has been implemented in Bagnai and Manzocchi (1996). The rationale of this procedure is based on the contribution of Gundlach and Sinn (1992), which has already been mentioned. According to Gundlach and Sinn (1992), one can rewrite the Feldstein–Horioka equation as (5.3): if the saving rate is integrated of order 1 (hence it is $I(1)$)[8] and the residual e_t is white noise, then ca_t can be $I(0)$ *if and only if* $\beta = 1$ – that is, if saving and investment follow the same stochastic pattern. Gundlach and Sinn (1992) propose to test the null hypothesis of $ca_t \sim I(1)$:[9] if it is *not* rejected by the data, saving and investment are not perfectly correlated in the long-run, hence there is capital mobility (although not necessarily *perfect* capital mobility).

Gundlach and Sinn argue that their empirical framework cannot be extended to the DCs:

> Of course there is the theoretical possibility that β equals one and e_t is not stationary. If this were true, one would have perfect capital immobility although our test procedure would indicate a unit root in the current account balance. As an example, consider the case of a

developing country which is closed to the international capital market, but irregularly receives aid in goods or financial assistance. Our test procedure would falsely identify such a country as being part of the world capital market. (Gundlach and Sinn, 1992, p. 619)

Let us define a new variable aid_t, 'net foreign aid flows': Gundlach and Sinn (1992) correctly argue that either aid_t is $I(0)$, or one *cannot* infer anything about capital mobility from the analysis of the order of integration of ca_t. To show their point, let us redefine the accounting identity in order to include foreign aid in the picture:

$$ca_t = s_t - i_t + aid_t \tag{5.4}$$

(where aid_t has been already defined). Subtracting i_t as defined in equation (5.1) from (5.4), one obtains:

$$\begin{aligned} ca_t &= -\alpha + (1-\beta)s_t + aid_t - e_t \\ &= -\alpha + (1-\beta)s_t + \varepsilon_t \end{aligned} \tag{5.5}$$

where $\varepsilon_t = -e_t + aid_t$ and e_t is a white noise as in (5.1).[10]

Equation (5.5) shows that, if ca_t is defined as in eq. (5.4), the residual differs by definition from e_t as it includes the variable aid_t which may follow either an $I(0)$ or an $I(1)$ process. According to equation (5.5) ca_t could be distributed as an $I(1)$ process even if $\beta = 1$ (i.e. even if s_t and i_t follow the same stochastic pattern), provided $aid_t \sim I(1)$: if this is the case, the Gundlach–Sinn (1992) test would lead to the incorrect conclusion that a country is 'open' to capital movements.

The Gundlach–Sinn procedure, however, can be adjusted to account for foreign aid flows. As a matter of fact, it is straightforward to define a new variable $ca_t^* = ca_t - aid_t = s_t - i_t$. From (5.5) we can derive:

$$ca_t^* = s_t - i_t = -\alpha + (1-\beta)s_t - e_t \tag{5.6}$$

Provided data on aid_t are available, we could then proceed exactly as suggested by Gundlach and Sinn (1992), substituting ca_t^* for ca_t and testing for the order of integration of ca_t^*.[11]

Once we have identified the relevant variable for the 'unit-root-test', another issue arises. Suppose the series of the current account corrected for aid flows is $I(0)$ but it has a *deterministic* trend and/or drift. This poses two different questions. First, how do we test for the presence of a unit root when such deterministic components exist? Second, what are the implications for the debate on capital mobility?

Consider the first question: if the data-generating process (hereafter, DGP) of the variable ca_t^* includes a deterministic trend and/or drift, testing the null hypothesis of a unit root *without* accounting for the deterministic components leads to *biased* results; the same is true if one includes a trend (drift) in the regression when it does not appear in the DGP.[12] One has hence to specify the correct DGP of the variable ca_t^* in order to get unbiased results on the order of integration of the series (see Section 5.4). Gundlach and Sinn (1992) neglect this problem as their specifications do not include a trend component: they argue that this choice is based on the *a priori* belief that 'the current account is one of the few economic time series which does not exhibit a trend' (Gundlach and Sinn, 1992, p. 619). However, this statement does not look appropriate at the stage of the statistical analysis of the data; moreover, why should we *a priori* exclude that the current account exhibits a deterministic trend *instead* of a unit root?

Dolado, Jenkinson and Sosvilla-Rivero (1990) develop a testing strategy that prevents this potential bias and at the same time reduces the pre-testing problems involved in the analysis of the DGP. Their suggestion is to adopt a 'general-to-specific' procedure where subsequent stages lead to the definition of the 'true' DGP: recall that the significance of the trend (drift) *under the null hypothesis of integration* cannot be ascertained with the values of the usual t and F distributions, but with the values of the asymptotic distributions tabulated in Fuller (1976) and Dickey and Fuller (1981).[13] The strategy by Dolado, Jenkinson and Sosvilla-Rivero (1990) is implemented in what follows. Both the Dickey–Fuller-test (DF) and the augmented Dickey–Fuller-test (ADF) are applied.[14]

The second point relates to the economic interpretation of the deterministic components in the current account series. As mentioned before, Gundlach and Sinn (1992) rule out the possibility that the DGP of ca_t contains a trend; insofar as the drift is concerned they 'do not attempt to explain why countries should have a persistent non-zero-mean current account balance' (Gundlach and Sinn, 1992, p. 619, n. 10). In principle, a country whose current account is given by $ca_t = \alpha + e_t$, with α a non-zero real constant and e_t white noise (so that $E(ca_t) = \alpha$) shows, on average, net capital inflows or outflows during the period under observation. Even in the case when ca_t moves along a deterministic *trend*, an individual country may experience net capital inflows or outflows in the long run.[15] Hence, Gundlach and Sinn (1992) are by definition oriented toward the rejection of the capital mobility hypothesis because they neglect the information contained in the deterministic components of the DGP.

While the subsequent discussion of the empirical results is especially focused on the presence of a unit root in the (modified) current-account series, as this feature points out to the lack of a long-run dynamic relation between saving and investment, we also stress that in some countries ca_t^* is trend-stationary or is stationary with a non-zero mean.[16]

Table 5.2 provides the results of the unit-root-tests on ca_t^* (current-account balance *less* official unrequited transfers, as a share of GDP) for 33 DCs over 1960–88, using the procedure suggested by Dolado, Jenkinson and Sosvilla-Rivero (1990). Details on the testing strategy and the sources and definitions of the variables can be found, respectively, in Sections 5.4 and 5.5. The time dimension of the sample has been chosen according to prior information on the length of a whole capital-flow cycle in DCs (see Chapter 2), spanning from the end of the 1950s (when world financial relations started to recover after a two-decade break) to the end of the 1980s (when the stagnation in capital transfers to DCs following the debt crisis of 1982–3 was bound to come to an end). The choice of 33 countries is dictated by the need of examining the same set of national units analysed also in Chapters 6 and 7.[17] The period under observation is slightly different across countries, owing to missing observations in the *International Financial Statistics*: however, it usually covers 1961–88. We adopt a conservative stance rejecting the null hypothesis of a unit root if the estimated statistic is smaller than the critical value at the 10 per cent level of statistical significance;[18] however, the results at the 5 per cent significance level are also reported in Table 5.2.

The null hypothesis of first-order integration of ca_t^* is rejected in 22 cases out of 33, hence in at least 11 remaining countries (Malawi, Tanzania, Tunisia, Brazil, Guatemala, Panama, Paraguay, Korea, India, Thailand and Israel) the hypothesis of no saving–investment correlation is not rejected by the data. Moreover, in six of the countries where ca_t^* is not $I(1)$ the modified current account balance has a (negative) deterministic trend (Argentina, El Salvador, Jamaica, Honduras, Mali and Zambia). Finally, there are ten cases in which ca is distributed as an $I(0)$ process, but we observe a significant non-zero mean (Bolivia, Costa Rica, Dominican Republic, Ecuador, Indonesia, Kenya, Mexico, Peru, Senegal, Sri Lanka).

If we assume that the presence of a deterministic component in the DGP can also be interpreted as evidence of a wedge between saving

Table 5.2 Results of the unit-root-tests on ca_t^*

Country	Years	τ_τ	Φ_3	$t(\beta)$	p	τ_μ	Φ_1	$t(\alpha)$	p	τ	p	$\alpha=0.05$	$\alpha=0.10$
Argentina	1961–88	−4.42		−2.69	1	−3.32						$I(0)$ T	$I(0)$ T
Bolivia	1962–88	−3.54	6.37	−1.21	0	−1.81	1.71	−2.69	0	−1.42	0	$I(0)$ D	$I(0)$ D
Brazil	1962–87	−1.80	1.67		0	−2.45	3.01		0	−1.71	0	$I(1)$	$I(1)$
Chile	1962–88	−2.55	3.39		0	−2.50	3.07		0	−1.90	0	$I(1)$	$I(0)$
Colombia	1961–88	−2.49	3.07		0	−2.70	3.66		0	−0.90	0	$I(1)$	$I(0)$
Costa Rica	1962–88	−2.61	3.57		0			−2.51	0			$I(1)$	$I(0)$
Dominican Rep.	1962–88	−3.37	7.21	0.37	0	−3.84		−3.31	0			$I(0)$ D	$I(0)$ D
Ecuador	1962–88	−3.40	5.81	−1.10	0	−3.21		−2.65	0			$I(0)$ D	$I(0)$ D
El Salvador	1961–88	−5.13		−2.25	0							$I(0)$ T	$I(0)$ T
Guatemala	1961–88	−1.73	1.57		2	−1.26	0.87		2	−0.11	2	$I(1)$	$I(1)$
Honduras	1961–88	−4.21		−3.02	1							$I(0)$ T	$I(0)$ T
India	1961–88	−1.92	2.13		0	−2.10	2.23		1	−1.18	1	$I(1)$	$I(1)$
Indonesia	1964–88	−3.89		0.48	0	−3.93		−2.68	0			$I(0)$ D	$I(0)$ D
Israel	1960–88	−3.68		−1.18	1	−1.76	1.55		2	−0.46	2	$I(1)$	$I(1)$
Jamaica	1961–87	−3.66		−3.12	1							$I(0)$ T	$I(0)$ T
Korea	1960–88	−0.29	1.03		2	0.23	0.64		2	−0.96	2	$I(1)$	$I(1)$
Kenya	1965–88	−3.04	4.69		0	−3.09		−2.66	0			$I(0)$ D	$I(0)$ D
Malawi	1966–88	−1.92	1.92		0	−1.84	1.75		0	−1.03	0	$I(1)$	$I(1)$
Malaysia	1962–88	−2.56	3.43		0	−2.65	3.55		0	−2.62	0	$I(1)$	$I(0)$
Mali	1965–88	−4.32		−1.95	1	−3.63		−0.60	0			$I(0)$ T	$I(0)$ T
Mexico	1961–88	−3.46	6.01	0.16	1	−3.53		−3.46	1			$I(0)$ D	$I(0)$ D
Panama	1962–86	−1.90	1.95		0	−1.51	1.48	−2.62	1	−1.57	0	$I(1)$	$I(1)$
Paraguay	1962–88	−3.01	4.62		0	−2.19	2.41		0	−0.86	0	$I(1)$	$I(1)$
Peru	1961–88	−4.12	−0.93		1	−4.03		−2.97	1			$I(0)$ D	$I(0)$ D
Philippines	1962–88	−2.20	2.47		0	−2.17	2.35		0	−1.64	0	$I(1)$	$I(0)$

		τ_τ	Φ_3	$t(\beta)$	τ_μ	Φ_1	$t(\alpha)$	τ	p		
Senegal	1970–88	−2.61	3.54		−2.64	3.51	−2.55	−0.63	0	$I(1)$	$I(0)$ D
Sri Lanka	1962–87	−3.20	5.13		−2.90	4.20	−2.37	−1.52	0	$I(1)$	$I(0)$ D
Thailand	1964–88	−2.57	3.39		−2.48	3.10		−1.33	0	$I(1)$	$I(1)$
Tanzania	1962–88	−2.98	4.46		−2.18	2.43		−1.22	0	$I(1)$	$I(1)$
Tunisia	1962–88	−2.26	2.87		−1.74	1.65		−1.25	0	$I(1)$	$I(1)$
Uruguay	1962–88	−2.89	4.19		−2.73	3.79	−1.34	−2.37	0	$I(0)$	$I(0)$
Venezuela	1966–87	−3.09	4.80		−3.17		0.61	−3.16	0	$I(0)$	$I(0)$
Zambia	1966–87	−3.97		−1.98	−3.26		−1.57	−2.80	0	$I(0)$	$I(0)$ T
5 per cent significance values		−3.60	7.24	2.07	−3.00	5.18	2.08	−1.95			
10 per cent significance values		−3.24	5.91	1.71	−2.63	4.12	1.72	−1.60			

Notes:

τ_τ, τ_μ and τ are the statistics for the unit-root hypothesis of the ADF testing procedure (Fuller, 1976, Table 8.5.2). Φ_3 and Φ_1 are the statistics of the Dickey–Fuller-tests (1981) for the significance of the deterministic trend and drift, respectively, under the assumption of a unit-root process.

$t(\beta)$ and $t(\alpha)$ are the t-statistics for the trend and the drift, respectively, when the unit-root hypothesis is rejected.

p is the number of lags in the ADF procedure.

$I(k)$ D (resp. $I(k)$ T) means that the series is integrated of order k with drift (trend).

The significance values in the last two rows relate to a sample of 25 observations.

and investment rates, we conclude that some degree of capital mobility was present in 27 out of the 33 DCs analysed. Obviously, this does not mean that perfect capital mobility occurred, but rather that a (possibly limited) amount of capital market integration emerged in several DCs over 1960–88.

The interpretation of the results must in any case be cautious. On the one hand, the proxy chosen for foreign aid flows is an imperfect one. On the other, the IMF classifies eight of the countries mentioned (Malawi, Tanzania, Tunisia, El Salvador, Jamaica, Honduras, Mali, Zambia) as 'official borrowers' – that is, countries whose external debt was owned at least two-thirds by international institutions in 1989. These countries benefit to a large extent from non-market loans, therefore the wedge between saving and investment may have a special origin (notice, however, that the series has been cleared of the official grant component). Finally, one should keep in mind that the quality of macroeconomic data on these economies is often unsatisfactory (Montiel, 1993).

Notwithstanding these caveats, these results indicate that in eleven developing countries saving and investment rates do not have a long-run stable relation, while in sixteen other the distance between the two variables is constant or increases over time. Compared with the finding by Gundlach and Sinn (1992) on industrial economies – namely, that only six out of 23 OECD countries have an integrated current account – this shows that in relatively many DCs saving and investment rates followed different statistical patterns in the period under observation. This outcome is broadly consistent with previous studies on developing countries (see Section 5.2). Only a few relevant differences appear.

- First, in one case not classified in other time-series studies (that of Argentina) the capital-mobility hypothesis is not rejected by our tests.
- Second, some of the countries for which the capital-mobility hypothesis is not rejected according to Table 5.1 (Chile, Colombia, Malaysia and Uruguay) *cannot* be classified as 'open' according to our tests.
- Third, the opposite is true for Honduras which anyway is included among the 'official borrowers' by the IMF.

Notice, however, that the studies mentioned in Table 5.1 do not always agree on the classification of individual countries.

It is important to remind ourselves that the testing procedure adopted here has several advantages over both the cross-section

Feldstein–Horioka (1980) approach and the traditional time-series regression, as well as over the Gundlach–Sinn (1992) testing strategy. This procedure suggests that the *absence* of a long run relation between saving and investment rates or the existence of a *different* mean or time trend in the two series are indications of (some degree of) capital market integration. One can therefore reasonably argue that almost all of 33 DCs examined have experienced some capital mobility over the period 1961–88, although this by no means implies perfect integration in world capital markets. Moreover, we cannot *a priori* exclude that potential capital mobility has been present in the countries where the adjusted current-account series appear to be stationary, even if in this case a persistent change in the net foreign asset position did not materialise. In Chapter 6 we turn to the issue of the determinants of net capital inflows across this set of developing economies.

APPENDIX 1: INTEGRATION AND COINTEGRATION

Integrated Stochastic Processes

A stochastic process is integrated of order d (hereafter, it is $I(d)$) if it admits a stationary and invertible ARMA representation after differencing d times (Engle and Granger, 1987); $I(d)$ processes are equivalent to the familiar ARIMA(p, d, q) processes:

$$\varphi_p(L)(1-L)^d y_t = \theta_q(L)\varepsilon_t \qquad (A5.1)$$

where $\varphi_p(L)$ and $\theta_q(L)$ are scalar polynomials of order p and q in the lag operator L (defined as $L^h x_t = x_{t-h}$) with all their roots outside the unit circle, and ε_t is a white noise (an identically and independently distributed stochastic process).

Integration Tests

If $q = 0$ in (A5.1), the order of integration d of a series generated by an $I(d)$ process can be ascertained with the ADF test of Dickey and Fuller (1981). This test will be carried out by estimating the regression:

$$\Delta y_t = \gamma y_{t-1} + \alpha + \beta t + \sum_{k=1}^{p} \theta_k \Delta y_{t-k} + \varepsilon_t \qquad (A5.2)$$

(where p lags of the endogenous variable are included in order to whiten the residuals ε_t) with the following associated system of hypotheses:

$$\begin{cases} H_0: \gamma = 0 & \Rightarrow \quad y_t \sim I(1) \\ H_1: \gamma < 0 & \Rightarrow \quad y_t \sim I(0) \end{cases} \tag{A5.3}$$

In order to do that, we use the t-statistic for γ. The critical values for this statistic are those reported by Fuller (1976): they are different depending on the inclusion in the regression (A5.2) of the trend and constant ('drift') terms. Hence there exist three critical values. The first one is for the regression with trend and drift ($\alpha \neq 0$, $\beta \neq 0$), whose values are tabulated in Fuller (1976) as τ_τ. The second is for the regression without trend but with drift ($\alpha \neq 0$, $\beta = 0$), named τ_μ. The third (simply τ) is for the regression without trend and drift ($\alpha = \beta = 0$).

If the trend and drift terms are included in the empirical regression (A5.2) but do not exist in the true generating process of the series y_t, the results of the integration test will be biased. The same is true in the opposite case (for instance, when the true process includes a trend, but the regression (A5.2) is estimated with $\alpha = \beta = 0$). Since the results of the integration test are conditional on the correct specification of the regression (A5.2), one should test the significance of the trend and the drift. If $\gamma = 0$ (namely, if the series y_t is integrated of order 1) the significance of α and β cannot be verified using their t-statistics; one should instead apply the Φ_1 and Φ_3 tests of Dickey and Fuller (1981). Moreover, the system of hypotheses (A5.3) compares the null hypothesis of $I(1)$ against the alternative of $I(0)$, but an economic time series can in principle be integrated of order greater than 1. In order to verify the null hypothesis of $I(d)$ against the alternative one of $I(d-1)$ the ADF test must be carried out after differencing the series $d-1$ times. We have also carried out ADF tests on differenced series, thus verifying the null of $I(2)$ against the alternative of $I(1)$; in no case was a series found $I(2)$.

The results reported in Table 5.2 were obtained following the procedure outlined in Dolado, Jenkinson and Sosvilla Rivero (1990) – that is, starting from the more general version of (A5.2) (that with $\alpha \neq 0$ and $\beta \neq 0$) and progressively simplifying the model with the appropriate Φ_i-tests (Dickey and Fuller, 1981) until the null hypothesis of integration or that of the absence of a deterministic component (trend or drift) are rejected.

Spurious Regression and Cointegration

Let us consider the regression model:

$$y_t = \beta x_t + z_t \tag{A5.4}$$

where z_t is the regression residual. If the variables y_t and x_t are $I(d)$ ($d > 0$) (A5.4) is defined a *spurious* regression (Granger and Newbold, 1974). In this case the t-statistic of β diverges asymptotically in absolute value towards infinity even though y_t and x_t are stochastically independent. A regression conducted on (A5.4) will therefore in any event appear highly significant, even if it is completely misspecified (in particular, even if it omits relevant variables).

The series y_t and x_t are cointegrated of order d and b (in short $CI(d,b)$) if the linear combination $z_t = y_t - \beta x_t$ defined by (A5.4) is $I(d - b)$. Since most economic time series are $I(1)$, the most frequent case is that of $CI(1,1)$ series – namely, $I(1)$ series with an $I(0)$ linear combination. In this case the stochastic trends of the series evolve jointly in the long run, without drifting too far apart. In other words, the random-walk component of the two variables cancel each other, so that the residual z_t of the regression (A5.4) does not keep persistently away from zero. The spurious regression (A5.4) does in this case express a true long-run economic relationship between the variables involved. The same concepts can be extended to the general case of n variables ($n > 2$).

APPENDIX 2: DEFINITIONS AND SOURCES OF THE EMPIRICAL VARIABLES

The unit-root-tests reported in Table 5.2 are performed on annual observations of the variable ca_t^* defined as $ca_t^* = (CA_t - OUT)/GDP_t$. CA_t and OUT_t are the series of the current account balance and the official unrequited transfers, respectively, expressed in current US dollars and provided by the IMF, *International Financial Statistics* (series codes: 77a.d and 77agd); GDP_t is gross domestic product in current dollars from Summers and Heston (1991). ca_t^* is meant to be the empirical counterpart of the left-hand-side variable of (5.6).

The use of OUT_t as a proxy for foreign aid flows needs some comments. No annual data on foreign aid flows covering a large number of DCs over the whole period 1960–88 are available, to our knowledge, from the international agencies. Therefore, while the item 'Official unrequited transfers' accounts for only a portion of foreign aid, it seems a reasonable proxy for aid_t. The item '*Private* unrequited transfers' has been dropped, as it includes labour incomes from some categories of emigrants, which of course cannot be assimilated to foreign aid.

6 Determinants of Net Capital Flows in Developing Countries

A fundamental question concerning capital movements in developing economies is tackled in this chapter. After suggesting a (qualified) positive answer to the question: 'Were developing countries (DCs) open to international capital movements during 1960–88?' in Chapter 5, we now ask: 'What determined the distribution of net capital flows across DCs in the same period?' While Chapter 5 addresses an issue which is preliminary with respect to the central topics of this volume, this chapter goes right to core of the growth-theoretical approach to capital flows – indeed, it would not be arbitrary to view it as the empirical counterpart of Chapter 3.

The chapter reports the outcome of empirical researches carried out in three directions. It starts from an introductory econometric evaluation of the theoretical predictions of the main representative-agent models outlined in Sections 3.1 and 3.2 of Chapter 3, after a digression on the conceptual difficulties involved therein (Section 6.1). It then describes the findings of a more detailed assessment of the 'augmented' neoclassical model with partial capital mobility. Finally, the demographic influences on net capital flows suggested, for instance, by the overlapping-generations (OLG) model are empirically tested (Section 6.2).

Our analysis is exploratory rather than assertive, because the econometric literature on these themes is surprisingly scarce if compared, for example, with cross-country studies on the sources of growth. However, we stick here to a few principles that we believe can improve the quality (and credibility) of our results. The first one is *parsimony*, in the sense of Occam's razor. We will not, in an eclectic attitude, plug into the regressions any sort of (potentially) significant explanatory variables, but we will rather operate an *a priori* discrimination. This will be done according to a *consistency* requirement *vis-à-vis* the theoretical models we adopt as reference. The third rule we follow is meant to cope with what we think is the most serious limitation of cross-country econometrics – namely, endogeneity and reverse causation. Instead of undertaking the route of fixing (complex) statistical remedies, we try to solve the problem at its origin introducing *initial conditions* as independent variables as extensively as possible. Finally, we test for *sensitivity* and robustness of our results, to the extent that this does not violate the parsimony and consistency principles stated above.

6.1 DISCRIMINATING AMONG GROWTH-THEORETICAL APPROACHES TO CAPITAL MOVEMENTS

This section illustrates the outcomes of an introductory empirical evaluation of theoretical predictions on the determinants of net capital flows in a cross-section of DCs. More specifically, we consider as a yardstick the sign of the partial correlations between the marginal product of (physical) capital – MPK – on the one hand, and the 'fundamentals' listed in Table 3.1 of Chapter 3, on the other. However, as no reliable empirical measure of the MPK is available, we regress the *per capita* amount of net capital inflows on the fundamentals. The rationale is that the distribution of capital flows across DCs should respond to international arbitrage incentives connected with country-specific relative conditions (physical and human capital endowments, scale effects, and so on) which are synthesised in the concept of MPK.

A short digression about the problems inherent in any attempt at discriminating among growth models is appropriate at this point. In general, the capacity of the applied economist of discriminating among alternative models is directly related to the availability and quality of the data and inversely associated with the 'observational equivalence' of the models themselves – or, in other words, with the affinity of their predictions. The latter point was made already in Section 3.5: take the case of the 'augmented' neoclassical and the Lucas (1988) models. If we make the assumption of partial capital mobility, therefore preventing an external financing of human capital accumulation, and if there are no 'scale effects' (as in the original Lucas paper), the qualitative predictions of the two models about the determinants of the MPK do not differ (see Table 3.1). Only if one allows for economywide scale economies does a positive correlation between the MPK and size appear that allows us to distinguish between the two. However, both the augmented and the Lucas model predict a negative partial correlation between the MPK and *per capita* income if the regression controls for human capital stocks, as well as a positive partial correlation between MPK and h.

Insofar as the quality of human capital data is concerned, a few caveats can be mentioned.

- First, the concept of human capital is of course a metaphor of the different human ability to perform an activity – in our case, a productive (marketable) activity; in other words, there is no directly measurable 'human capital' (see OECD, 1998, for an overview). The concept of human capital is so elusive and hard to translate into empirical measurement that Paul Romer concluded his essay on human capital and growth with the following statement (1990, p. 282):

[The results] should not be taken as a strong confirmation of the model considered here because there is little reason to believe that these data discriminate strongly between different models.

- Second, in most of the empirical studies of the relation between human capital and growth only 'education' has been used as a proxy for human capital: this is questionable as one can argue that other factors such as 'health-care' or 'social norms' enter the definition of human capital, which is by definition a multi-dimensional concept.[1]
- Third, while proxies for the 'investment in education' such as enrolment rates have been available for a long time, reliable proxies for the 'stock of education' have become accessible only recently.[2]
- Fourth, the issue of *quality* standards in education is largely neglected (OECD, 1998, p. 82).

The scarcity of reliable long time series has remarkably limited the scope of international comparisons of the growth effect of human capital based on time-series analysis, although attempts in this direction have been made – for instance, in the context of the 'growth-accounting' literature (see Maddison, 1987). As a consequence, the bulk of the recent revival of empirical research is based on cross-section or panel-data analysis. Another restriction, which is binding even in a cross-section context, has until recently been imposed by the lack of *stock* data on human capital: even in 1991, Robert Barro regretted that he had to use flow instead of stock data (Barro, 1991, p. 414).

The reason why insufficient data on the stock of human capital seriously limit the empirical researcher can be perceived looking at the growth rate of y in the 'augmented' neoclassical and the 'modified' Lucas models, as shown by (3.18) and (3.25). One can check that in both equations the right-hand-side variable affecting the growth rate of *per capita* output is the rate of change of h, which in general is *not* equal to the rate of investment in human capital, s_h. In order to use s_h (a flow variable) instead of the rate of change of h one has to assume that *every* economy included in the cross-section is sufficiently close to its steady-state position (on this point, see Benhabib and Spiegel, 1994, p. 154). The steady-state assumption justifies the choice of Mankiw, Romer and Weil (1992, p. 423) and Knight, Loayza and Villanueva (1993) of estimating an equation like (3.18) with investment rates in physical and human capital as independent variables, but not the procedure of Barro (1991) as he does not assume that each individual economy is necessarily in the neighbourhood of its steady state. The steady-state assumption is obviously inconsistent with endogenous-growth equations such as (3.25): in this case, one must necessarily estimate the empirical relation using stock data for the rate of growth of h.

A different class of endogenous growth models relate *per capita* income growth to the *level* of human capital (instead of its rate of change), through a mechanism of 'endogenous innovation' (see Romer, 1990; Benhabib and Spiegel, 1994). The underlying intuition is that the national rate of technical innovation and the capability of technological adoption from the leading countries depends on the existing level of human capital rather than on its rate of change. In principle, it would be feasible to assess the empirical performance of the augmented neoclassical setup versus that of this 'endogenous-innovation' model: all one should do is to check if the growth rate of y is positively associated with either the rate of change (augmented model) or the level of human capital (endogenous-innovation model). Unfortunately, while the evidence provided by Romer (1990)[3] and Benhabib and Spiegel (1994) is supportive of the endogenous-innovation model, the evidence produced by Mankiw, Romer and Weil (1992) and by Levine and Renelt (1992) lends support to the augmented model. As trivial at it may sound, all one can infer from this literature is that there exists only a *general* presumption that human capital positively affects growth: attempts at discriminating among different approaches may sometimes turn out to be inconclusive.[4]

However, the predictions concerning the MPK do not replicate this dichotomy 'levels vs. rates-of-change': both (3.19) and (3.28) point out to a relation between the stock of h and the marginal product of physical capital, the only distinctive *qualitative* feature of the modified Lucas model being a positive effect of the size of the economy on the MPK (see Chapter 3).

Determinants of Net Capital Flows in Developing Countries 109

Let us now describe our approach to the empirical evaluation of different models of capital movements in a cross-section of DCs. We regress *per capita* net capital inflows, cumulated over the relevant period, on the determinants of the MPK, as listed in Table 3.1. One would like to find a direct proxy for the marginal product of capital. Unfortunately, no comprehensive and easily comparable measure of the MPK exists, so we resort to the *indirect* strategy of using (*per capita*) cumulated net capital inflows in DCs as the dependent variable, to be regressed against the fundamentals affecting the MPK according to different models.

This strategy has some clear limitations: first, the link between net capital inflows and the fundamentals is theoretically correct only if international arbitrage occurs in such a way that all variation in the MPK across national economies is *instantaneously* eliminated by the operation of capital movements; otherwise, the contribution of other variables must be accounted for – as argued, for instance, in Section 3.3. It is clear that immediate factor price equalisation conflicts with our choice of cumulating net capital flows over a long interval of time; in another respect, however, this allows us to remove all cyclical influences and to focus on long-run factors. Second, working with a cross-country sample does not permit us to evaluate the determinants of the absolute amount of *per capita* net capital flows in DCs but instead of their *distribution* among national economies (an equiproportional rise in all countries would be captured by an increase in the constant term without affecting other features of the cross-sectional regression). Incidentally, this means that our analysis cannot lead to a judgement about the *quantity* of foreign capital flowing into a developing economy (too little or too much, see Lucas, 1990), but rather to an evaluation of the consistency of the distribution of capital flows among DCs with respect to the predictions of the models.

Among the explanatory variables, we include *per capita* income (which is equivalent to a measure of the stock of physical capital, see Section 3.1 and 3.2), proxies for the stock of human capital and the size of population as a measure of the dimension of the economy. As already stressed, one of the most serious problems of growth regressions in a cross-section setup is reverse causality – namely, the possibility that the estimated correlations are wrongly interpreted because in reality the left-hand-side variable does not depend on, but rather 'causes', some of the right-hand-side variables. This problem can be addressed with causality tests in a time-series setup, but not in a cross-section framework. When *period averages* of the left-hand-side variable and of (some of) the right-hand-side regressors are computed over the same time interval, as is often the case in cross-country growth regressions, the possibility of causality tests is largely precluded. Alternatively, instrumental variables can be introduced, but only when good enough instruments are available. Here we follow a different approach to cross-section analysis that overcomes the reverse causality bias (as emphasised by Rodrik, 1996a; Sarel, 1996). We regress the dependent variable on the *initial values* of the explanatory variables, which are predetermined with respect to net capital inflows, rather than on their period averages. In other words, we estimate the impact of the relevant initial conditions on the distribution of net capital inflows across DCs, which we assume is driven by international variability in the MPK at the beginning of the period.

Per capita income is obtained from the Summers–Heston (1991) database. As mentioned above, finding satisfactory proxies of human capital stocks is more complex; here we opt for a multidimensional measure of h relying both on the rather common practice of including educational attainments and on an international standard of healthcare capacity. In the first case we use secondary educational attainments, in the second the ratio of the number of physicians over population (see the Appendix on p. 131 for further details).

Another question is how to measure scale effects. Backus, Kehoe and Kehoe (1992) use either total GDP or total output of manufacturing sectors to test whether the growth rate of *per capita* output (alternatively, productivity growth in manufacturing) is positively affected by scale. They also construct scale and intensity variables to account for human capital. Overall, their empirical findings do not support simple endogenous growth models based on scale effects, while they are consistent with a role of intra-industry trade in enhancing productivity growth. Jones (1995a, 1995b) argues that total investment or investment in producer durables is a good proxy for scale effects in Romer (1986)- or Rebelo (1992)-type models of endogenous growth, while an indicator of the amount of resources devoted to R&D (for example the number of scientists or real R&D expenditure) can reveal the presence of scale effects according to endogenous-innovation models. In both cases Jones rejects the hypothesis that scale positively affects growth. Here we do not consider R&D-based models, and we take total population as a measure of the size of the economy.[5]

Our dependent variable is cumulated over 1960–88 – that is, a whole capital-flow cycle, in order to analyse the pattern of net capital movements over a complete recovery–insolvency–stagnation sequence.

Determinants of Net Capital Flows in Developing Countries 111

Although the choice of 1960 as the initial year has been primarily dictated by the availability of the data, we have also checked that the foreign debt and direct investment stocks of most DCs in 1960 were negligible with respect to the stocks accumulated thereafter (both in absolute and in *per capita* terms, and even accounting for nominal depreciation). The choice of 1988 as the end-point of the analysis is based on the consideration that in 1988 a full cycle of international capital flows to DCs, starting with the slow revival in capital flows after the Second World War and ending with a stagnation after the crisis of the early 1980s, was concluded (see Section 2.2). 1960–88 is therefore a sensible periodisation within which a study of the determinants of the distribution of capital flows across DCs can be conducted; nonetheless we also test the models in a shorter sub-period.

The country sample is the same as in Chapter 5: it includes seven African, ten South American, eight Central American, and eight Asian economies. Merely 'oil-based' economies and pure financial centres have been excluded, as well as other countries for which data on human capital stocks or the current account balance were not available from 1960 (see the Appendix for further details). During this period, the DCs have generally been net capital importers, and the sign of the current-account balance is usually negative for the countries considered here (see Table A6.1 in the Appendix). The incomplete coverage of the country sample implies that the results relate just to these economies and no claim of universality is made;[6] nonetheless, the sample includes the large majority of developing *market* economies in terms of either population or GDP.

Column (1) in Table 6.1 shows that *per capita* income displays a positive partial correlation with net capital inflows, which is in contrast with the prediction of the Solow model but could instead support the Romer endogenous-growth model; however, column (3) shows that the scale variable (population in 1960) has a negative significant correlation with net inflows, which is not what one would expect according to the Romer model.[7] The sign of the partial correlation between *per capita* income and net inflows becomes negative if one adds proxies for the stock of human capital in 1960: this is true both for the augmented neoclassical model of Mankiw, Romer and Weil (1992) and for the 'modified' Lucas model including a scale variable. The coefficient of the health-care proxy is significant at the 5 per cent level, but that of secondary education is not; however, both coefficients are correctly signed, while the scale variable displays a negative coefficient which is in contrast with the prediction of basic endogenous-growth theory.

Table 6.1 Regression of *per capita* net inflows, 1960–88, on the determinants of the MPK in 1960 according to different models
Dependent variable: *per capita* cumulated net capital inflows over 1960–88

	Solow (1956) (1)	Mankiw, Romer and Weil (1992) (2)	Modified Romer (1986) (3)	Modified Lucas (1988) (4)
Constant	269.5 (1.06)	343 (1.27)	341.8 (1.28)	439 (1.57)
Per capita income, 1990	1.02 (1.37)	−0.49 (−0.74)	0.953 (1.25)	−0.67 (−1.0)
Secondary education, 1960		17.7 (1.17)		20.9 (1.4)
No. of physicians, 1960		935969 (2.11)**		929998 (2.11)**
Population, 1960			−0.001 (−2.74)**	−0.002 (−1.22)
Adjusted R^2	0.1	0.28	0.09	0.29
F-statistic	4.72 [0.04]	5.05 [0.00]	2.59 [0.09]	4.23 [0.00]

Notes:
T-values in parentheses.
Probability values in brackets.
* Significant at the 10 per cent level; ** Significant at the 5 per cent level.
Estimation method: OLS. Standard errors adjusted according to White (1980) if the hypothesis of homoscedasticity is rejected.

The inclusion of some measures of human capital improves the fit of the regression, but the coefficient of *per capita* income is always estimated very imprecisely and is never significant even at the 10 per cent level.

In Table 6.2 we perform some sensitivity analysis. Among the additional explanatory variables we include the openness ratio in 1960 (it is plausibly argued that trade openness favours the inflows of capitals as it reduces the incentive to default: see for instance Aizenman, 1991);[8] a measure of political instability (more instability should command a higher risk premium hence, *ceteris paribus*, curtail net inflows); and a dummy for the countries classified as official borrowers. The regressions essentially replicate those of Table 6.1. Among the additional explanatory variables, only the proxy for political instability turns out to be significant at the 10 per cent level.

Table 6.3 reports the sensitivity regressions run with two regional dummies for African and Asian countries.[9] Once again, the signs of the coefficients are unaltered relative to Table 6.1 but, quite interestingly, the inclusion of regional dummies improves the fit of the regressions in columns (2) and (4) – namely, those accounting for human capital stocks. Moreover, the parameter of *per capita* income is now estimated rather precisely in the augmented neoclassical- and Lucas-type regressions (in both cases, it is negative and significant at the 10 per cent level). Notice that both regional dummies display negative coefficients indicating that African and Asian economies have, *ceteris paribus*, received less *per capita* inflows relative to Latin American ones.

One of the limitations of these estimates is that explaining net inflows with the determinants of the MPK is likely to be more effective the closer one is to the initial date when the determinants of the MPK are evaluated. Indeed, if international arbitrage does not immediately equalise the MPK across countries, one can predict that other variables affect net capital flows even in a growth-theory framework. We therefore replicate our exercise of empirical discrimination among theoretical models over the sub-period 1960–72 – that is, the period ending before the first oil crisis of 1973–4 which partly reshaped international financial relations (see Section 2.2). The growth models accounting for human capital performs better over 1960–72: about one-third of the variability of net *per capita* inflows is explained by the regressions in columns (2) and (4), and the coefficients of the 'fundamentals' are often significant and correctly signed (Table 6.4). However, the hypothesis of positive scale effects is rejected.

Table 6.2 Regression of *per capita* net inflows, 1960–88, on the determinants of the MPK in 1960 according to different models
(Sensitivity analysis regressions)
Dependent variable: *per capita* cumulated net capital inflows over 1960–88

	Solow (1956) (1)	*Mankiw, Romer and Weil (1992)* (2)	*Modified Romer (1986)* (3)	*Modified Lucas (1988)* (4)
Constant	133 (0.3)	226 (0.65)	202.4 (0.36)	322.5 (0.77)
Per capita income, 1960	1.1 (1.66)*	−0.22 (−0.4)	1.06 (1.46)	−0.29 (−0.46)
Secondary education, 1960		76.6 (1.36)		72.5 (1.25)
No. of physicians, 1960		934286 (2.1)**		966989 (2.08)**
Population, 1960			−0.6 E-3 (−0.67)	−0.001 (−0.44)
Openness ratio	12.4 (0.91)	7.2 (0.74)	11.3 (0.75)	5.8 (0.56)
Political instability	−661.2 (−1.4)	−741.5 (−1.96)*	−673 (−1.4)	−762 (−1.87)*
Dummy for official borrowers	−25.6 (−0.1)	271.2 (0.77)	−44.5 (−0.16)	243.7 (0.67)
Adjusted R^2	0.15	0.38	0.12	0.36
F-statistic	2.41 [0.07]	4.3 [0.00]	1.89 [0.13]	3.58 [0.01]

Notes:
T-values in parentheses.
Probability values in brackets.
* Significant at the 10 per cent level; ** Significant at the 5 per cent level.
Estimation method: OLS. Standard errors adjusted to White (1980) if the hypothesis of homoscedasticity is rejected.

Table 6.3 Regression of *per capita* net inflows, 1960–88, on the determinants of the MPK in 1960 according to different models
(Sensitivity analysis regressions: regional dummies)
Dependent variable: *per capita* cumulated net capital inflows over 1960–88

	Solow (1956) (1)	Mankiw, Romer and Weil (1992) (2)	Modified Romer (1986) (3)	Modified Lucas (1988) (4)
Constant	352.3 (0.49)	1018 (2.25)	418.9 (0.78)	1016.6 (2.09)
Per capita income, 1960	0.87 (1.6)	−1.16 (−1.74)*	0.83 (1.47)	−1.16 (−1.7)*
Secondary education, 1960		78.1 (1.44)		78.2 (1.36)
No. of physicians, 1960		1296404 (2.89)**		1296025 (2.82)**
Population, 1960			−0.9E-3 (−0.4)	0.19E-4 (0.01)
Openness ratio	13.8 (1.27)	7.3 (0.84)	12.4 (1.07)	7.37 (0.79)
Political instability	−792.8 (−1.66)*	−1203.6 (−3.03)**	−793.8 (−1.64)	−1203.3 (−2.79)
African dummy	−393.8 (−0.85)	−493.9 (−1.29)	−405.7 (−0.85)	−493.5 (−1.26)
Asian dummy	−119.4 (−0.3)	−812.8 (−2.34)**	−70.6 (−0.17)	−814 (−2.17)**
Adjusted R^2	0.14	0.46	0.11	0.44
F-stastic	2.05 [0.1]	4.93 [0.00]	1.69 [0.16]	4.14 [0.00]

Notes:
T-values in parentheses.
Probability values in brackets.
* Significant at the 10 per cent level; ** Significant at the 5 per cent level.
Estimation method: OLS. Standard errors adjusted according to White (1980) if the hypothesis of homoscedasticity is rejected.

Table 6.4 Regression of *per capita* net inflows, 1960–72, on the determinants of the MPK in 1960 according to different models
Dependent variable: *per capita* cumulated net capital inflows over 1960–72

	Solow (1956) (1)	Mankiw, Romer and Weil (1992) (2)	Modified Romer (1986) (3)	Modified Lucas (1988) (4)
Constant	31.6 (0.61)	65.1 (1.1)	42 (0.63)	79.9 (1.3)
Per capita income, 1960	0.16 (0.9)	−0.22 (−1.7)*	0.15 (0.86)	−0.23 (−1.68)*
Secondary education, 1960		15.8 (1.3)		15.1 (1.2)
No. of physicians, 1960		258244 (2.5)**		265024 (2.5)**
Population, 1960			−0.2 E-3 (−1.6)	−0.26 E-3 (−0.7)
Adjusted R^2	0.04	0.33	0.01	0.31
F-statistic	2.24 [0.14]	6.1 [0.00]	1.19 [0.32]	4.6 [0.00]

Notes:
T-values in parentheses.
Probability values in brackets.
* Significant at the 10 per cent level; ** Significant at the 5 per cent level.
Estimation method: OLS. Standard errors adjusted according to White (1980) if the hypothesis of homoscedesticity is rejected.

Table 6.5 Regression of *per capita* net inflows, 1960–72, on the determinants of the MPK in 1960 according to different models
(Sensitivity analysis regressions)
Dependent variable: *per capita* cumulated net capital inflows over 1960–72

	Solow (1956) (1)	Mankiw, Romer and Weil (1992) (2)	Modified Romer (1986) (3)	Modified Lucas (1988) (4)
Constant	−15.6 (0.15)	18.6 (0.24)	−18.7 (−0.14)	21.6 (0.24)
Per capita income, 1960	0.15 (0.98)	−0.21 (−1.67)*	0.15 (0.92)	−0.21 (−1.54)
Secondary education, 1960		16.2 (1.3)		16.04 (1.54)
No. of physicians, 1960		270032 (2.77)**		271057 (2.7)**
Population, 1960			0.29 E-3 (0.11)	−0.24 E-3 (−0.06)
Openness ratio	4.46 (1.23)	3.1 (1.4)	4.51 (1.02)	3.04 (1.3)
Political instability	−123 (−1.41)	−148.8 (−1.8)*	−122.4 (−1.38)	−149 (−1.78)*
Dummy for official borrowers	−55.6 (0.76)	17.6 (0.2)	−54.2 (−0.73)	16.7 (0.21)
Adjusted R^2	0.1	0.43	0.07	0.41
F-statistic	1.9 [0.14]	5.06 [0.00]	1.47 [0.23]	4.2 [0.00]

Notes:
T-values in parentheses.
Probability values in brackets.
* Significant at the 10 per cent level; ** Significant at the 5 per cent level.
Estimation method: OLS. Standard errors adjusted according to White (1980) if the hypothesis of homoscedasticity is rejected.

Table 6.6 Regression of *per capita* net inflows, 1960–72, on the determinants of the MPK in 1960 according to different models
(Sensitivity analysis regressions: regional dummies)
Dependent variable: *per capita* cumulated net capital inflows over 1960–72

	Solow (1956) (1)	Mankiw, Romer and Weil (1992) (2)	Modified Romer (1986) (3)	Modified Lucas (1988) (4)
Constant	11.4 (0.1)	187.16 (1.93)	20.7 (0.17)	181.9 (1.75)
Per capita income, 1960	0.1 (0.86)	−0.4 (−2.8)**	0.1 (0.79)	−0.4 (−2.7)**
Secondary education, 1960		13.9 (1.2)		14.5 (1.18)
No. of physicians, 1960		342661 (3.6)**		34966 (3.5)**
Population, 1960			−0.12 E-3 (−0.25)	0.64 E-4 (0.16)
Openness ratio	4.78 (1.94)*	3.17 (1.7)*	4.58 (1.75)*	3.26 (1.64)
Political instability	−140.5 (−1.3)	−247.4 (−2.9)**	−140.7 (−1.3)	−247.2 (−2.86)**
African dummy	−130.1 (−1.2)	−163.9 (−2.0)*	−131.8 (−1.2)	−162.4 (−1.94)*
Asian dummy	22.5 (0.25)	−145.6 (−1.97)*	29.3 (0.31)	−149.8 (−1.87)*
Adjusted R^2	0.13	0.52	0.1	0.49
F-statistic	1.98 [0.11]	5.8 [0.00]	1.6 [0.19]	4.95 [0.00]

Notes:
T-values in parentheses.
Probability values in brackets.
* Significant at the 10 per cent level; ** Significant at the 5 per cent level.
Estimation method: OLS. Standard errors adjusted according to White (1980) if the hypothesis of homoscedasticity is rejected.

Determinants of Net Capital Flows in Developing Countries 119

These findings are confirmed, and even reinforced, by the sensitivity regressions reported in Table 6.5, which shows that the inclusion of the openness ratio, of the proxy for political instability and of the official-borrower dummy does not remarkably modify the coefficients of the fundamentals.

Testing for the statistical significance of regional dummies induces some alterations in the response of the empirical models (see Table 6.6). The coefficient of initial *per capita* income is now significant at the 5 per cent level in both the Mankiw, Romer and Weil (1992) and the 'modified' Lucas (1988) models. The openness ratio, the political instability variable and the regional dummies are almost always significant at the 10 per cent or 5 per cent level in these two specifications.

The main conclusion we draw from this exploratory investigation of the empirical response of growth-theory predictions concerning capital flows, is that models incorporating human capital perform better than models which rely only on *per capita* income (and scale effects). This result is in line with other econometric findings on the role of human capital in the process of economic growth (Barro and Lee, 1994; Benhabib and Spiegel, 1994). As we show in Chapter 3, there is a sort of duality between the predictions on capital movements and the determinants of the growth rate of the economy, so it is not surprising that human capital stocks provide a positive contribution both in enhancing growth and in attracting capital flows (see Lucas, 1990). An econometric comparison between the neoclassical and the (modified) endogenous-growth model reveals that the size of a developing economy, as proxied by population or GDP, played no discernible role in affecting net capital flows in DCs over 1960–88 (or 1960–72), so the hypothesis of scale effects is not supported by the data. The neoclassical model featuring human capital as an additional factor of production therefore looks the best candidate for an explanation of the determinants of net capital inflows in DCs. In Section 6.2 we accomplish a deeper econometric investigation of this model.

6.2 AN EMPIRICAL ASSESSMENT OF THE NEOCLASSICAL MODEL, WITH PARTIAL CAPITAL MOBILITY, 1960–88

This section reports the outcome of various empirical tests conducted on the basis of an 'augmented' Solow model of capital flows (with capital mobility restricted to physical assets) in a cross-section of 33

DCs, taking 1960 as the starting year and 1988 as the end one. The analysis conducted here is different from that of Section 6.1 in two main respects: first, not only initial conditions but also variables affecting the steady-state position of an individual economy are contemplated; second, we recognise that factor-price equalisation does not occur instantaneously and try to account for this in the regressions. The reason we adopt the assumption of partial capital mobility is that the capital market integration of DCs is likely to have been neither null nor perfect over 1960–88 (see Section 5.3).

The reference model is that of Section 3.3, and the equation to be tested is an empirical version of (3.43) which is reproduced here as (6.1) for convenience:

$$b^* - b(0) = \left\{ \frac{\alpha A}{r+\delta} \left(\frac{s_h A}{n+\delta} \right)^{\frac{\beta}{1-\beta}} \right\}^{\frac{1-\beta}{1-\alpha-\beta}}$$

$$- \left\{ \frac{y(0)}{A(h(0))^\beta} \right\}^{\frac{1}{\alpha}} - \int_0^T s(y-rb)_t \qquad (6.1)$$

In brief, (6.1) suggests that the distribution of net capital inflows (on a *per capita* basis) depends on the so-called 'capital requirement' – namely, the distance between the initial and steady-state level of physical capital (the first two terms on the right-hand side of 6.1), and on domestic saving capacity over the time interval that is needed to complete the transition to the steady state (the third term in 6.1). As stressed in Section 3.5, (6.1) is not a true 'reduced-form' as the integral on its right-hand side is the summation of the product of net *per capita* income and the saving rate in some periods after $t(0)$: obviously these variables are not fully predetermined with respect to cumulated capital flows, so a problem of endogeneity may arise. To overcome this pitfall we stick to the rule stated before, even if we are aware that it provides only an imperfect fixing in this case: the domestic saving rate evaluated at the beginning of the period ($s(0)$) is included among the right-hand-side variables.[10]

In terms of empirical explanatory variables (6.1) thus suggests that the following should be included: the initial stock of human capital ($h(0)$) and the investment rate in secondary education (a proxy for s_h) (positively associated with net capital flows); initial income ($y(0)$), the rate of growth of population and the domestic saving rate (s) which are negatively associated with net capital inflows. The dependent variable is defined as in Section 6.1. Definitions and sources of all empirical variables can be found in the Appendix (pp. 129–32). We also test for sensitiveness and robustness of the coefficients including other regressors as in Section 6.1. Furthermore, we evaluate whether the demographic composition of population can affect net capital flows via its influence on investment and saving rates: to do so, we estimate an empirical formulation where *both* the rate of growth of population *and* a proxy for the dependent share over total population are present together (as suggested for example by Higgins and Williamson, 1996).

Table 6.7 presents all results relative to the whole capital-flow cycle of 1960–88. Column (1) shows the outcome of the basic regression stemming from a linear empirical version of (6.1.) Although the signs of all coefficients are consistent with the neoclassical model, they are estimated very imprecisely and none of them is significant at the 10 per cent level. Column (2) provides a sensitivity analysis regression identical to the ones performed in Section 6.1. The reader can check that only in one case (that of the secondary education enrolment rate) the sign of the 'structural' coefficient changes after additional variables are included. Nonetheless the explanatory capacity of the model is unsatisfactory. Column (3) displays the behaviour of the empirical equation when two control variables which had turned out to be extremely powerful in the sensitivity regressions of Section 6.1 are added to the basic model. A proxy for political instability and a dummy for Asian DCs are both significant at the 5 per cent level and contribute to a substantial reduction of the variability associated with the coefficients of $y(0)$ and $h(0)$. Initial *per capita* income has a negative effect on *per capita* net inflows (significant at the 10 per cent level) as predicted by the augmented model, while the number of physicians (as a share of total population) has a positive impact (significant at the 5 per cent level). The interpretation of these findings is that Asian economies behaved somehow differently with respect to other DCs as far as the inflows of foreign capital over 1960–88 is concerned (namely, they received *lower per capita* flows on a comparative basis), and the inclusion of an Asian dummy improves the efficiency of the estimates.

Higgins and Williamson (1996) suggest that demographic elements exert a strong influence on the saving and investment rate of individual DCs, and that transitional phenomena (particularly demographic transitions) might matter more than initial and steady-state conditions in shaping the long-run behaviour of the balance of payments. We argued extensively in Section 3.4 that different theoretical models and even

Table 6.7 An econometric evaluation of the augmented neoclassical model in a cross-section of 33 DCs Dependent variable: *per capita* cumulated net capital inflows over 1960–88

	(1)	(2)	(3)	(4)
Constant	512.2 (0.65)	1227.2 (1.4)	1360 (1.95)	−3267 (−1.29)
Per capita income, 1960	−0.46 (−0.66)	−0.3 (−0.49)	−1.18 (−1.8)*	−0.02 (−0.03)
Secondary education, 1960	52.6 (0.79)	87.7 (1.44)	79.7 (1.43)	105.5 (1.68)*
No. of physicians, 1960	804697 (1.15)	1108118 (2.31)**	1263244 (2.78)**	14177075 (2.85)**
Rate of investment in secondary education, 1960	12.1 (0.66)	−11.9 (−0.65)	14.1 (0.81)	0.41 (0.02)
Rate of growth of population	−5523 (−0.22)	−30493 (−1.22)	−15545 (−0.73)	−71605 (−2.0)**
Saving rate, 1960	−4.24 (−0.37)	−16.2 (−1.4)	−8.37 (−0.86)	
Openness ratio		21.8 (1.72)*		
Political instability		−895.8 (−2.6)**	−1103 (−2.99)**	−884.7 (−2.33)**
Dummy for official borrowers		27.6 (0.07)		
Asian dummy			−832 (−2.5)**	
Share of population under 15, 1960				12389 (1.82)*
Adjusted R^2	0.21	0.39	0.45	0.4
F-statistic	2.48 [0.05]	3.29 [0.01]	4.33 [0.00]	4.16 [0.00]
Bera–Jarque-test of normality of the residuals	2.62 [0.27]	2.16 [0.34]	0.38 [0.83]	11.6 [0.00]
Chi square-test of homoscedasticity	0.95 [0.33]	0.04 [0.84]	0.26 [0.6]	0.13 [0.71]

Notes:
T-values in parentheses.
Probability values in brackets.
* Significant at the 10 per cent level; ** Significant at the 5 per cent level.
Estimation method: OLS. Standard errors adjusted according to White (1980) if the hypothesis of homoscedasticity is rejected.

specific assumptions regarding the age composition of population and the labour force lead to different predictions about saving and net capital flows. One should track the dynamics of population and trace the development of any demographic transition episode (à la Kuznets) in each country of the sample, so that saving rates can be fully explained by demography (provided this is feasible). We follow a less ambitious programme here: drawing on Higgins and Williamson (1996), we verify whether two demographic variables (the rate of growth of population and the share of population under 15 at the beginning of the period) can capture the variability in saving rates across our country sample. We would also like to see whether demographic variables can (partially) account for the 'Asian peculiarity' mentioned above. The regression reported in column (4) of Table 6.7 yields mixed responses. Demographic proxies behave rather well: both coefficients are significant and correctly signed, as one would expect that the steady-state capital stock is reduced in the presence of a higher rate of growth of population while the dependency rate, proxied by the share of population under 15, depresses the saving rate enhancing foreign capital dependence.[11] However, capital flows appear no longer related to initial *per capita* income. Moreover, a violation of the normality assumption is revealed by the Bera–Jarque-test: we interpret this as a signal of the presence of outliers which in turn means that the empirical model does not correctly apply to all countries in the sample. We also tested an alternative specification where not only the initial dependency rate, but also the rate of variation of the dependency rate over the relevant period, is included to capture the transitional effect of demographic change on the saving rate (see Bloom and Williamson, 1997): this specification, however, does not bear improvement in any of the intervals considered.

Table 6.8 replicates the analysis for the sub-period 1960–72: the rationale for shortening the time span is that we get closer to the year when the initial conditions are evaluated, so if the transition to the steady state is faster the model should perform better in a smaller sub-period. Besides, the years 1973–74 witnessed the first oil-shock which triggered a wide adjustment process involving international financial relations and especially the pattern of capital movements to DCs. It could thus be that 1960–72 is a more uniform time interval for estimating the model.

As a matter of fact, the global performance of the regressions of Table 6.8 is better, while it turns out that the rate of investment in secondary education and the saving rate in 1960 have a higher

Table 6.8 An econometric evaluation of the augmented neoclassical model in a cross-section of 33 developing countries
Dependent variable: *per capita* cumulated net capital inflows over 1960–72

	(1)	(2)	(3)	(4)
Constant	−89.2 (−0.46)	5.87 (0.03)	102.6 (0.46)	−530.1 (−1.06)
Per capita income, 1960	−0.27 (−1.46)	−0.24 (−1.96)*	−0.47 (−2.89)**	−0.25 (−1.9)*
Secondary education, 1960	2.58 (0.19)	9.28 (0.76)	7.88 (0.9)	
Number of physicians, 1960	190354 (1.44)	235342 (2.45)**	287222 (2.4)**	317743 (2.88)**
Rate of investment in secondary education, 1960	9.99 (2.13)**	5.78 (1.59)	10.9 (2.82)**	7.6 (2.35)**
Rate of growth of population	4528.5 (0.75)	−70.4 (−0.01)	2187 (0.44)	−6144 (−0.74)
Saving rate in 1960	−2.3 (−1.67)*	−4.68 (−2.03)**	−2.9 (−2.8)**	
Openness ratio		4.59 (1.81)*		
Political instability		−127 (−1.69)*	−191 (−2.2)**	−122.26 (−1.53)
Dummy for official borrowers		−0.33 (0.00)		
African dummy			−340 (−0.45)	
Asian dummy			−204.5 (−2.58)**	
Share of population under 15, 1960				1626 (1.14)
Adjusted R^2	0.43	0.52	0.59	0.49
F-statistic	5.05 [0.00]	4.83 [0.00]	6.1 [0.00]	6.07 [0.00]
Bera–Jarque-test of normality of the residuals	0.88 [0.64]	0.76 [0.68]	0.46 [0.79]	6.55 [0.04]
Chi square-test of homoscedasticity	7.19 [0.00]	0.87 [0.36]	5.1 [0.02]	5.73 [0.02]

Notes:
T-values in parentheses. Probability values in brackets.
* Significant at the 10 per cent level; ** Significant at the 5 per cent level.
Estimation method: OLS. Standard errors adjusted according to White (1980) if the hypothesis of homoscedasticity is rejected.

explanatory power. The latter outcome is quite reasonable if one consider that these variables do *not* approximate initial stocks but rather flow variables associated with the process of convergence to the steady state, whose values are likely to change during the transition (see Section 3.3). It is then obvious that if the dependent variable is evaluated closer to 1960, these right-hand-side proxies can be more effective. Column (3) shows that the empirical model including a proxy for political instability and the Asian dummy explains 60 per cent of the variability of *per capita* net inflows, with almost all right-hand-side variables correctly signed (the exception being the rate of growth of population) and many of them significant at the 5 per cent level. In particular, initial *per capita* income displays a strongly significant negative coefficient and human capital proxies positive coefficients, which is what one would predict on the basis of a neoclassical model yielding *conditional* convergence. The exercise of testing to what extent demographic variables can be substitutes for the saving rate in 1960 (and for the Asian dummy) is reported in column (4): in the 1960–72 period the equation performs slightly better than in the whole capital-flow cycle, but the demographic variables are not significant and an outlier problem possibly arises (as signalled by the rejection of the normality assumption at the 5 per cent level in the Bera–Jarque-test). The inclusion of the rate of variation of the dependency proxy does not improve the regression. Actually, it could be that 1960–72 is too short a period for demographic phenomena to unfold their effects; in general, a more careful assessment of demographic influences on net capital flows in DCs is a topic for future research.

Section 2.2 suggests that 1982 is another turning point in international capital markets, with the breakout of the Third World debt crisis whose consequences were felt for at least six years on worldwide scale. Table 6.9 reports the estimates conducted on 1960–82, that is before the crisis induced a dramatic drought in capital transfers to DCs. It has been suggested that the pattern of capital flows to developing economies was completely altered after 1982, with (few) capital inflows intended only to avoid widespread default. In this sense, Savvides (1991) argues that in the years following the debt crisis foreign lending to the DCs has been to a large extent 'defensive' – that is, aimed at preventing explicit default; he also provides empirical evidence supporting this conjecture. This could imply that the structural relations suggested by the augmented Solow model do not provide useful indications on the pattern of net capital flows in DCs after 1982, while the performance of the empirical model is satisfactory before the debt crisis.

Table 6.9 An econometric evaluation of the augmented neoclassical model in a cross-section of 33 developing countries
Dependent variable: *per capita* cumulated net capital inflows over 1960–82

	(1)	(2)	(3)	(4)
Constant	−207.25 (−0.36)	349.5 (0.6)	546.1 (2.85)	−974 (−0.53)
Per capita income, 1960	−0.38 (−0.75)	−0.3 (0.68)	−0.96 (−2.12)**	−0.28 (−0.59)
Secondary education, 1960	39.2 (0.82)	63.3 (1.47)	59.7 (1.53)	46.2 (1.05)
No. of physicians, 1960	559765 (1.43)	794748 (2.33)**	920321 (3.02)**	927936 (2.23)**
Rate of investment in secondary education, 1960	21.6 (1.63)	2.23 (0.17)	21.04 (1.90)*	10.56 (0.83)
Rate of growth of population	13203 (0.73)	−8789 (−0.17)		−14244 (−0.47)
Saving rate, 1960	−2.03 (−0.24)	−12.1 (−1.48)		
Openness ratio		19.69 (2.19)**		
Political instability		−662.9 (−2.36)**	−789.6 (−3.2)**	−656.9 (−2.26)**
Dummy for official borrowers		−103 (−0.39)		
Asian dummy			−615.9 (−2.67)**	
Share of population under 15, 1960				3656 (0.7)
Adjusted R^2	0.36	0.52	0.59	0.46
F-statistic	4.09 [0.00]	6.98 [0.00]	8.66 [0.00]	5.03 [0.00]
Bera-Jarque-test of normality of the residuals	2.32 [0.31]	0.42 [0.8]	0.2 [0.9]	2.7 [0.26]
Chi square-test of homoscedasticity	2.43 [0.12]	0.00 [0.99]	0.73 [0.39]	1.42 [0.22]

Notes:
T-values in parentheses.
Probability values in brackets.
* Significant at the 10 per cent level; ** Significant at the 5 per cent level.
Estimation method: OLS. Standard errors adjusted according to White (1980) if the hypothesis of homoscedasticity is rejected.

Column (3) in Table 6.9 shows that the hypothesis that an augmented-neoclassical equation, also featuring a proxy for political turmoil and the Asian dummy, explains *per capita* net flows from 1960–82 cannot be dismissed. Consistent with conditional convergence, the neoclassical model with partial capital mobility predicts that initial *per capita* income displays a negative coefficient while human – capital measures positive coefficients (see Table 6.9). The 'demographic' specification featuring the rate of growth of population and a proxy for the dependency rate in 1960 (the share of population under 15), yields a worse empirical fit (see column (4) in Table 6.9).

The empirical findings of this chapter have to be considered with caution. They relate a limited set of DCs (although one representing the majority of population and GDP in developing market economies). One can also question whether the empirical proxies we selected to assess the predictions of growth models are the most adequate and reliable for this purpose. Even the periodisation can be questioned, although the choice of 1960 is dictated by data availability and 1988 is commonly identified as a nadir in capital transfers to DCs. The option of cumulating net capital over a long time interval can also be disputed. More important, perhaps, one can argue that the augmented Solow model analysed in Section 3.3, and especially (6.1) used here as a benchmark for the empirical regressions, provide a rough representation of the interplay among initial conditions, steady-state solutions and transitional elements.

Notwithstanding these limitations, the econometric evidence reported in this chapter points to some strong findings.

- First, growth models incorporating human capital as a production factor perform better than other models in accounting for the pattern of net capital flows in DCs over 1960–82. After 1982, the implications of the debt crisis probably altered the pattern of international capital movements.
- Second, within that class of models, the augmented neoclassical setup (with partial capital mobility) is supported by the data while an alternative setup featuring scale effects is not (as shown by the 'modified' Lucas model). In particular, initial income appears to be negatively, and human capital proxies positively, related to *per capita* net inflows in Dcs.
- Third, among additional regressors suggested by recent theoretical advances, a measure of political instability turns out to be negatively (and significantly) associated with *per capita* inflows. Furthermore

the coefficients of the regional dummies indicate that residents in Asian economies have comparatively received *less* capital from abroad than in the rest of the sample. This finding can be given alternative explanations: for instance, one can conjecture that large countries (as many of the Asian countries of the sample are) have been less open to capital movements than small ones, though this should be captured also by the *trade* openness variable already included. Otherwise, capital controls could have been more effective in Asian DCs that elsewhere (but our study of capital mobility in these countries does not lead to such a conclusion: see Chapter 5).
- Finally, demographic conditions could have determined the peculiar behaviour of Asian economies *vis-à-vis* the rest of the country set. In order to test for this possibility, we have simultaneously included the rate of growth of population and a proxy for the dependency rate in the regressions. Although the theoretical predictions concerning the sign with which these variables enter the regressions are supported by the data, their coefficients are almost always estimated with large standard errors and their inclusion worsens the global fit of the empirical model.

We can therefore conclude this chapter with a positive assessment of the explanatory power of the augmented neoclassical model, though it is fair to admit that more will have be done to provide a satisfactory empirical representation of demographic influences on capital movements. Chapter 7 moves forward to the issue of the *consequences* of capital flows in DCs – in general, finding that a growth model can explain the determinants of capital movements does not ensure that the effect of capital flows is consistent with the predictions of such a model.

APPENDIX: COUNTRY SAMPLE – DEFINITIONS AND SOURCES OF THE EMPIRICAL VARIABLES

Composition of the Sample

The DC sample that has been selected includes DCs classified as 'intermediate' by Mankiw, Romer and Weil (1992) for which the IMF provides current-account data from 1960 without relevant gaps. The 'intermediate countries' sample is considered a reliable one by Mankiw, Romer and Weil (1992), because it excludes economies based only (or almost only) on the oil sector, and very small economies. The sample selected here also excludes financial centres (such as the Bermudas, Singapore, and others), and those countries for which only incomplete or no data are available in the Barro and Lee (1993) data set on education.

The sample consists of the following 33 countries: Kenya, Malawi, Mali, Senegal, Tanzania, Tunisia, Zambia (seven African countries); Costa Rica, Dominican Republic, El Salvador, Guatemala, Honduras, Jamaica, Mexico, Panama (eight Central American countries); Argentina, Bolivia, Brazil, Chile, Colombia, Ecuador, Paraguay, Peru, Uruguay, Venezuela (ten South American countries); India, Indonesia, Korea, Malaysia, the Philippines, Sri Lanka, Thailand and Israel (eight Asian countries). Averaged data on net capital inflows and *per capita* income relative to the USA are reported for these countries in Table A6.1.

Eight countries are classified as 'official borrowers' by the IMF (*World Economic Outlook*, October 1994 issue) – that is, countries whose external debt in 1989 was at least two-thirds owned by governmental agencies and international organisations (Malawi, Mali, Tanzania, Tunisia, Zambia, El Salvador, Honduras, Jamaica).

Definition and Sources of the Data

(1) The dependent variable in the regressions of Chapter 6 – *per capita* cumulated net capital inflows – is the empirical counterpart of $(b^* - b(0))$ in (6.1). It is constructed as the sum, over the relevant time interval, of the negative of the current account of the balance of payments (expressed in current US dollars) divided by the size of the population. Yearly data on the current-account balance are available from the IMF (*International Financial Statistics*, CD-ROM version). In a few cases, the coverage of the current account data set is incomplete: individual countries have been excluded from the sample if some observations were missing. Further details are available from the author upon request.

(2) Data on the *size of population* are taken from the Summers and Heston (1991) data set.

(3) *Per capita income* (an empirical proxy for $y(0)$ in (6.1)) is defined as a country's *per capita* GDP measured in current 'international dollars' – that is, evaluated with the PPP index computed within the UN International Comparison Project. The source of the data is Summers and Heston (1991), variable *CGDP*. In the case

Table A6.1 Net capital inflows (NCI) and relative *per capita* income in 33 developing economies, 1960–88

Country	NCI			Income ratio		
	1960–72	1973–82	1983–8	1960–72	1973–82	1983–8
Africa						
Kenya	2.4718	23.3315	9.7902	0.0592	0.0679	0.0523
Malawi	6.0103	20.6482	11.5681	0.0412	0.0414	0.0332
Mali	3.6243	11.7989	14.8774	0.0375	0.0311	0.0287
Senegal	5.4203	36.5489	42.4807	0.0993	0.0797	0.0690
Tanzania	0.8871	16.7435	14.7640	0.0316	0.0333	0.0297
Tunisia	13.4337	54.4152	56.1480	0.1321	0.1774	0.1793
Zambia	−12.7390	54.9544	41.7586	0.1194	0.0866	0.0456
Central America						
Costa Rica	29.8963	154.4092	112.1272	0.2237	0.2540	0.2209
Dominican Rep.	9.6794	51.6888	32.7852	0.1346	0.1562	0.1306
El Salvador	4.1955	18.9433	25.6981	0.1411	0.1400	0.1037
Guatemala	5.4755	27.5846	35.2833	0.1711	0.1683	0.1330
Honduras	6.7708	47.9868	66.5743	0.0906	0.0901	0.0748
Jamaica	40.5083	97.5850	101.6125	0.2009	0.1920	0.1461
Mexico	10.9841	80.7109	−23.1810	0.3044	0.3496	0.3028
Panama	26.7380	90.7181	−147.9914	0.1859	0.2221	0.2216
South America						
Argentina	1.6795	31.5128	79.3863	0.3364	0.3089	0.2438
Bolivia	5.0065	27.6796	43.5802	0.1168	0.1288	0.0898
Brazil	5.3325	73.9868	20.5874	0.2205	0.1890	0.2433
Chile	13.0060	114.4743	91.9489	0.3290	0.2735	0.2317
Colombia	9.0776	17.1135	34.3446	0.1814	0.2077	0.2005
Ecuador	9.0174	58.0599	42.2151	0.1394	0.1915	0.1603
Paraguay	6.8862	51.9204	83.4998	0.1172	0.1395	0.1379
Peru	4.3345	46.4246	38.7129	0.2240	0.2192	0.1705
Uruguay	2.4447	83.4675	23.3892	0.3888	0.3642	0.2904
Venezuela	−15.9349	−42.5416	−107.1817	0.3097	0.4414	0.3470
Asia						
India	1.4701	0.2232	5.4041	0.0536	0.0438	0.0425
Indonesia	2.2562	3.5598	17.7990	0.0530	0.0820	0.1001
Israel	70.8565	259.1115	79.7379	0.4445	0.5767	0.5657
Korea	8.0665	59.6300	−97.0018	0.1123	0.1941	0.2486
Malaysia	1.3960	36.4747	20.7649	0.1792	0.2563	0.2786
Philippines	0.6459	25.3188	12.3226	0.1163	0.1296	0.1120
Sri Lanka	3.9318	14.1754	20.4836	0.1125	0.1037	0.1160
Thailand	2.0818	24.4304	26.9340	0.1115	0.1342	0.1547

Notes:
NCI is the average value of *per capita* net capital inflows per year (in current dollars).
Income ratio is the average value of *per capita* income (expressed in current 'international' dollars) as a share of the US *per capita* income of the same year.
Sources:
NCI: IMF.
Income ratio: Summers and Heston (1991).

of Indonesia, as this variable is not available for 1960, we have taken its value in the year 1962.

(4) Data on the stock of *secondary education* can be obtained from the database by Barro and Lee (1993), which is available upon request at the World Bank Growth Project. Barro and Lee provide data for a large sample of countries over 1960–85 at five-year intervals. We have checked the statistical significance of many of the stock variables provided by Barro and Lee, and it has turned out that the share of people aged 25 or more who have completed secondary education has a good explanatory power against net capital flows in DCs. It is well known, and has been recognised by Barro and Lee (1993) who provide the data, that this proxy does not account for the 'quality' of education in different countries, but only for the 'amount' of education received. Nonetheless, it represents an improvement with respect to other proxies such as the literacy rate (Benhabib and Spiegel, 1994). Other kinds of proxies – for instance, the primary educational attainment or the average years of total schooling – are less significant than measures of secondary educational attainments (similar results in cross-sectional growth regressions have been found by Barro and Lee, 1994).

(5) Human capital is commonly associated not only with skills but also with health, and this is especially true for DCs. We therefore introduce a second type of proxies for the initial stock of human capital that is related to health-care. The available information on DCs is extremely unsatisfactory and incomplete in this case, especially for the 1960s. We have opted for the *number of physicians (normalised for total population)* at the beginning of the 1960s, for which data are available for each country of the sample, as an admittedly rough index of the capacity of national health-care systems. Data on the number of physicians over total population are derived from the *World Development Report* of the World Bank, and the year of observation for each country is chosen as close as possible to 1960.

(6) As far as the *investment rate in secondary education* (a proxy for the rate of investment in human capital, s_h) is concerned, we have used as a proxy the rate of secondary education enrolment evaluated in 1960. This measure is likely to be exogenous with respect to net capital inflows in the following periods. Moreover, secondary enrolment rates appear to be 'robustly' correlated with growth according to Levine and Renelt (1992). Data on secondary education enrolment rates are taken from the *World Development Report* of the World Bank: the variable is defined as the ratio of the number of people of *all ages* enrolled in secondary school to the size of the population of secondary school age (12–17 years).

(7) The *openness ratio* is defined as exports *plus* imports over income at current international prices; data on the openness ratio are taken from Summers and Heston (1991). Other trade-related variables may in principle matter for the distribution of net capital flows in DCs – such as measures of the variability of the terms of trade which could be associated with a reduced incentive to export capital (Ghosh and Ostry, 1994), or measures of the long-term tendency of primary commodity prices (Grilli and Wang, 1990) which might affect expected rates of returns in DCs. Some regressions including other trade-related variables indicate that they have no additional explanatory power within our framework.

(8) As a measure of *political instability* we have included the number of revolutions and coups over 1960–70 already employed in Barro (1991). Notice that this variable is not fully predetermined with respect to net capital inflows. We have tried alternative measures of social instability (the number of assassinations) or of economic distortion (the black market premium on the exchange rate) which, however, enter the regressions with non-significant coefficients.

(9) The dummy for *official borrowers* covers the following countries: Malawi, Mali, Tanzania, Tunisia, Zambia, El Salvador, Honduras and Jamaica.

(10) The *rate of growth of population* is computed on the basis of the data contained in Summers and Heston (1991).

(11) The *saving rate* is *per capita* net income *less* (private and public) consumption, as a share of *per capita* income. It is obtained after some elaborations from the Summers–Heston (1991) database.

(12) The *share of population under 15* years is also computed from date available in Summers and Heston (1991).

7 Capital Movements, Economic Growth and Investment in Developing Countries

The neoclassical growth model, in both its basic and its augmented version, provides an optimistic view of the consequences of capital movements for a developing economy: as foreign inflows are used to finance investment in physical capital, opening to capital mobility should make a developing country (DC) an attractive location for international investors (provided it is endowed with, and will accumulate, enough human capital according to the augmented model with partial mobility). Consequently, the main predictions of the neoclassical theory are that:

- First, the integration in international capital markets will foster the speed of convergence to the steady state and therefore raise the growth rate for those developing economies that become net capital importers.
- Second, the larger the (*per capita*) inflow of net foreign capital, the higher the *ex ante* marginal product of capital hence the more the underlying fundamentals of a DC are conducive to economic growth (see Section 4.1).

Other theoretical frameworks predict that not only the relative attractiveness of investment (measured by the marginal product of capital) but also the domestic saving capacity of a backward economy matters for the rate of investment and economic growth – for instance, when borrowing abroad is constrained to be a fraction of current income (see Section 4.2). However, even in this case the inflow of foreign resources supports capital accumulation, productivity growth and the rise of *per capita* income over time. Less optimistic perspectives, however, may be derived from models in which residents in the DC have the option of either investing (part of) net capital inflows in such a way as to increase future productivity and output, or using them to raise current consumption standards at the expense of future ones (an example is offered in Section 4.3). If the second option is selected, there is actually no contribution of capital movements to economic growth and investment in developing economies, and the conditions are set for the emergence of liquidity and solvency problems. Of course, difficulties in the repayment of foreign debt and the possibility of capital account crises are not ruled out *even* if the first option (investing foreign capital in productive activities) is picked: in this case it might happen that although external resources are used to finance investment projects in DCs, the *ex post* profitability of these ventures is low and the association between capital flows and economic growth is weak or even absent.

The aim of this chapter is to assess the contribution of foreign capital to growth and investment in developing economies, so to provide an empirical evaluation of the various theoretical propositions just noted. The set of countries we analyse is the same as in Chapters 5 and 6; however, we focus more on the years 1960–82 than on the whole capital-flow cycle (1960–88): the reason is that, as shown in Chapter 6, the pattern of *per capita* net inflows in DCs during 1983–8 is not consistent with the predictions of growth models but is likely to be shaped by the 'defensive' attitude of international lenders (and institutions) engaged in preventing generalised default (Savvides, 1991). Clearly, under these conditions it does not make sense to ask whether capital movements that *did not* respond to international arbitrage opportunities dictated by the relative productivity of investment across countries were effectively contributing to economic growth. Hence, while the fall in growth rates in DCs after the debt crisis of 1982–3 is described, we concentrate our attention on the consequences of capital movements for growth and investment over 1960–82 – a period when the distribution of net capital inflows across DCs seems consistent with our model of relative *ex ante* investment profitability (see Section 6.2). The remainder of the chapter is organised as follows: Section 7.1 considers the impact of foreign capital on growth rates of *per capita* income in a cross-section of 33 DCs, drawing on the predictions of the neoclassical and the overlapping-generations (OLG) models, and on existing empirical literature on the sources of economic growth. Section 7.2 looks at the correlations among external capital flows, consumption and investment in this sample of countries, as well as in regional sub-samples, over 1960–88 and shorter sub-periods. An Appendix (p. 152) records the description and origin of the empirical variables.

7.1 FOREIGN CAPITAL AND ECONOMIC GROWTH IN A CROSS-SECTION OF DEVELOPING COUNTRIES, 1960–82

The empirical literature on the determinants of – or, more modestly, on the conditions associated with – economic growth is immense. Following a hiatus between the golden age of growth-accounting studies in the 1960s (see Maddison, 1987, for an overview) and the revival of growth theory in the mid-1980s (Romer, 1986), an impressive amount of econometric work has been accomplished in the 1990s on the relations between growth on the one side, and factor endowments, macroeconomic and financial conditions, trade regimes, political stability and other variables, on the other. Among the outstanding studies in this field, one can mention Barro (1991); Levine and Renelt (1992); Mankiw, Romer and Weil (1992); Dowrick (1992); Fischer (1993); King and Levine (1994); Barro and Lee (1994); De Gregorio and Guidotti (1995); Bloom and Williamson (1997); Durlauf and Quah (1998). Another group of excellent studies focus on economic growth in developing economies, using both comparative analysis and cross-country econometrics (see, for instance, Reynolds, 1983, 1986; Chenery, Robinson and Syrquin, 1986; IMF, 1996). Other works specialise on growth empirics in a sub-set of DCs: De Gregorio (1992) on Latin America; World Bank (1993), Young (1994) on Asia; Easterly and Levine (1997) on Africa.

This section is not designed as an incremental contribution to this literature, its more limited object being to investigate the relationship between foreign capital and growth in 33 DCs. This issue is relevant for at least three reasons:

- First, assessing the impact of foreign capital on growth may allow one to perform another test of alternative theoretical models.
- Second, the effectiveness of foreign capital in promoting long-run growth is clearly a key argument when the choice of a political attitude towards capital liberalisation is at stake.
- Finally, the sustainability of foreign-capital dependence is related to the growth performance of a transforming economy (and particularly to the growth performance of the tradable sector as argued in Chapter 8).

We focus here on the first aspect, but some policy indications can perhaps be derived from our empirical findings.

Although confined to the empirical relation between external capital and growth, the object of this section is by no means less ambitious:

several authors have underlined the difficulties inherent in disentangling the role of foreign capital as an independent factor in the process of development. The following quotation well represents this position:

> The interaction between policies and financing is complex, and it has typically been difficult to identify a robust association between external financing and growth from cross-section or time-series studies ... Causation probably acts in both directions, since faster growth may also attract capital inflows, including foreign direct investment. (IMF, 1996, p. 49)

Evidence exists on the growth consequences of specific types of capital transfers, and on their mechanics. For instance, Balasubramanyam, Salisu and Sapsford (1996) show that foreign direct investment (FDI) has been more effective in promoting growth in export-oriented DCs with respect to countries following import-substitution strategies. Borensztein, De Gregorio and Lee (1998) argue that FDI positively affects growth only in those developing economies which have overcome a threshold in human-capital accumulation. Mosley, Huson and Horrell (1987) focus on aid flows to DCs and their relationship with growth; they find that aid did not contribute to growth either in the 1960s or in the 1970s, and argue that a model of government behaviour that allows for 'non-productive' expenditure can account for this evidence. Boone (1996) reports that the effectiveness of foreign aid as an instrument for raising investment rates (and human-development indicators) in DCs is very limited, while the main effect of external aid is to foster private, and especially government, consumption.

De Gregorio (1992) concludes that foreign capital had a positive impact on growth in Latin American countries over 1950–82, while Cohen (1994) finds that foreign debt contributed substantially to investment in a sample of DCs over the 1970s, but only marginally in the 1980s. Unfortunately, it is not clear what is the definition of 'foreign capital' implicit in these two studies.[1]

The world debt crisis of 1982–3 has stimulated an extensive theoretical and empirical literature on a closely connected, yet distinct, topic – namely, the burden of outstanding debt on the growth performance of DCs. The core of the so-called 'debt overhang' hypothesis (Krugman, 1988) states that domestic investment can be prevented in the presence of high stocks of external debt (relative to GDP or exports), because an excessive share of any future income generated by current investment will be devoted to the service of the debt. Several empirical studies have tried to evaluate this conjecture in different countries using different data and techniques, with mixed results. While Werner (1992) claims that the debt crisis did not cause the investment collapse of the 1980s in DCs, Sachs (1985); Cohen (1993); Kaminsky and Pereira (1996) argue that the burden of servicing the debt actually lowered investment and output growth in DCs, particularly those of Latin America. Moreover, Cohen (1997) constructs a proxy for the likelihood of debt rescheduling that is employed to account for the reduction in Latin American growth rates over the 1970s and 1980s. Although very interesting, this literature does not deal with our main object, as it is not concerned with the consequences of capital flows in DCs but rather with the consequences of facing an external debt when net capital transfers from abroad have withdrawn, or are on the point of withdrawing. True, the building of an unsustainable stock of debt can be tracked looking at the past investment and growth behaviour of DCs, but estimating the impact of the debt *stock* on investment is a conceptually distinct question from evaluating the effects of net capital *flows*. We already showed in Chapter 6 that the augmented neoclassical model could not explain the distribution of capital inflows after 1982, most likely because of the outbreak of the crisis. The debt-overhang literature indicates that after 1982 growth and investment in DCs were possibly affected by an unsolved debt problem: this reinforces our argument in favour of limiting to 1960–82 the econometric study of the consequences of foreign capital on growth.

Before turning to econometrics, though, let us introduce some descriptive statistics on economic growth in DCs. Table 7.1 shows the unweighted average of logarithmic growth rates for our sample of 33 DCs as well as for regional sub-samples over 1960–88 and three sub-periods. It also presents the coefficients of variations associated with those growth rates.

The average growth rate of *per capita* income in the 33 countries rises of 2.5 percentage points in the second sub-period (after the oil-shock and before the debt crisis) and then declines markedly over the period 1983–8, mainly as a consequence of the crisis itself. Hence the slowdown in economic growth that affected industrial countries in the 1970s (see Maddison, 1987) did not have a counterpart in this sample of DCs, possibly because some of them gained from the boom in commodity prices;[2] on the other hand, the decline in growth rates was striking after 1982. Both the rise of 1973–82 and the fall of 1983–8 are most evident in the eight Asian economies (almost 5 and 7 percentage

Table 7.1 Descriptive statistics on economic growth in 33 developing countries over 1960–88
Average logarithmic growth rates and coefficients of variation

	1960–88	1960–72	1973–82	1983–8
All 33 developing countries	0.062	0.06	0.085	0.029
	(0.22)	(0.3)	(0.33)	(0.69)
7 African countries	0.053	0.054	0.069	0.025
	(0.27)	(0.38)	(0.55)	(0.47)
18 Latin American countries	0.06	0.062	0.079	0.025
	(0.15)	(0.23)	(0.23)	(0.71)
8 Asian countries	0.074	0.062	0.11	0.4
	(0.21)	(0.38)	(0.2)	(0.67)

Notes:
Unweighted average growth rates of *per capita* income over each period. Coefficients of variation in parentheses.

points, respectively); however, growth rates in these economies are constantly above the global average of DCs after 1972.

The growth performance of Latin American economies was altogether below that of the Asian countries, and particularly so after 1972; De Gregorio (1992, p. 62) reports that *per capita* income growth in some large Latin American economies (with the exception of Brazil) was lower than in developed countries over 1950–85. *Per capita* income growth accelerates in Latin America during 1973–82, but then declines, approaching rates comparable with those of the African countries after the debt crisis. The variation in growth rates is also remarkably changed after 1982, with a coefficient of variation of almost 0.7 in the full sample, in Latin America and Asia. Quite interestingly, growth accelerates during the 1970s in both Latin American economies – which, according to the regressions of Chapter 6 received more *per capita* net inflows from abroad – and in Asia, where net capital transfers from abroad were lower on a comparative basis (see Tables 6.7–6.9). However growth rates remained higher in Asian countries after the debt crisis.

Turning to the relationship between growth and net capital flows, Table 7.2 suggests that the simple correlation between the two variables across our country samples was positive during the 1960s (although very low in African countries) but negative during the 1970s, while mixed results are obtained for the years 1983–8 – when, however, the distribution of net capital flows across DCs was not consistent with the augmented Solow model.

Table 7.2 Cross-country correlation coefficients between average growth rates and average *per capita* net capital inflows, 1960–88

	1960–72	1973–82	1983–8
All 33 developing countries	0.45	–0.17	0.00
7 African countries	0.01	–0.27	–0.62
18 Latin American countries	0.4	–0.28	0.41
8 Asian countries	0.58	–0.36	–0.63

Notes:
Unweighted average growth rates of *per capita* income as in Table 7.1.
Average *per capita* net capital inflows as in Table A6.1.

To evaluate the contribution of foreign capital to growth more carefully, we conduct the following exercise. We consider two alternative empirical setups – the 'investment-led' growth model of Levine and Renelt (1992) and the 'demographic' growth model by Bloom and Williamson (1997). We check whether slightly modified versions of these equations perform well with cross-sectional data for 33 DCs; we also introduce foreign capital as an independent variable to see whether it can act as a substitute for the variables used by the original authors or as an additional regressor that raises the explanatory capacity of the model. In this sense, we do not suggest a new framework in which growth is generated by foreign capital, but we manipulate two existing, and rightly eminent, empirical setups to appraise the incremental contribution of foreign capital to economic growth, according to the spirit of the theoretical models of Chapter 4.

Empirical analysis of economic growth based on cross-section data is problematic for several reasons. One might ask whether it is feasible to make useful generalisations over such a largely heterogeneous universe as that of existing nations (Reynolds, 1983, p. 945). Durlauf and Quah (1998, pp. 42–52) point out to a number of conceptual and statistical problems involved in cross-section (and even panel-data) growth regressions: above all, they question the ability of the linear model to capture complex dynamics, the common attitude of applied researchers of adding control variables or using orthogonal instruments, the finite-sample interpretation of asymptotic properties and the causal economic interpretation of statistical results. Nonetheless, they admit that their alternative research programme based on distribution dynamics and cross-country interactions, 'while formalising certain facts about the patterns of cross-country growth, does not yet provide an explanation for those patterns' (Durlauf and Quah, 1998, p. 59). We therefore stick to our econometric strategy, already employed in Chapter 6, of implementing cross-country regressions but trying to keep the empirical analysis as consistent as possible with underlying theoretical models.

Levine and Renelt (1992, pp. 945–7) suggest that *per capita* income growth is explained by the initial level of income, the average rate of growth of population, the initial secondary enrolment rate and the average investment share of GDP. Together these variables account for 46 per cent of the variability of growth rates in a sample of 101 countries over 1960–89; moreover, initial income, secondary enrolment and the investment share display statistically significant coefficients. This model is consistent with conditional convergence (and hence with the augmented neoclassical model: see Mankiw, Romer and Weil, 1992) as the coefficient of initial income is negative. Sensitivity tests conducted using other explanatory variables indicate that the investment share has a remarkably 'robust' positive correlation with growth.[3] We estimate a modified version of the Levine–Renelt (1992) equation, based on the following conjecture: domestic investment is driven by the marginal product of capital which can be approximated by initial income levels and human-capital proxies; at the same time, investment can be financed either by domestic saving or by foreign capital inflows (see, for instance, Section 3.3). One can therefore substitute the domestic *saving* share (evaluated in 1960 to avoid the endogeneity bias) and *per capita* net inflows for the investment share into the Levine–Renelt equation and test the performance of this model in a cross-section of 33 DCs.

This approach, as well as that of the original Levine–Renelt paper, can be blamed for 'capital fundamentalism' according to the definition of King and Levine (1994), who argue that there is not much sense in explaining 'growth' with the rate of 'investment' for several reasons.

- First, growth-accounting econometrics had already revealed in the 1960s that the contributions of investment and of labour force growth can account for a only low fraction of the long-run increase in *per capita* output in industrial economies, while the largest share of such increase – the so-called 'residual' – remains largely unexplained and is usually attributed to (unmeasurable) technological improvements.
- Second, even if recent cross-country or panel-data show a significant statistical correlation between growth and investment, this is

indeed a correlation – the direction of causation is uncertain. This is even more true when the both the growth rate and the investment share in the empirical regressions are averaged over the same time interval, as there can be no attempt at testing exogeneity in this case.
- Third, it is argued that while investment comes along with growth, the burden of the explanation of *both* variables must be placed in deeper fundamentals such as technology, demography, geographical and social conditions, institutions and political regimes (see, for instance, Abramovitz, 1986; North, 1994).

We basically agree with these arguments, nonetheless we believe that our exercise is not meaningless for a few reasons:

- First, it has been shown that the role of investment in growth-accounting is typically larger in developing than in industrial economies (Dowrick, 1992; King and Levine, 1994; Young, 1994).
- Second, devices can be found that partly avoid the endogeneity bias as mentioned above.
- Finally, although finding a significant correlation need not mean that investment 'causes' growth, it possibly means that the economic and social conditions favouring growth also affects investment and that investment is a major channel for the implementation of a growth potential (Temple and Voth, 1998, argue that equipment investment and growth are the joint outcome of industrialisation, prompted by human capital).

As a matter of fact, our approach to the determinants of capital flows is not in contrast with the views critical of the 'capital fundamentalist' approach: we tried to relate net inflows to a set of fundamentals such as the initial gap with leading economies, human capital and political stability indicators that *jointly* affect the incentive to invest (the marginal product of capital) and the growth rate of *per capita* income (see Chapters 3 and 6). Here, we do not ask: 'Is investment the origin of growth?', but rather: 'Are higher saving rates and capital inflows positively associated with growth, as it is investment in a larger cross-section of countries?'

The results of this exercise for the period 1960–82 are shown in the first two columns (1) and (2) of Table 7.3 (column (2) also includes three additional regressors – the openness ratio, a measure of political instability and the log of the black market premium on the exchange rate as a proxy of economic distortions). Only the coefficient of the rate of enrolment in secondary school is significant at the 10 per cent level, while that of initial income is significant only when other regressors are included in column (2). The performance of this Levine–Renelt-type equation is clearly unsatisfactory in this cross-section of DCs over 1960–82; more relevant for our purposes, the saving rate and *per capita* net inflows do *not* appear significantly correlated with economic growth.[4]

The second empirical model we take as benchmark is the 'demographic' one by Bloom and Williamson (1997), who forcefully argue that the evolution of the size and composition of population is the main driving force of economic growth in the long run, and is especially apt for explaining the growth performance of East Asian economies in the past thirty years. Bloom and Williamson (1997) suggest that only capturing at least part of the complex dynamics of population – labour force and dependency rates – can explain the behaviour of saving and investment and hence *per capita* growth. In particular, population growth can *positively* be associated with *per capita* growth if at the same time one controls for the composition of population (dependent vs. working shares) and the change in dependency rates which are negatively related to *per capita* income. Their empirical model, once adjusted for the distance between initial and steady state conditions, shows that 'transitional' demographic phenomena explain growth-rate differentials in a large cross-section of countries over 1965–90. This model can be viewed as a sort of antidote against 'capital fundamentalism', because the growth process is driven by fundamental demographic phenomena from which saving and investment dynamics originate.

We replicate their analysis with some modifications, in columns (3) and (4) of Table 7.3. In column (3) we check whether a more complete representation of demographic variables can add explanatory power to the basic regression of column (1): the answer is rather negative, although one of the demographic variables suggested by Bloom and Williamson (1997) – namely, the rate of change of the dependent share of population[5] – is negatively associated with growth and strongly significant. In column (4) we present the result of the demographic-growth model adjusted for net capital inflows and a measure of economic distortion (the average value of logarithm of the black-market premium on the exchange rate over the period considered: see also Grilli and Milesi-Ferretti, 1995). This equation performs well across our 33 DCs, accounting for half of the variability of average growth rates, with almost all variables correctly signed and significant.[6] Therefore,

Table 7.3 An econometric evaluation of the growth effect of net capital inflows in a cross-section of 33 developing countries Dependent variable: logarithmic growth rate of *per capita* income over 1960–82

	(1)	(2)	(3)	(4)
Constant	0.05 (3.7)	0.06 (4.32)	0.1 (2.23)	0.13 (3.3)
Per capita income, 1960	−0.15E-4 (−1.33)	−0.23E-4 (−2.15)**	−0.2E-4 (−1.75)*	−0.26E-4 (−2.6)**
Rate of growth of population	0.73 (1.47)	0.66 (1.43)	1.23 (1.64)	1.23 (1.93)*
Rate of investment in secondary education, 1960	0.6E-3 (1.7)*	0.55E-3 (1.71)*	0.11E-4 (0.3)	
Saving rate, 1960	−0.16E-3 (−0.7)	0.2E-3 (0.9)	−0.15E-3 (−0.72)	
Per capita cumulated net capital inflows over 1960–82	0.17E-5 (0.34)	0.64E-5 (1.32)	0.29E-5 (0.17)	0.27E-5 (0.82)
Openness ratio		0.4E-3 (−1.79)*		
Political instability, 1960–80		0.01 (0.9)		
Share of population under 15, 1960			−0.14 (−1.12)	−0.19 (−1.89)*
Rate of change of the share of population under 15 years			−2.91 (−3.5)**	−2.81 (−4.39)**
Logarithm of the black-market premium on the exchange rate		−0.03 (−2.25)**		−0.03 (−2.98)**
Adjusted R^2	0.04	0.25	0.3	0.49
F-statistic	1.25 [0.31]	2.37 [0.05]	3.0 [0.02]	6.15 [0.00]
Bera–Jarque-test of normality of the residuals	0.9 [0.63]	0.76 [0.68]	0.57 [0.75]	0.47 [0.79]
Chi square-test of homoscedasticity	0.59 [0.47]	0.16 [0.69]	0.95 [0.33]	0.01 [0.94]

Notes:
T-values in parentheses. Probability values in brackets.
* Significant at the 10 per cent level; ** Significant at the 5 per cent level.
Estimation method: OLS. Standard errors adjusted according to White (1980) if the hypothesis of homoscedasticity is rejected.

the 'demographic'-growth model works better than the 'investment-led' model within this set of developing economies over 1960–82; in this context, the impact of foreign capital on growth is not significant although its coefficient remains positive as in columns (1) and (2).

However, these findings referred to the whole period leading to the debt crisis hide different results over 1960–72 and 1973–82. Table 7.4 suggests that the 'investment-led' model with the initial saving rate and *per capita* net inflows as proxies for the investment share of GDP has superior explanatory power relative to the demographic model over 1960–72. Both the saving rate and *per capita* inflows are positively and significantly associated with income growth before the oil-shock, and they contribute together with the growth rate of population to account for the diversity of development paths during the 1960s. A reason why the initial value of *per capita* income is not significantly correlated with the dependent variable can be that *per capita* net inflows are themselves negatively related to initial income (see Section 6.2), hence part of the conditional convergence effect is captured by the capital inflow variable which appears to be positively associated with growth.[7] Nevertheless, the comparative performance of the 'investment-led' model is superior as the 'demographic' equations of columns (3) and (4) do not provide an alternative explanation of growth patterns over 1960–72.[8]

This conclusion is reversed if we estimate our growth equations in the subsequent sub-period (Table 7.5). In this case the modified Levine–Renelt (1992) model does not account for growth patterns in our set of DCs, and both the saving rate in 1973 and cumulated capital inflows are wrongly signed and statistically not significant. In contrast, the Bloom–Williamson (1997) framework seems well suited to provide a representation of the underlying sources of economic growth across developing nations over 1973–82: the conditional-convergence hypothesis is supported as well as the conjectures on the impact of the demographic conditions on *per capita* income (positive effect of population growth, negative effects of the dependency rate and its growth rate). Within this framework, the positive association between net capital inflows and growth vanishes: the coefficient on the capital transfer is negative and always insignificant.

Overall, the perception one draws from the simple correlation coefficients of Table 7.2 is supported by the econometric analysis: foreign capital looks positively associated with *per capita* growth during the 1960s and until the first oil-shock of 1973, but negatively related to growth in the following decade. This does not mean that foreign capital can *explain* growth in the first interval and not in the second. It just

Table 7.4 An econometric evaluation of the growth effect of net capital inflows in a cross-section of 33 developing countries Dependent variable: logarithmic growth rate of *per capita* income over 1960–72

	(1)	(2)	(3)	(4)
Constant	0.03 (2.06)	0.03 (1.88)	0.01 (0.32)	0.02 (0.5)
Per capita income, 1960	−0.86E-5 (−0.77)	−012E-4 (−1.02)	−0.84E-5 (−0.62)	−0.37E-5 (−0.28)
Rate of growth of population	0.84 (1.75)*	0.94 (1.91)*	0.32 (0.41)	0.6 (0.76)
Rate of investment in secondary education, 1960	0.18E-3 (0.47)	0.2E-3 (0.52)	0.77E-4 (0.19)	
Saving rate, 1960	0.46E-3 (2.0)**	0.6E-3 (2.2)**	0.49E-3 (2.13)**	
Per capita cumulated net capital inflows over 1960–72	0.37E-4 (2.03)**	0.45E-4 (2.3)**	0.4E-4 (2.18)**	0.41E-4 (2.74)**
Openness ratio		−0.17E-3 (−0.7)		
Political instability, 1960–70		0.01 (1.03)	0.07 (0.53)	0.04 (0.31)
Share of population under 15, 1960			−1.28 (−1.27)	−1.21 (−1.16)
Rate of change of the share of population under 15 years				
Adjusted R^2	0.31	0.3	0.3	0.22
F-statistic	3.91 [0.00]	3.0 [0.02]	3.0 [0.02]	2.8 [0.03]
Bera-Jarque-test of normality of the residuals	3.2 [0.2]	1.8 [0.4]	1.09 [0.58]	0.16 [0.45]
Chi square-test of homoscedasticity	0.25 [0.61]	0.67E-3 [0.98]	0.09 [0.76]	0.05 [0.83]

Notes:
T-values in parentheses.
Probability values in brackets.
* Significant at the 10 per cent level; ** Significant at the 5 per cent level.
Estimation method: OLS. Standard errors adjusted according to White (1980) if the hypothesis of homoscedasticity is rejected.

Table 7.5 An econometric evaluation of the growth effect of net capital inflows in a cross-section of 33 developing countries
Dependent variable: logarithmic growth rate of *per capita* income over 1973–82

	(1)	(2)	(3)	(4)
Constant	0.06 (1.76)	0.09 (3.28)	0.18 (2.28)	0.24 (4.7)
Per capita income in 1973	−0.7E-5 (−0.57)	−0.11E-4 (−1.22)	−0.88E-5 (−0.72)	−0.15E-4 (−1.85)*
Rate of growth of population	0.59 (0.53)	0.85 (0.98)	2.07 (1.61)	1.78 (2.03)**
Rate of investment in secondary education, 1970	0.84E-3 (1.24)	0.78E-3 (1.54)	0.51E-4 (0.07)	
Saving rate, 1973	−0.32E-3 (0.89)	0.22E-3 (0.74)	−0.33E-3 (0.99)	
Per capita cumulated net capital inflows over 1973–82	−0.92E-5 (0.67)	0.44E-6 (0.01)	−0.1E-4 (−0.83)	−0.67E-5 (−0.71)
Openness ratio		−0.9E-3 (−2.5)**		
Political instability, 1970–80		−0.01 (−1.03)		
Share of population under 15, 1973			−0.34 (−1.71)*	−0.4 (−2.87)**
Rate of change of the share of population under 15 years			−2.65 (−2.27)**	−2.06 (−3.17)**
Logarithm of the black-market premium on the exchange rate		−0.08 (−3.97)**		−0.09 (−4.76)**
Adjusted R^2	−0.07	0.43	0.11	0.52
F-statistic	0.58 [0.77]	3.98 [0.00]	1.54 [0.2]	6.08 [0.00]
Bera–Jarque-test of normality of the residuals	0.6 [0.74]	1.5 [0.47]	0.96 [0.62]	0.97 [0.62]
Chi square-test of homoscedasticity	2.43 [0.12]	0.16 [0.68]	0.64 [0.42]	1.56 [0.2]

Notes:
T-values in parentheses. Probability values in brackets.
* Significant at the 10 per cent level; ** Significant at the 5 per cent level.
Estimation method: OLS. Standard errors adjusted according to White (1980) if the hypothesis of homoscedasticity is rejected.

means that while a neoclassical growth model can account for the distribution of net capital flows in DCs over the *whole* 1960–82 period (Chapter 6), a compatible model in which investment is proxied by domestic saving and capital inflows can account for growth patterns only in the first sub-period but performs poorly over 1973–82. The contribution of foreign capital to growth apparently vanished after 1972, although we know from Chapter 2 that global capital transfers to developing economies rose substantially during the 1970s. Another notable evidence is, that the Asian countries of our sample that received *lower per capita* amounts of foreign financing on comparative grounds (that is, accounting for their income levels, human-capital endowments and political situations; see Section 6.2), were able to raise their average growth rates far more during 1973–82 and to maintain a faster growth pace than other DCs after 1982 (Table 7.1).

Hence, the two predictions of the (augmented) neoclassical model recalled at the beginning of this chapter – namely, that foreign capital promotes growth and that countries receiving larger *per capita* inflows should grow faster (on a comparative basis, controlling for other sources of growth), are partially in contrast with the findings of this section. This casts some doubts on the effective destination of foreign capital (consumption or investment?) or the actual profitability of investment ventures financed with external resources in DCs, particularly in the post-1972 period. Section 7.2 introduces further stylised facts that may help provide an answer.

7.2 CAPITAL INFLOWS, INVESTMENT AND CONSUMPTION

In his detailed study of the effectiveness of foreign aid, Boone (1996, p. 315) concludes that 'most or all aid goes to consumption, it increases the size of the government, but it has no significant impact on poverty indicators'. The reason is that aid flows, apart from some directed aid programmes, are usually fungible so that the donor is not really able to ensure that the original destination of the funds is maintained *ex post*. Boone finds that the marginal propensity to consume out of aid revenues is not statistically different from one, while the propensity to invest is not different from zero, when one controls for other determinants of consumption and investment rates in DCs. Moreover the marginal impact on government consumption is larger (it amounts to almost 70 per cent of aid receipts) than the impact on private consumption in most specifications (Boone, 1996, p. 311).[9]

The fungibility of capital flows in general is likely to be at least as high as that of foreign aid, with the possible exception of direct investment when the foreign company has majority control of the assets located in the developing country. Hence fungibility is an issue when the impact of foreign capital on the recipient economies is under evaluation, and it is worthwhile studying the correlation between capital inflows, consumption and investment as this may help clarify the question posed at the end of Section 7.1. Table 7.6 displays the cross-country correlation coefficients between investment, private consumption and government consumption rates, on the one hand, and *per capita* inflows of foreign capital, on the other, all averaged over three six-years periods to smooth out possible anomalies in the data. It turns out that *per capita* inflows were positively correlated with investment rates over 1960–5 and 1972–7, although the correlation coefficient is halved in the second period relative to the first. The correlation turns negative over 1983–8. Although no causal relationship is involved here, it is clear that the cross-section association between larger foreign inflows and higher investment rates is loosening over time. Consistent with this, we observe a rising correlation between external financing and government consumption from 1960–5 to 1972–7. Finally the correlation between foreign capital and private consumption is negative in the first two periods and becomes positive after the debt crisis.

It must be mentioned that the allocation of available resources between investment and consumption depends on many variables other than capital inflows, which are not considered here. Moreover, the

Table 7.6 Cross-country correlation coefficients between average consumption and investment rates and average *per capita* net capital inflows (all 33 developing countries), 1960–88

	1960–5	1972–7	1983–7
Investment rate and net capital inflows	0.42	0.23	−0.25
Private consumption rate and net capital inflows	−0.006	−0.22	0.27
Public consumption rate and net capital inflows	0.14	0.39	0.17

Notes:
Average investment, private and public consumption rates over each five-year period (see the Appendix on p. 152).
Average *per capita* net capital inflows as in Table A6.1.

figures in Table 7.6, being *cross-country* correlation coefficients, do not convey information about the *evolution* of investment and consumption over time as compared with capital flows. Tables 7.7 and 7.8 show the absolute changes in investment and consumption rates, respectively, from 1960–5 to 1972–7 and from 1972–7 to 1983–8. What is striking in Table 7.7 is the global reallocation from private to government consumption in the mid-1970s as compared with the early 1960s. Another remarkable feature is the differential increase in investment rates in Asian *vis-à-vis* other DCs (about 4 percentage points if we take the Latin American economies as a benchmark): the superior growth performance of the Asian countries in the 1970s had therefore a counterpart in a substantial surge in investment rates, that grew of about 15 percentage points in countries such as Indonesia and Korea.[10] In the Western Hemisphere investment rates increased much less from 1960–5 to 1972–7, and actually fell in Chile, Colombia, Peru and other countries.

Table 7.8 shows that the Asian economies of our sample were on average able to preserve such higher investment rates after the debt crisis of the early 1980s, which was not the case in Africa and Latin America and is consistent with the superior growth performance of Asia after 1982.

We now consider the cross-section correlation between the *change* in investment and consumption rates, on one side, and foreign inflows, on the other, which can provide indications on the solvency and sustainability conditions related to the accumulation of foreign debt: these

Table 7.7 Change in average investment and consumption rates, 1960–5 to 1972–7

	Change in average investment rate	Change in average private-consumption rate	Change in average government-consumption rate
All 33 developing countries	1.93	–10.2	10.59
7 African countries	0.23	–12.37	14.8
18 Latin American countries	1.16	–8.71	8.86
8 Asian countries	5.17	–11.64	10.8

Notes:
Unweighted averages of investment and consumption rates as defined in the Appendix (p. 152).

Table 7.8 Change in average investment and consumption rates, 1972–7 to 1983–8

	Change in average investment rate	Change in average private-consumption rate	Change in average government-consumption rate
All 33 developing countries	−3.69	0.34	1.83
7 African countries	−5.6	4.07	1.26
18 Latin American countries	−4.37	−0.1	2.37
8 Asian countries	−0.49	−1.92	1.12

Notes:
Unweighted averages of investment and consumption rates as defined in the Appendix (p. 152).

conditions are more likely to be fulfilled (violated) if investment and growth move (do not move) together with external borrowing.[11] Table 7.9 links the change in investment and consumption to cumulated *per capita* inflows over 1972–7 and 1983–8.

The correlation coefficient between the change in investment rates from the early 1960s to the mid-1970s, and cumulated *per capita* inflows over 1972–7 suggests that larger inflows were *not* associated with larger increases in investment rates: indeed, quite the opposite happened as more resources flowed into countries where investment rates were rising less (or falling). The mirror-image of this evidence is the correlation between the change in government consumption and capital inflows which is positive and rather strong, suggesting that larger inflows during 1972–7 were associated with larger increases in public-sector consumption relative to 1960–5.[12]

Overall, the stylised facts discussed in this section seem to indicate that the size of foreign inflows was not positively associated with the rise in investment rates during the 1970s, hence one could conjecture that a weak contribution of external capital to growth after 1972 (see Section 7.1) can be partly ascribed to a diversion of resources from investment to consumption, and particularly to government consumption. We claimed in Section 7.1 that although the *distribution* of net capital flows across DCs from 1960 through 1982 looks consistent with an augmented neoclassical model (see Chapter 6), the predictions of the same model about the *consequences* of foreign capital for economic

Table 7.9 Cross-country correlation coefficients between the change in average consumption and investment rates and cumulated *per capita* net capital inflows (all 33 developing countries)

	Change from 1960–5 to 1972–7, and capital inflows over 1972–7	Change from 1972–7 to 1983–8, and capital inflows over 1983–8
Investment rates and net capital inflows	−0.43	0.17
Private-consumption rates and net capital inflows	0.2	0.13
Government-consumption rates and net capital inflows	0.45	0.14

Notes:
Average investment, private and government consumption rates over each five-year period (see the Appendix of p. 152).
Cumulated *per capita* net capital inflows as defined in the Appendix (p. 152).

growth are not fulfilled over 1973–82. An explanation for this failure of the theoretical model is that external resources were oriented to finance government consumption more than investment after 1972; moreover, the Asian countries that received comparatively lower inflows fared better in terms of economic growth during the 1970s, and hence were better equipped to face the financial turmoil of the 1980s.

This chapter therefore yields mixed responses on the contribution of foreign capital to economic progress in DCs: while there is evidence of a positive impact of external finance on growth over 1960–72, this effect vanishes over the following decade. This in turn appears to be associated with a weak correlation between foreign capital inflows and rising investment rates, and to a shift of resources towards government consumption, although we do not claim to have unveiled any causal links. We argued in Chapter 4 that alternative growth models can explain why foreign capital is mainly consumed rather than invested (Section 4.3 provides an example).[13] What should be clear is that a vaning relation between net capital inflows, on the one side, and investment and growth, on the other, is a clue of forthcoming sustainability problems and possibly of financial instability: in this sense, the lacking contribution of foreign capital to growth in DCs after 1972 could have set the conditions for the debt crisis of 1982–3.

APPENDIX: DEFINITIONS AND SOURCES OF THE EMPIRICAL VARIABLES

The Composition of the Country Sample

The same as in Chapters 5 and 6 (see the Appendix on p. 129 for a list of the DCs included).

Definition and Sources of the Data

(1) The *growth rate* is the logarithmic growth rate of *per capita* GDP measured in current 'international dollars' (Summers and Heston, 1991, variable *CGDP*).

(2) *Per capita income* is defined as a country's *per capita* GDP measured in current 'international dollars' (Summers and Heston, 1991).

(3) The average *rate of growth of population* is computed on the basis of the data contained in Summers and Heston (1991).

(4) As far as the *investment rate in secondary education* (a proxy for the rate of investment in human capital, s_h) is concerned, we have used as a proxy the rate of secondary education enrollment evaluated in 1960 (World Bank, *World Development Report*, 1975).

(5) The *saving rate* is *per capita* net income *less* (private and public) consumption, as a share of *per capita* income. It is obtained after some elaborations from Summers and Heston (1991).

(6) *Per capita cumulated net capital inflows*, used in Tables 7.3–7.5 and 7.7, is defined as in the Appendix on p. 129, while *average per capita* net inflows is defined as average yearly inflows defined as in Table A6.1.

(7) As a measure of *political instability* we have included the number of revolutions and coups from Barro (1991).

(8) The *openness ratio* is the sum of exports and imports over income at current international prices; data on the openness ratio are taken from Summers and Heston (1991).

(9) The *share of population under 15 years and its (logarithmic) rate of change* are also computed from data available in Summers and Heston (1991).

(10) The *log of the black-market premium* averaged over a decade is taken from Barro (1991).

(11) The *(private and government) consumption rate and the investment rate* are taken from Summers and Heston (1991).

8 External Finance and Foreign Debt: A Study of the Transition Economies of Central and Eastern Europe

The empirics of Chapters 5–7 are centred on developing *market* economies, because these economies have been part of the world capital market for a long enough time to allow an application of growth models to the determinants and consequences of foreign capital. Other transforming economies have (re)joined international financial relations in the 1990s: the so-called *transition* economies of Central and Eastern Europe and Asia. This chapter deals with the determinants and the sustainability of foreign capital inflows in a sub-set of these economies.

The large investment requirements and the fall in domestic saving in transition economies suggest that there exists a strong potential for external finance in enhancing the growth of *per capita* output and the improvement of welfare in these countries. Beyond the motivations commonly offered in international economics, the integration in world capital markets can mitigate some special problems of liquidity or information shortage, market access and institution-building that are particularly severe in transition economies. To the extent that the transition process is associated with the emergence of liquidity constraints not fully overcome by domestic bank lending, access to foreign capital markets may limit the dimension of output decline. Moreover, foreign direct investment can allow easier access to Western export markets and a reduction in the uncertainty associated with investment projects, and therefore favour domestic investment. The increasing dependence of transition economies on external trade with Western economies also stresses the need for convertible currency reserves in transition economies, and capital inflows can provide a solution for incipient foreign exchange shortages. Finally, direct and portfolio investment by foreign entities can affect regulatory policies and support legislation aimed at improving the efficiency of domestic capital markets (possibly, through the adoption of Western standards of monitoring and property rights enforcement). Nevertheless, foreign capital inflows in these countries are strictly related to the progress in economic transformation and, as we will show, to the stock of outstanding external liabilities.

The nature of the empirical study presented in this chapter is different from those of Chapters 6 and 7. First, the time dimension implied here is so short (six years) that we opt for a panel-data approach. Second, we do not search for long-run *determinants* of capital inflows but for medium-run factors affecting the demand and supply of financial resources in transition economies. Third, as far as the *consequences* of foreign capital are concerned, we do not try to establish the growth impact of net inflows using the techniques adopted in Chapter 7, but we assess the sustainability of foreign debt in relation with predicted or actual growth patterns.

The chapter is organised as follows: we first review the literature on, and analyse the developments in, external borrowing in ten Central and Eastern European economies (the ones that have signed 'Europe Agreements' with the European Union, that is the Visegrád countries plus Slovenia, Romania, Bulgaria and the Baltic countries) (Section 8.1). We then apply panel-data analysis in order to evaluate the determinants of net foreign financing and to assess the impact of outstanding foreign liabilities on the borrowing capacity of these countries (Section 8.2). The issue of the sustainability of external debt is revisited in Section 8.3, with some indexes based on the ratio of foreign debt to GDP and export. The main conclusion is that the sustainability of foreign borrowing in Central and Eastern European countries crucially depends on the ability to generate quickly a sustained growth process and to successfully reshape and enlarge the export base: some predictions on the excessive 'foreign-debt burden' of individual economies, formulated in the early 1990s, should therefore be reconsidered in this light.

8.1 THE ROLE OF EXTERNAL FINANCE IN THE TRANSITION PROCESS: AN OVERVIEW

External finance can contribute to the transition process and enhance welfare in former centrally planned economies, especially when domestic saving has not fully recovered after the contraction of the early post-communist period. However, some authors (for instance, Borensztein and Montiel, 1991; Cohen, 1991b) have pointed out at the beginning of the transition that foreign debt could exert a severe constraint on the borrowing capacity of some Central and Eastern European Countries (CEECs). As a matter of fact, net capital inflows in CEECs have been lower than most scholars had predicted in the first two–three years of the post-communist period, despite the new overall surge in capital flows to developing (especially middle-income) economies. Since 1993 net capital flows to CEECs as a whole increased substantially (Calvo, Sahay and Vegh, 1995) and a peak has been reached in 1995; however, the amount and the composition of inflows differed substantially across individual countries, while the financial fragilities and banking crises that plagued some CEECs might have partially reduced the confidence of foreign investors. The contribution of external capital to the growth and welfare of CEECs has become more relevant, although a recovery in domestic saving is considered as the main channel for the financing of large investment needs in these economies (EBRD, 1996, p. 78). It is important to underline that even when it is rather limited in quantitative terms,[1] external capital not only can have multiplicative effects on investment and economic activity, but can also favour the selection of more profitable projects to which additional domestic resources can then be channelled, therefore raising *per capita* output.

There exist a number of specific reasons why integration in world capital markets could favour economic growth and improvement of welfare in transition economies, in addition to those traditionally stressed by the theory of international economics (namely, the decoupling of domestic investment from national saving; the possibility of smoothing consumption in the face of country-specific shocks; the availability of a worldwide pool of financial instruments that allows a more efficient insurance against risk and lower borrowing costs).

The first set of reasons deals with the (mis)functioning of *credit markets* in transition economies. Adopting a cash-in-advance setup, some authors have suggested that output decline in Eastern Europe might have been worsened by imperfections in domestic credit markets: the transition process is associated with the emergence of liquidity constraints, as the reduction in the firms' real monetary balances due to a jump in the price level in the early phases of liberalisation has not been mitigated by an adequate supply of bank lending (for an overview, see Coricelli, 1995). It can be argued that under these conditions the access to foreign capital markets may improve the outcome – that is, it may limit output decline if firms can (partially) overcome their credit-constraint problems. Other authors point out to the (mis)functioning of credit markets in the selection of investment projects, suggesting that distortions in the initial distribution of wealth in a transition economy can be magnified under incomplete information on the profitability of the projects themselves (Kletzer and Roldos, 1996). In this case one could think of a positive role for foreign direct investment (FDI) as, provided some conditions are fulfilled, FDI favours access to Western export markets and leads to a reduction in the uncertainty of investment projects. Moreover, FDI can trigger further domestic investment if production linkages require the establishment of local output capacity in intermediate-goods sectors in host countries.

Another kind of consideration emerges if we turn to the developments in the *external trade* of Central Eastern European transition economies. A deep reorientation of foreign trade has been involved in the passage from previous planned patterns to the present ones dictated by new incentives and the underlying structure of comparative advantage in world markets. The redirection of external trade has both a geographical and a qualitative dimension, as CEECs have increasingly moved towards trade with OECD countries and have changed their product specialisation. Hoekman and Djankov (1996) show that Central European transition economies have become strongly dependent on the European Union (EU) as far as import of intermediates and machinery is concerned, while at the same time they have reoriented their exports to Western Europe. It is likely that the increasing dependence on external trade with Western – and, particularly, EU – economies has stressed the need for convertible currency reserves in transition economies.[2] As foreign exchange reserves were at very low levels in the early 1990s in several CEECs (the Czech and Slovak Republics, Bulgaria, Slovenia), the integration in world financial markets and the inflow of foreign capital could provide a solution to the foreign exchange shortage.

While the integration in international capital markets can have many other beneficial effects in transition economies, we would like to point out briefly the impact on the system of property rights and *corporate governance*. Each of the various methods of privatisation adopted in former centrally planned economies has pros and cons when judged in the long-term perspective of building a sound framework of corporate governance and a self-sustaining support for economic and political reform (Gray, 1996). The contribution of direct and portfolio investment by foreign entities in this field goes beyond the quantitative terms of foreign involvement in the privatisation process, as joint ventures and acquisitions can affect regulatory policies and support legislation aimed at improving the efficiency of domestic capital markets (Kogut, 1994). This is especially true in the case of financial institutions in transition economies, as the participation of foreign partners in these institutions can trigger the adoption of Western standards of monitoring and property-rights enforcement (Rapaczynski, 1996).

The ten countries in transition considered here have been selected on the basis of their historically belonging to the European political and economic space, which has been reaffirmed by their special economic ties with the EU (the 'Europe Agreements'). However, these countries are substantially different from the viewpoint of their advancement in the transition process and of their external financial relations. In 1996, the so-called Visegrád countries (the Czech Republic, Hungary, Poland, Slovakia) and Slovenia were classified among the economies at relatively advanced stages of transition by the *Transition Report* (EBRD, 1996, p. 15). All this countries have a land border in common with the EU and are members of the main regional free-trade area (CEFTA). The Baltic countries were also included among those at a relatively advanced stage of transition by the *Transition Report*, but their liberalisation programme started with some delay with respect to the Visegrád countries. The Baltic economies are very small and do not have land borders with the EU, nor are they part of CEFTA. Finally, Bulgaria and Romania were classified among the countries at intermediate stages of transition by the *Transition Report* (EBRD, 1996, p. 21), and lagged behind in many aspects of the transformation process such as privatisation and price liberalisation (Bulgaria), competition policy (Romania) and enterprise restructuring (both countries).

The external financial situations of these economies are quite different, too. Three of them (Poland, Hungary and Bulgaria) were running large foreign debts at the beginning of the 1990s, in both absolute and *per capita* terms. However, while the external debt of Poland was predominantly towards official creditors, the other two countries were mostly indebted to commercial banks. Moreover, Hungary has never declared a moratorium on its debt nor it has rescheduled it, while Bulgaria and Poland have undergone several episodes of debt-servicing difficulties during the 1980s and early 1990s, and obtained significant debt reduction and rescheduling from the Paris and London Clubs in 1994 and 1995 (Begg, 1996, p. 65).[3] In the first half of the 1990s, therefore, the stock of external debt *net* of foreign exchange reserves, evaluated in current US dollars, has been stable in Hungary, and has declined in Bulgaria and more steeply in Poland.

Gross foreign debt in 1990 was very low in Romania and the former Czechoslovakia; since then, it has increased in these countries but while Romania has accumulated official reserves at a slow pace, the growth of foreign exchange reserves in the Czech and Slovak Republics has been spectacular, leading to a very limited increase in net foreign debt until 1996. The case of Slovenia and the Baltic states is different, as these countries were part of larger federal entities that eventually split. The Baltic Republics never acknowledged the legitimacy of the agreements concerning the foreign assets and liabilities of the former Soviet Union, and therefore inherited neither debt nor foreign exchange reserves at the time of their independence. Since then they have accumulated reserves at a faster pace than gross debt, so their net financial asset position has been positive (although it turned negative in Lithuania in 1995). Slovenia, as a part of the former Socialist Federal Republic of Yugoslavia, inherited a portion of the foreign debt of that entity, the so-called 'allocated' component, but virtually no reserves. Since 1992 Slovenia has accumulated reserves and negotiated the attribution of the 'unallocated' debt of former Yugoslavia, as well other agreements concerning its share of the former Yugoslavia's debt, with the Paris Club (1993) and London Club (first half of 1996).

Current-account convertibility and repatriation of capital and profits by foreign investors are officially in force in most of the countries of Central and Eastern Europe. However, some restrictions on current-account convertibility were adopted in Romania in March 1996, while temporary and selective limitations on repatriation of capital and profits were imposed in Bulgaria in 1996–7. Full capital-account convertibility holds in the Baltic states, and progress towards it has been made in the Visegrád countries and Slovenia (EBRD, 1996, pp. 136–84), although a whole range of (temporary) measures have been employed during episodes of capital inflow surges or currency instability and capital-account reversals.[4]

The overall picture of capital flows in CEECs was rather stagnant in 1990–1, when these economies as a whole were actually running capital-account deficits and were mainly receiving official loans, especially from the International Monetary Fund (IMF) (Calvo, Sahay and Vegh, 1995, p. 12; UN Economic Commission for Europe, 1996, p. 144). Notice that the worsening of the capital account in CEECs was occurring at a time when a new surge in capital flows to developing countries was materialising. An improvement in the external financial situation of CEECs started in 1992, became relevant in 1993, and was consolidated in 1994. In 1995, net capital inflows to Central and Eastern Europe reached a peak of more than 30 billion dollars, almost totally from private sources. However, the regional distribution of these inflows was not homogeneous, with the Czech Republic, Poland and Hungary accounting for about 90 per cent of the inflows, and Slovakia, Romania and, above all, Bulgaria receiving marginal shares (about 3–4 per cent of GDP *vis-à-vis* more than 10 per cent in the other three countries).

The composition of the inflows has also been heterogeneous across countries: Hungary, Estonia, the Czech Republic, Latvia and Slovenia have recorded large cumulative inflows of FDI since 1989 (on a *per capita* basis), while portfolio flows have been mainly directed to Hungary and the Czech Republic, and more recently to Slovakia and Poland. Medium- and long-term borrowing from commercial banks has been concentrated in Hungary, Poland and the Czech Republic, with some relevant loans to Bulgaria in 1994 and Romania in 1995.[5]

Therefore, after a period of financial semi-autarky (mitigated by the intervention of official lenders), some of the transition countries of Central and Eastern Europe have started to benefit from sizeable capital inflows, and in a medium–long-run perspective this is likely to be particularly welcome for the reasons mentioned above.[6] However, other countries still remain in a marginal position as far as international financial flows are concerned. Before turning to an econometric model of the determinants of foreign borrowing in these countries, it is useful perhaps to remind ourselves that at the beginning of the transition the outstanding foreign debt had been regarded by some authors as exerting a severe limitation on the creditworthiness of some CEECs and on their ability to attract new financial resources.

As soon as the collapse of the communist regimes occurred in Central and Eastern Europe, Western economists begun to evaluate the growth prospects and the investment requirements of the transition economies. Their task was made considerably hard by the lack of data on these economies, especially of data comparable with those on market economies, and by the difficulty of assessing the nature, length and costs of liberalisation, stabilisation and reform. Nevertheless, a number of path-breaking studies were published in the early 1990s on the growth capacity and financial needs of the transition economies. Among them, Collins and Rodrik (1991) estimated the capital needs of Eastern Europe (defined in different ways, namely with or without

East Germany and the former-USSR) under two hypotheses: in the first case, they assumed an average 'target' annual rate of growth of 7 per cent, a capital–output ratio of 2.5 and, given their estimates of initial *per capita* income in former communist countries, computed the cumulative capital requirements of these economies. In the second scenario, their forecasts of capital needs were made under the hypothesis of catching-up of labour productivity with Western levels. In both cases, the prediction was that investment rates should rise to exceptionally high levels. Borensztein and Montiel (1991) argued that the capital–labour ratio in CEECs was likely to be significantly lower (and the marginal product of capital higher) than what Collins and Rodrik (1991) had suggested: their conclusion therefore was that reasonably high growth rates of GDP (ranging from 3 to 7 per cent) could be achieved with an average investment rate of 22 per cent per year. Neither of these studies took full account of the distortions and inefficiencies that could hamper the growth performance of transition economies. Taking into account the predictable rate of technical progress, the degree of 'general factor inefficiency' (a measure of the distortion in the use of resources) and a coefficient of labour hoarding, Boote (1992) found that unrealistically high rates of investment were required to catch-up with Western Europe by 2002. However, if all inefficiencies could have been removed by that year, the average investment rate would have been about 30 per cent per year.

Regardless of the individual predictions of each study, this early debate indicated that a formidable amount of resources was needed, together with a radical improvement in the functioning of markets and enterprises, in order to support the growth performance expected in, or rather hoped for, these economies. The domestic financing of such investment needs was immediately perceived as a dramatic problem (Borensztein and Montiel, 1991, pp. 14–21) and the fall in aggregate savings experienced by transition economies since 1990 confirmed those fears (EBRD, 1996, Chapter 6). On the other hand, the contribution of foreign finance was viewed as potentially relevant, but severe doubts were expressed on the creditworthiness of CEECs (and the former Soviet Union) and on their ability to attract substantial capital flows from abroad. Three main concerns were mentioned:

- First, how fast would transition countries proceed along the reform path?
- Second, how much would a bad growth performance affect net capital inflows?

- And, third, what would the legacy of external debt represent for their creditworthiness?

The burden of foreign debt was considered a relevant constraint on the capacity to attract external capital (net lending and FDI) by Borensztein and Montiel (1991, p. 24), who argued that 'in the case of Hungary and Poland it is unlikely that significant foreign savings would be available on a commercial basis', but also that an improvement in the fiscal situation of the two countries could have improved their creditworthiness. Cohen (1991b) concluded his detailed study on the solvency of Eastern Europe, based on growth-adjusted indexes of *per capita* indebtedness in 1989, by suggesting that 'the burden of East European debt appeared to be quite substantial by all the measures that we came up with'; he also suggested that the external position of Hungary, and to a lesser extent, those of Poland and Bulgaria, were difficult to sustain (Cohen, 1991, p. 276).

Nonetheless, few years after these predictions were made the contribution of foreign capital to welfare (and possibly growth) in Central and Eastern Europe became relevant, as net capital inflows in some transition economies were close in 1995 to the upper range of some of the early forecasts. As mentioned above, there was an extreme variability in these inflows across countries and over time. Moreover, it is not clear whether the stock of external liabilities has been, *ceteris paribus*, one of the elements affecting the CEECs' borrowing ability. Although some of the indebted economies of Central Europe had obtained a partial cancellation and a rescheduling of their debts, *per capita* liabilities were still high in a few countries; nonetheless, some of them (notably, Hungary) were able to attract considerable amounts of new funds. One has to distinguish, of course, between debt-creating and non-debt-creating flows (mostly FDI in transition economies until 1995), as the two categories respond to different motivations and incentives.[7] While the determinants of FDI in CEECs have been analysed (Wang and Swain, 1994; Meyer, 1995; Lansbury, Pain and Smidkova, 1996), Section 8.2 focuses on net external borrowing.

8.2 FOREIGN FINANCIAL FLOWS IN CENTRAL AND EASTERN EUROPE: A PANEL-DATA ANALYSIS

The new surge in capital flows to middle-income developing countries (DCs) after 1989 has motivated new research on the determinants of these flows (Calvo, Leiderman and Reinhart 128, 1993; Fernandez-Arias and Montiel, 1996; Fernandez-Arias, 1996). As discussed in Chapter 2, these studies have generally found that a large part of the upturn in net capital flows to developing countries can be explained by 'external' factors – namely, the changing conditions in world financial markets and the timing of the business cycle in OECD countries – although the weight of external factors has not been the same in different regions (Chuhan, Claessens and Mamingi, 1993). Of course, another part of the variation of capital inflows is likely to be country-specific – it is likely to depend on the creditworthiness of individual borrowers and the divergence in domestic rates of return across individual countries. Unfortunately these country-specific effects are more difficult to measure over a short time horizon, and have been usually proxied in rather tentative ways (for a discussion of this issue, see Fernandez-Arias and Montiel, 1996, pp. 60–2).

One related branch of the literature focused on the short- and long-run dynamics of the current account (see among others, Ghosh and Ostry, 1995; Elliott and Fatàs, 1996; Debelle and Faruqee, 1996; see also Chapter 6 of this volume) while another dealt with the sustainability of current account deficits (Milesi-Ferretti and Razin, 1996a, 1996b). A main concern of these authors is the definition of a set of 'fundamentals' that can account for the country-specific behaviour of the current-account balance, either in a time-series framework or in a cross-section or panel-data setup. Although the dependent variables used in these empirical studies differ from those of the previously mentioned works on capital flows, there is a correspondence between the evolution of a country's overall net capital inflows, its components (debt and non-debt flows) and its current account (provided the change in net reserve assets does not systematically offset the current-account balance).

In this section we focus on some fundamental domestic variables that can explain the variability, over time and across countries, in net foreign borrowing in CEECs. Relative to the analysis of Chapter 6, the time horizon examined here is quite short (six years) and the frequency of the data is annual. We do not search for long-run but for medium-term determinants of net *financial* inflows in CEECs: nonetheless, it is implicit in this approach that some of these medium-run variables such as the rate of growth of GDP or exports depend on the same long-run determinants identified in Chapter 6.

A simplifying assumption is that 'external factors' (for instance, US interest rates) are given: this can be mainly justified by the short temporal dimension of our sample; moreover, the large switch in external conditions that has contributed to the new surge in inflows to middle-income countries is dated to 1989–90 by most authors – that is, at the beginning of the period considered here.[8] The dependent empirical variable is a *proxy* for net foreign borrowing over GDP and is obtained subtracting the series of net foreign direct investment (FDI) exceptional financing and IMF lending from net capital flows. The reason why exceptional financing is excluded is that this item often records cancellations and restructuring of foreign debt arrears, which do not necessarily reflect saving–investment imbalances or the capacity to attract new funds. As far as IMF lending is concerned, although it can be conditional on the progress in liberalisation and macroeconomic reform, it also depends on a different set of considerations.[9]

Our set of explanatory variables is meant to capture two kinds of potential effects on net foreign borrowing, that could be synthetically defined as 'demand-' and 'supply-side' effects. On the one hand, we have looked for some proxies of the imbalance between national saving and domestic investment. The rationale for including these proxies is that in a small open economy an excess of investment over saving, if not fully matched by a fall in official reserves, may trigger an inflow of external financial resources (alternatively, FDI provides another channel for closing the gap between national saving and domestic investment). Unfortunately, reliable and comparable measures of the saving–investment imbalance in the *private* sector are difficult to find for all CEECs. Insofar as the *public* sector is concerned, the ratio of fiscal surplus to GDP, on which there exist broadly comparable data, is a proxy for the contribution of the government to the overall saving–investment imbalance. Notice that, if Ricardian equivalence holds perfectly, any fiscal surplus (deficit) should be offset by a correspondent private-sector deficit (surplus) with no impact on net foreign borrowing: here we are implicitly ruling out this possibility.[10] Furthermore, the ratio of FDI to GDP has been included in the regressions to check whether FDI has acted as a substitute for net foreign borrowing in filling the saving–investment gap in Central and Eastern Europe.[11]

On the other hand, we have selected some variables that are in principle related to the *incentive to lend* to CEECs. A fall in the incentive to lend could affect net foreign borrowing in two distinct ways: first, directly, through some sort of international credit constraint imposed on a country's residents; second, indirectly, through an increase in the premium on the world interest rate the residents are requested to pay on their borrowing abroad. In both cases, a likely outcome of the fall in the incentive to lend is a decrease in the amount of net foreign borrowing (although in the case of a higher premium, the assumption of a downward-sloping demand schedule for net borrowing is required). We consider two distinct kinds of proxies for the incentive to lend. The first is intended to capture the extent and probability of capital losses on national currency-denominated assets: the higher the (probability of) capital losses, the lower the incentive to lend. The rates of inflation or, alternatively, of *nominal* exchange rate depreciation are used to evaluate this effect, under the hypothesis that the investors believe these phenomena are persistent.[12] Begg (1996, p. 75) also argues that the behaviour of the *real* exchange rate matters for the pattern of capital flows in transition economies, as it affects the current account and thus the investors' expectations on the future level of the nominal exchange rate. An overvalued real rate can lead to the deterioration of the trade balance and eventually to a depreciation of the nominal rate.[13]

A second type of variables reflects the (macroeconomic) sustainability of external debt and the solvency prospects of CEECs. Drawing on some basic measures of the foreign-debt burden, such as the net debt–GDP ratio and net debt–export ratio,[14] and adjusting them for the growth rates of output or exports (see Cohen, 1991b) one can argue that the incentive to lend is *negatively* related to the current debt ratios (unless involuntary or 'defensive' lending prevails: see Section 6.2). Furthermore, the incentive to lend is *positively* related to the growth rates of GDP and export (higher growth rates, if maintained in the future, signal a potential decline in the debt burden over time).[15] The inclusion of the rate of growth of GDP among the explanatory variables poses some problems, however. First, there is an issue of interpretation as more growth could also be associated with larger investment–saving imbalances (at least in the short run), hence the growth rate could affect the *demand* for foreign credit. Second, as argued below, a simultaneity bias might arise.

We construct a so-called 'unbalanced' panel for ten CEECs (the countries with 'Europe Agreements' with the EU) over 1990 through 1995: there are six annual observations on Bulgaria, the Czech Republic (until 1993, we use data related to Czechoslovakia), Hungary, Poland, Romania and Slovenia, while only three observations (1993–5) are available for the Slovak Republic, Estonia, Latvia and Lithuania. The empirical model we estimate is a so-called 'fixed-effects model' (for a description, see for instance Greene, 1993, pp. 466–9). The reason we use fixed, instead of random, effects is that our cross-sectional units are the entire set of CEECs we are interested in (and not a sample drawn from a larger population), and that we do not consider the individual effects to be uncorrelated with other regressors.[16] Moreover, valuable information can be drawn from the estimates of a country's fixed-effect parameter. In brief, our 'eclectic' model of net foreign borrowing can be written in a single-equation format as (8.1):

$$(\text{net borrowing over GDP})_{it} = \beta X_{it} + \mu_i + u_{it}$$
$$i = 1, \ldots, 10;$$
$$t = 1990, \ldots, 1995 \quad (8.1)$$

where X is a matrix of explanatory variables, i is the country index, t is the time index, μ_i is the country-specific effect and u_{it} is a normally and independently distributed residual.

The estimated correlation matrix of the explanatory variables is reported in Table 8.1. A strong positive correlation is detected, as one might expect, between the rates of inflation and nominal depreciation, and between the debt–GDP ratio and debt–export ratio. We will therefore use the rates of inflation and of nominal exchange rate change as alternative proxies for the expected capital losses to be incurred by investors, and similarly the debt–GDP and debt–export variables as alternative measures of the sustainability of a country's stock of foreign liabilities.

The estimation techniques adopted are the ordinary least squares (OLS; in the case of fixed effects, usually referred to as 'within-estimator'), and the instrumental variables two-stage least squares estimator (IV-2SLS) to account for a possible simultaneity bias. The

Table 8.1 Estimated correlation matrix of the explanatory variables

Growth rate of GDP	1.0							
Fiscal balance over GDP	0.1	1.0						
Inflation	−0.5	0.07	1.0					
Nominal exchange rate devaluation	−0.38	0.007	0.82	1.0				
Rate of growth of export	−0.13	0.31	0.18	−0.20	1.0			
Foreign debt–exports ratio	−0.013	−0.64	0.07	0.21	−0.39	1.0		
Foreign debt–GDP ratio	−0.11	−0.74	0.12	0.28	−0.38	0.90	1.0	
FDI over GDP	0.05	0.04	−0.25	−0.33	0.29	−0.26	−0.25	1.0

Source: Author's elaborations from data obtained by the publications listed in the Appendix on p. 178.

results of the regressions when the debt–GDP ratio is included among the explanatory variables are summarised in Table 8.2. The regression in column (1) shows that, as expected, net foreign borrowing over GDP is positively (and significantly) related to the rates of growth of GDP and exports, while the fiscal balance (as a proportion of GDP) is negatively related to net foreign borrowing, but with a non-significant parameter. Finally the coefficient of the inflation rate is not significant (and has the wrong sign, if we assume that a more stable price level enhances the incentive to lend to CEECs). The interpretation of the positive correlations between net borrowing and the rates of growth of GDP and exports is rather straightforward from the perspective of the incentive to lend: for a given stock of liabilities, higher growth rates tend to dynamically reduce the burden of the debt (measured by the debt–GDP ratio or debt–export ratio) and therefore increase the sustainability of foreign borrowing (see Milesi-Ferretti and Razin, 1996b, for a similar argument related to Asian and Latin American current-account experiences). However column (1) also shows that, in contrast to what expected, the stock of foreign debt is *positively* (but insignificantly) correlated with net foreign borrowing.

The regression of column (1) is plagued by an outlier problem which is signalled by the non-normal distribution of the residuals. The outlier is the observation on Bulgaria in 1990, and this is due to the very high level of exceptional financing received by that country, which leads to a large negative value of net foreign borrowing once this component is subtracted from the series.[17] We thus run a new regression on the same explanatory variables, but excluding the outlying observation (column (2) in Table 8.2). The overall fit of the regression is substantially improved, and the statistical significance of some coefficients is altered: the rate of growth of GDP is now insignificant, while the parameter of the fiscal balance–GDP ratio is now significant at the 5 per cent level and that of net foreign debt has the correct sign (although its standard error is still high). The response of the dependent variable to inflation and export growth is almost unaffected. Most important, the exclusion of the outlier resolves the normality problem (as the Bera–Jarque test shows).

Replacing the rate of inflation with the rate of devaluation of the nominal exchange rate (column (3)), we obtain the expected negative sign of the coefficient (more devaluation implies a lower incentive to lend), but the parameter is still not significant. Moreover, there is no relevant impact on the coefficients of the other variables (or on their standard errors).[18]

Table 8.2 Determinants of net foreign borrowing in CEECs
Dependent variable: net foreign borrowing over GDP

Estimation method	OLS with fixed effects (1)	OLS with fixed effects (2)	OLS with fixed effects (3)	Instrumental variables 2SLS (4)	OLS with fixed effects (5)	OLS with fixed effects (6)
Growth rate	0.003 (2.2)	0.0017 (1.43)	0.0015 (1.33)	−0.13E-4 (−0.07)		
Fiscal balance–GDP	−0.41 (−1.12)	−0.7 (−2.45)	−0.66 (−2.24)	−0.66 (−2.21)	−0.66 (−2.26)	−0.74 (−2.65)
Inflation	0.15E-4 (0.15)	0.24E-4 (0.03)				
Nominal exchange rate devaluation			−0.32E-4 (−0.37)			
Rate of growth of export	0.12 (3.03)	0.09 (3.06)	0.09 (3.11)	0.08 (2.47)	0.08 (2.77)	0.08 (2.8)
Foreign debt–GDP ratio	0.033 (0.37)	−0.1 (−1.42)	−0.089 (−1.19)	−0.14 (−1.77)	−0.13 (−2.18)	−0.15 (−2.49)
FDI–GDP				0.44 (0.89)	0.44 (0.91)	
Adjusted R^2	0.294	0.481	0.483	0.448	0.47	0.47
Bera–Jarque-test of normality of the residuals	21.32 [0.00]	0.76 [0.68]	0.71 [0.7]	0.29 [0.86]	0.34 [0.84]	0.04 [0.98]
F-test of homoscedasticity	0.18 [0.75]	0.33 [0.57]	0.06 [0.8]	0.18 [0.66]*	0.2 [0.65]	0.016 [0.9]
F-test for the fixed-effects specification	2.73 [0.017]	3.72 [0.00]	4.83 [0.00]		5.24 [0.00]	5.2 [0.00]
Wald-test for the fixed-effects specification				42.7 [0.00]		
No. of observations	48	47	47	47	47	47

Notes:
T-statistics in parentheses. Probability levels in brackets (the values refer to the probability of falsely rejecting the null hypothesis of, respectively, normality, homoscedasticity and joint zero restrictions on the individual countries' fixed effects).
* Chi^2-test of homoscedasticity.

A crucial problem with the correlation between the rate of growth of GDP and net foreign borrowing is that causation may go both ways. More growth might enhance solvency and creditworthiness (or it might increase the current-account deficit), therefore leading to larger borrowing. Conversely, higher levels of foreign lending could relax the liquidity and foreign exchange constraints in a transition economy, and thus have a positive impact on the growth rate. A solution to this simultaneity problem is to run an instrumental variables regression (column (4)). We could employ instruments for all explanatory variables; however, reverse causation from net foreign borrowing to the fiscal balance, the rate of growth of export and the debt–GDP ratio is less likely to occur,[19] while it is difficult to find good instruments. Hence, while the lagged growth rate is used as an instrument for the current growth rate, the current values of the other explanatory variables are still included in the regression. The results show that the growth rate has no longer the expected sign, and its coefficient is not significant; there is an improvement in the statistical performance of the foreign debt–GDP ratio, while no impact is detected on the coefficients of fiscal balance and the growth rate of exports.

The ratio of FDI–GDP is also included in the regression of column (4), to check whether FDI and net borrowing have been substitutes or complements in transition economies over 1990–5. On the one hand, for a *given* saving–investment imbalance, larger inflows of FDI could imply a lower resort to foreign credit; on the other hand, some authors suggest that a high FDI–GDP ratio can enhance creditworthiness and trigger more foreign lending to a middle-income economy.[20] The sign of the coefficient indicates that complementarity is likely to occur in CEECs, but the standard error is too large to draw any sound conclusion.

Finally, in columns (5) and (6) we exclude the rate of growth of GDP from the regression. In this case, the coefficients of the fiscal balance, the growth rate of exports and the foreign debt–GDP ratio have the expected signs and are statistically significant (while that of FDI is positive, but insignificant). Overall, these three variables account for about 50 per cent of the dispersion of the dependent variable in the fixed-effects regression. Net foreign borrowing in CEECs appears to be *positively* related to fiscal deficits (an increase of 1 per cent in the fiscal deficit–GDP ratio raises net foreign borrowing over GDP by 0.7 percentage points), and to the rate of growth of exports (an increase of 10 per cent in exports raises net financing from abroad over GDP by 0.8 percentage points). The stock of foreign debt has a *negative* impact on new lending, as expected (a rise of 10 per cent in the debt–GDP ratio lowers the borrowing ratio by 1.5 percentage points).

The F-statistics (and the Wald-test in column (4), always lead to a clear-cut rejection of the joint zero restrictions on the parameters of the individual country effects (the country dummies). The fixed-effects model is therefore clearly preferred to the plain OLS model in this case. Bulgaria has the highest intercept (foreign borrowing has been larger than what was granted by fundamentals, for an amount equal to 12 per cent of GDP), followed by Hungary, the Czech Republic and Slovakia. At the other end of the range, the Baltic countries have, *ceteris paribus*, borrowed systematically less than the other CEECs (see Manzocchi, 1977). The fixed effects capture either some unobservable country-specific features or the different policy options *vis-à-vis* foreign indebtedness pursued in each economy. An attempt has been made to check whether the country dummies could be replaced by the Cumulative Liberalisation Index (CLI, see De Melo, Denizer and Gelb, 1995) – that is, a measure of the progress made by a transition economy along the reform path. Although this index has some explanatory power, the fixed-effects model performs better than the alternative model featuring the CLI. Possibly, the high positive intercept for Bulgaria might capture a large relative component of official (concessional) lending that is not strictly related to the economic incentive to lend. The negative values for the Baltic Republics could reflect the additional uncertainty owing to their geographical position, or alternatively a very cautious domestic attitude towards foreign borrowing. Finally, the low intercept term for Poland relative to the other Visegrád countries might be due to the rescheduling arrangements negotiated by this country, which on the one hand have contributed to reduction in the debt–resources ratio (whose impact on net borrowing is captured in the regressions), but on the other could have negatively affected the creditors' perception of the country (this qualitative effect can be captured by the individual intercept term).

Table 8.3 summarises the results of the regressions where the debt–GDP ratio has been replaced by the debt–export ratio: as the reader can check, no relevant changes are visible relative to Table 8.2 (notice that only three regressions are shown in Table 8.3). Therefore, given the very high correlation between these two variables (Table 8.1), an increase in either debt–GDP ratio or debt–export ratio yields a similar (negative) effect on net foreign borrowing, as a consequence of the reduced sustainability of the stock of external liabilities. In detail, net foreign borrowing in transition economies is *positively* related to fiscal

Table 8.3 Determinants of net foreign borrowing in CEECs
Dependent variable: net foreign borrowing over GDP

Estimation method	Instrumental variables 2SLS	OLS with fixed effects	OLS with fixed effects
Growth rate	−0.24E-3 (−0.13)		
Fiscal balance–GDP	−0.7 (−2.13)	−0.7 (−2.19)	−0.79 (−2.65)
Inflation			
Nominal exchange rate devaluation			
Rate of growth of export	0.076 (2.36)	0.078 (2.67)	0.079 (2.7)
Foreign debt–Exports	−0.04 (−1.56)	−0.04 (−1.7)	−0.05 (−2.1)
FDI–GDP	0.43 (0.81)	0.42 (0.83)	
Adjusted R^2	0.41	0.44	0.45
Bera–Jarque-test of normality of the residuals	0.02 [0.99]	0.03 [0.98]	0.08 [0.96]
F-test of homoscedasticity	0.14 [0.7]*	0.21 [0.65]	0.05 [0.85]
F-test for the fixed-effects specification		4.68 [0.00]	4.7 [0.00]
Wald-test for the fixed-effects specification	40.3 [0.00]		
No. of observations	47	47	47

Notes:
T-statistics in parentheses.
Probability levels in brackets (the values refer to the probability of falsely rejecting the null hypothesis of, respectively, normality, homoscedasticity and joint zero restrictions on the individual countries' fixed effects).
* Chi^2-test of homoscedasticity.

deficits (in this case, an increase of 1 per cent in the fiscal deficit–GDP ratio is associated with a rise in net foreign borrowing over GDP of 0.8 percentage points), and to the rate of growth of exports (an increase of 10 per cent in exports raises net financing over GDP by 0.8 percentage points). Foreign debt has the expected *negative* impact on new lending (a rise of 10 per cent in debt over export lowers the borrowing ratio by 0.5 percentage points).

From a statistical viewpoint, the regressions featuring debt–GDP ratio (Table 8.2) are perhaps slightly preferred to those including the debt–export ratio. However, given the strong correlation between two variables, the main qualitative conclusions are unaltered – about half of the variability of foreign borrowing in CEECs is accounted for by a measure of the public-sector imbalance (fiscal surplus over GDP), and by two proxies of the incentive to lend (a stock-of-debt index, and the rate of growth of exports). In conclusion, export growth appears to play a relevant role in enhancing the sustainability of foreign financing in CEECs: Section 8.3 reconsiders the debate on the solvency of Eastern Europe in this light.

8.3 THE SUSTAINABILITY OF FOREIGN DEBT IN CENTRAL AND EASTERN EUROPE

We stressed in Chapter 7 that net foreign liabilities are viable if and only if they broadly evolve together with national output. There exist two main approaches to the sustainability of foreign debt: one is based on the concept of intertemporal solvency, and approximately states that (*per capita*) net borrowing cannot follow non-stationary rising paths (Sawada, 1994). The second approach considers a target ratio of foreign debt to GDP or exports (Cohen, 1985). We draw on the latter approach which is perhaps less controversial and can be easily translated into an empirical criterion.

The econometric estimates discussed in Section 8.2 may be viewed in the perspective of the sustainability of Central and Eastern European debt. For instance, the links between fiscal policy, external debt and net foreign borrowing could be reinterpreted in the following way:

- First, the impact effect of a deterioration in a country's fiscal position can be larger foreign borrowing, because of a wider saving–investment imbalance in a context where Ricardian equivalence does not perfectly hold.
- Second, the worsening of the fiscal position can have indirect consequences on the incentive to lend to the country (on its credit worthiness): to the extent that larger foreign borrowing is not counterbalanced by a proportional expansion in GDP (or exports) over time, a worsening of the fiscal balance can lead to higher debt–GDP (–export) ratios, and *through this channel*, reduce a country's ability to maintain its credit standards in the future. Interestingly, in recent studies on the sustainability of current-account deficits (Milesi-Ferretti and Razin, 1996a, 1996b) one cannot find clear-cut indications that persisting fiscal imbalances are necessarily associated with balance of payments crises. The evidence of Section 8.2 indicates that the medium-run effects of fiscal policy on the creditworthiness of CEECs (and possibly on the sustainability of their

172 Empirical Studies

external deficits) might be very different depending on whether rapid growth occurs or not. Clearly, the *composition* of government expenditures, whether it is oriented towards growth-enhancing investment or merely unproductive transfers, is likely to be a decisive issue in this case.[21]

Another set of issues concerns the relevant measure(s) of the burden of the debt that is (are) selected when assessing its sustainability. We will briefly consider three facets of the question:

- First, the issue of gross vs. net foreign debt.
- Second, the preferable way of weighing the stock of the debt (which normalisation of the outstanding stock of debt one should use).
- Third, the matter of the composition of the debt.

Defining 'net' foreign debt as 'gross' debt *minus* the stock of foreign exchange reserves owned by a country's central bank, net foreign debt is probably a more reliable indicator of sustainability than gross debt, as it takes into account the dynamics of external reserves (there is a widespread consensus that, *ceteris paribus*, larger stocks of foreign exchange reserves limit the probability of financial crises, and therefore increase creditworthiness). Although the comparison among the CEECs does not change much if relative indebtedness in *1990* is evaluated by gross or net debt, things are quite different if the situation is assessed in *1995*: Bulgaria is *the* most indebted country taking the net debt-over-export criterion; Hungary and Poland are clearly below the World Bank threshold for moderately indebted countries according to the net debt index; net debt in the Czech and Slovak Republics is significantly smaller than gross debt; two of the Baltic Republics show largely negative net debts (see Table 8.4).

More interesting, perhaps, is a comparison among debt-burden indicators computed according to alternative definitions of the resources available for the service of the debt (Table 8.5).

Column (1) in Table 8.5 reproduces the estimates of the burden of the debt in five CEECs in 1989, according to Cohen (1991b, p. 275). The underlying assumption is that each economy is populated by infinitely lived agents which every period pay a constant interest rate of 10 per cent on their outstanding foreign obligations (there is no further borrowing), and whose *per capita* output grows at a constant rate (estimated by Cohen under the hypothesis that the underlying long-run determinants of growth in CEECs in 1989 were the same as in

Table 8.4 A comparison of gross vs. net debt–exports ratios in CEECs (per cent), 1990 and 1995

	1990 Gross debt–exports	1990 Net debt–exports	1995 Gross debt–exports	1995 Net debt–exports
Bulgaria	328	328	149	131
Czech Republic	63	57	68	9
Slovak Republic	110	103	41	13
Hungary	243	231	187	116
Poland	398	361	162	108
Romania	-28	15	73	55
Slovenia	25	25	24	11
Estonia[a]	6	–18	10	–10
Latvia[a]	6	1	19	–7
Lithuania[a]	4	0	29	3

Memorandum items:
(a) World Bank threshold ratio for moderately indebted countries: more than 132.
(b) World Bank threshold ratio for severely indebted countries: more than 220.
Notes:
[a] 1992 instead of 1990.
Source: UN Economic Commission for Europe (1996).

a cross-section of market economies over 1965–85). Cohen's formula for the debt burden is the following:

growth-adjusted *per capita* debt = $(1 - g/r)(\text{per capita debt})$ (8.2)

where g is the rate of growth of real *per capita* output and r is the interest rate.

Columns (2) and (3) show alternative measures of the burden of the debt based, respectively, on the gross (net) debt–export ratio in 1990. Similarly to Cohen (1991b), we assume that a fixed share of a country's *exports* is devoted to interest payments on outstanding debt. Moreover, this share is consistent with the stabilisation of the debt–export ratio over an infinite horizon, provided the interest rate is constant at 10 per cent and the growth rate of export takes a constant value (assumed equal, for simplicity, to its actual average value over 1990–5).[22] The growth adjusted debt–export ratio can be written as:[23]

$$\text{growth-adjusted debt–export ratio} = (1 - z/r)(\text{debt–export ratio}) \quad (8.3)$$

Table 8.5 Alternative measures of the burden of the debt adjusted for economic growth

	Cohen's (1991b) per capita debt (adjusted for the rate of growth of GDP) (in US dollars, 1989)	Gross debt–export ratio in 1990, adjusted for the rate of growth of exports (per cent)	Net debt–export ratio in 1990, adjusted for the rate of growth of exports (per cent)
Bulgaria	1573	339.5	339.5
Czechoslovakia	757*	..	..
Czech Republic	..	37.8	34.2
Slovak Republic	..	–88	–82.4
Hungary	3041	109.35	103.9
Poland	1704	79.6	72.2
Romania	80	21	11.25

Notes:
* Not adjusted for growth.
.. Not available.
Sources: Cohen (1991b); and author's calculations based on UN Economic Commission for Europe (1996).

where z is the rate of growth of exports. The assumption that no country undertakes net borrowing, but that all existing (gross or net) liabilities are fully serviced, is maintained throughout. Therefore, the growth-adjusted measures of columns (2) and (3) tell us what was the debt burden that an observer could have estimated in 1990 had she correctly predicted the actual rate of growth of exports over 1990–5, and assuming that this rate is an approximation of the long-run one. Clearly, all this is rather heroic and this exercise must not be taken at face value.

While Hungary was the most indebted economy according to Cohen's (1991b) criterion (column (1)), Bulgaria can be considered the only severely indebted country of Central and Eastern Europe according to the adjusted debt–export measures. Hungary, Poland, the Czech Republic (the data are related to Czechoslovakia until 1993) and Romania appear to be less than moderately indebted (according to the World Bank classification), while the adjusted debt–export ratios of the Slovak Republic would look *negative* (under the assumption of no more foreign borrowing). There is not much economic content in projecting the current rate of growth of exports into the future (even assuming this rate could be correctly anticipated). Nonetheless, Table 8.5 shows that one could have reached different conclusions on the sustainability of foreign borrowing at the beginning of the transition, by considering a measure of the debt burden based on *exports* and its growth rate, instead of GDP (after all, exports are the resource base through which foreign debt obligations are mainly serviced).[24] According to the figures in columns (2) and (3), one can see that the external positions of Hungary and Poland are not inconsistent (from an incentive-to-lend perspective) with net foreign borrowing after 1990 despite the huge initial stocks of liabilities. As argued before, the sizeable fiscal deficits incurred by these economies since the start of the transition could provide a complementary explanation from the demand side.

Let us turn to the composition of external debt. Table 8.6 shows the relative shares of CEECs' gross debts in 1990 and 1995, according to the term structure and the relative role of financial markets (including commercial bank lending *plus* bonds, but not export credits). In 1990, Romania, Poland and Bulgaria had the lowest shares of long-term debt, and hence they were in principle more exposed to sudden changes in credit market conditions. Romania and the Baltic Republics relied more on concessional debt than any other CEEC; only in Hungary was a non-negligible share of debt covered by bonds. By the end of 1995, Bulgaria and Romania managed to significantly lengthen the average maturity of their debts, partly through rescheduling operations, while in the case of Poland the term structure only marginally changed. The Czech and Slovak Republics, and to a less extent Slovenia and the Baltics, display a shorter average maturity of debt (however, recall that *net debt* is relatively small in each of these countries). Interestingly, there is no clear overall trend in the share of debt accounted for by Western financial markets (but notice that export credits, which account for a large share of external debt in Poland, Romania and Estonia, were not recorded under this item).

Overall, the reduction in net debt–export ratios over 1990–5, the sustainability measures showed in Table 8.5 and the lengthening of the term structure of outstanding liabilities (except for those countries with the lowest net debt), indicate that the external solvency prospects for CEECs could be positively assessed with the possible exception of Bulgaria, *provided* these economies are able to maintain (or to achieve) high growth rates, especially in the tradable goods sector, and to pursue the reorientation of their external trade towards high-income and dynamic markets.

The stock of foreign debt exerted a negative impact on net foreign borrowing, as predicted by some studies of the early 1990s; for

Table 8.6 The composition of gross external debt in Central and Eastern Europe (percentage points), end-1990 and 1995

Country	1990 Long-term debt	1990 Concessional debt	1990 Debt due to financial markets	1990 Bonds	1990 Short-term debt	1995 Long-term debt	1995 Debt due to financial markets	1995 Short-term debt
Bulgaria	77	0	37.5	1	23	88	41	12
Czech Republic[a]	81.5	0.5	56	4.5	18	66	45	34
Slovak Republic[b]	92	0	5.5	0	8	71	32	29
Hungary	92	0.4	72	22	8	92	72	8
Poland	67	3	21	0	33	71.5	12	28
Romania	52[c]	11	37	0	16[c]	84	5.5	16
Slovenia[b]	81	4.5	11.5	0	19	75	35	25
Estonia[b]	96.5	19	17	0	3.5	89.5	8	10.5
Latvia[b]	99	24	0	0	1	87	0	13
Lithuania[b]	96	26	0	0	4	90	0	10

Notes:
[a] Data referred to former Czechoslovakia for 1990.
[b] Data referred to 1993 instead of 1990.
[c] Short- and long-term debt does not add up to 100 owing to other non-classified liabilities.
Source: OECD, *External Debt Statistics* (Paris: OECD, various issues).

instance, the reduction and rescheduling of Poland's debt in 1994 probably favoured the surge in net borrowing the year after. However, what matters is a measure of the burden of outstanding liabilities that establishes a correspondence between debt and the resources used to implement its service. In this case, we show how different indices lead to different rankings of relative indebtedness among CEECs at the beginning of the transition, depending on what variables are used (gross or net liabilities, GDP or exports). Moreover, if one looks at the debt burden *adjusted* for the rate of growth of domestic resources, different conclusions are reached if *per capita* GDP (and its growth rate) is taken as a reference, or if exports (and their growth rate) are chosen. In the first case, Cohen (1991b) found that Hungary and Poland were the most seriously indebted countries in 1989; in the second, our calculations show that Bulgaria was clearly in the most problematic condition in 1990.

This leads us to a final remark. The attractiveness of Hungary – and, more recently, Poland – as destinations of financial flows despite their remarkable foreign debts seems to be related to the rapid growth of their export base (and, of course, to the compliance with existing foreign obligations in Hungary and the reduction in the debt stock in Poland). A high growth rate of exports, which is a common feature in several 'successful' transition economies, is associated with an improvement in creditworthiness and the ability to attract new funds in CEECs, as shown by the empirical estimates. Furthermore, from the standpoint of dynamic sustainability the growth rate of exports can be considered a crucial variable when evaluating the burden of outstanding liabilities.

APPENDIX: DEFINITIONS AND SOURCES OF THE EMPIRICAL VARIABLES

The dependent variable is a proxy for net foreign borrowing (over GDP), obtained by subtracting the series of net FDI, exceptional financing and IMF lending from net capital flows. Errors and omissions are included in the UN definition of net capital flows, on the basis that they could reflect unrecorded financial transactions (capital flight); however, it must be mentioned that in some instances errors and omissions are likely to include unrecorded *current-account* transactions (for example, unregistered cross-border trade in Poland). The definition of the explanatory variables is the conventional one. All stock and flow variables are expressed in current dollars. The sources of the data are the following:

(1) *Net capital flows (including errors and omissions)*: UN Economic Commission for Europe (1996).
(2) *Net foreign direct investment flows*: UN Economic Commission for Europe (1996).
(3) *Exceptional financing and net IMF lending*: International Monetary Fund, *International Financial Statistics* (Washington, DC) (October 1996); *Balance of Payments Statistics Yearbooks* (Washington, DC) (1996).
(4) *Gross domestic product*: EBRD (1996) (defined as GDP in national currency converted to US dollars at the yearly average nominal exchange rate).
(5) *Growth rate of GDP*: EBRD (1996).
(6) *Rate of inflation*: EBRD (1996).
(7) *Rate of change of the nominal exchange rate vis-à-vis the dollar*: EBRD (1996).
(8) *General government fiscal balance over GDP*: EBRD (1996).
(9) *Net foreign debt (gross debt less foreign exchange reserves):* UN Economic Commission for Europe (1996).
(10) *Exports and rate of growth of exports (in current US dollars)*: UN Economic Commission for Europe (1996).

Notes and References

2 Recovery, Insolvency and Stagnation: The Flow of Foreign Capital to Developing Economies in Historical Perspective

1. Of course, the USA, Canada and Australia were also catching up with Europe in the nineteenth century, and were net capital importers (Taylor and Williamson, 1994).
2. See Grilli and Wang (1990) for a study of the secular behaviour of commodity and other traded goods prices.
3. Note that partial convertibility of capital account transactions, in addition to current account ones, was introduced only in Germany and the UK.
4. Calvo and Mendoza (1996) argue that this was a feature of the Mexican economy before 1994.

3 Growth Theory and the Determinants of Capital Flows

1. In the original Solow (1956) model the coefficient A moves according to the exogenous rate of technical progress x and the rate of growth of *per capita* income equals x in the steady state (*exogenous* growth); see Barro and Sala-i-Martin (1995, Chapter 1).
2. See Section 4.1 for a summary of the implications of partial capital mobility according to Barro, Mankiw and Sala-i-Martin (1995).
3. Romer assumes that physical capital and 'knowledge' are used in fixed proportions and 'the variable $k(t)$ can be interpreted as a composite capital good' (1986, p. 1019). Unlike Romer, we assume that $k(t)$ exhibits constant marginal productivity.
4. The consistency problems involved in the coexistence of increasing returns and a competitive equilibrium are not treated here (see Romer, 1986, 1989).
5. If α is larger than one (*increasing* marginal productivity of k), net capital inflows will be associated with high levels of the capital–labour ratio (see Romer, 1986, p. 1032–3).
6. For simplicity, we assume that u_t (the share of human capital employed in the output sector) is constant; for a detailed exploration of the Lucas model, see Barro and Sala-i-Martin (1995, Chapter 5).
7. We do not distinguish in this section between direct investment and lending from abroad, hence we treat the expressions 'capital inflows' and 'foreign borrowing' as synonymous.
8. An asterisk denotes the steady-state value of the variables.
9. If there are no impediments to capital mobility (restricted to physical assets) nor adjustment costs then (3.35) implies that the MPK is instantaneously equalised across countries once the economy becomes open to capital movements. Nonetheless, one can argue that due to

various types of transaction costs the process of capital endowment equalisation takes place over a number of periods.
10. Ghosh and Ostry (1993) show that capital flows have played a relevant role in *consumption-smoothing* for several DCs. However they focus on *short-term*, not on long-term foreign borrowing, as in this work.
11. The exposition follows Obstfeld and Rogoff (1996, Chapter 3).
12. One could ask whether a deterministic formulation in which human capital is accumulated with no decreasing returns but according to given technological parameters is a true improvement over a formulation with exogenous technical change.

4 Growth Theory and the Effects of Capital Flows

1. This distinction holds within the concept of 'convergence in income levels' (the so-called beta-convergence); we are neglecting the concept of 'reduced dispersion of income levels' (the so-called sigma-convergence). See Barro and Sala-i-Martin (1995, pp. 26–31). On the evidence against absolute convergence, see Pritchett (1997).
2. Recall that for the sake of simplicity we set the rate of exogenous technical progress equal to zero as in Chapter 3.
3. See the Appendix (p. 75).
4. What are the consequences for DCs of capital mobility in models of *endogenous* growth? Provided the pattern of net flows depends on the assumptions of the model – namely, there is no guarantee that DCs are net capital importers – *if* capital mobility implies a lower rate of interest in DCs this leads to a higher rate of sustained growth (see, for instance, Lucas, 1988, p. 23; Eaton, 1993, p. 143–8). Of course there is no 'convergence' in the sense intended here as there is no steady state in models such as those of Section 3.2.
5. The existence of three 'growth clubs' consisting of high-, middle- and low-income countries was suggested by Baumol (1986); see also Abramovitz (1986).
6. See Chenery and Syrquin (1986, pp. 68–73); Dowrick and Gemmel (1991, p. 273). For a comprehensive survey of growth accounting techniques and TFP estimates, see Maddison (1987).
7. A list of such 'stylised facts' of growth is provided by Romer (1989).
8. This sort of structural instability is modelled by Azariadis and Drazen (1990); Spiegel (1995).
9. See Cho (1990a).
10. See Cooper and John (1988, p. 442) for a definition of 'coordination failures'.
11. Rodrik (1996b) develops a more detailed closed-economy model of economic transformation in the presence of coordination failures.
12. A third case, in which $(1/1+\rho)[p-1] > \gamma$ is rather trivial, as moving into the modern sector in period 2 is the dominant strategy for each worker.
13. One can easily check this statement substituting $(l_2^* - 1)$ for l_2 in (4.20b), and taking account of condition (4.22). If exactly l_2^* fellow-workers enter

the modern sector in period 2, a worker is indifferent between choosing strategy T or M.
14. Cooper and John (1988, p. 444).
15. Cooper and John (1988, p. 448).
16. This intertemporal 'bottleneck' is determined by condition (4.21).
17. This is true only of foreign borrowing, while direct investment from abroad could play an active role in the process of industrialization provided it has a 'dimension' sufficient to overcome the coordination gap: I am grateful to Giuseppe Bertola for raising this issue. Rodriguez-Clare (1996) provides a model in which multinationals can overcome underdevelopment traps due to increasing-returns technologies.
18. Recall that γ and θ are positive by assumption.
19. The solvency condition is fulfilled by assumption in this section, but could be violated in reality.
20. Rosenstein Rodan (1943, p. 249).
21. Of course, a model that incorporates such a market structure can differ on many other relevant points from the present one.
22. Scitovsky (1954, p. 306).
23. Taylor's theorem is summarised in elementary mathematical textbooks. See also Barro and Sala-i-Martin (1995, pp. 513–14).

5 Measuring Capital Mobility in Developing Economies

1. More on this topic in the book edited by Leiderman and Razin (1994).
2. Among other approaches, we signal those of *gross* capital flows (Golub, 1990), of international comovements in aggregate *consumption* (see Obstfeld, 1993, 1994) and of benchmark intertemporal optimising models (Ghosh, 1995; Dooley, Fernandez-Arias and Kletzer 1996).
3. See Appendix 1 (pp. 101–3) for the definitions of 'integration' and 'cointegration'.
4. See Ghosh (1995) for a different perspective on this issue.
5. Their findings are reproduced here (Table 5.1, column (1)) but only the countries we analyse in Section 5.3 are listed.
6. See paragraph 2.2.2 in Campbell and Perron (1991, p. 153).
7. They argue that the cointegration between saving and investment is the statistical counterpart of the intertemporal solvency requirement, or no-Ponzi-game condition (this position is also expressed by Jansen, 1996). However, these authors neglect that not every theoretical model imposes the no-Ponzi-game condition, hence the *statistical* hypothesis of cointegration must be tested.
8. The definition of 'integrated variable' and other technical definitions are in Appendix 1 (pp. 101–3). The saving rate has been found $I(1)$ in previous studies by Miller (1988) and Leachman (1991).
9. See Appendix 1 for the description of the system of hypotheses to be tested.
10. For the purpose of the empirical tests, the variable aid_t is defined in Appendix 2 (p. 104).

11. A similar argument is advanced by Montiel (1993, pp. 34–5). In order to account for non-market financing, Montiel proposes *also* to include the variation of the official reserves of the central bank as an additional independent variable in the Feldstein–Horioka equation. However, this is likely to generate new difficulties as the change in official reserves already contributes to the definition of public, hence of aggregate, saving.
12. See Dolado, Jenkinson and Sosvilla-Rivero (1990); Campbell and Perron (1991).
13. Further details on this procedure can be found in Appendix 1.
14. As suggested by Campbell and Perron (1991, p. 156) the DF test can be preferred to the Phillips–Perron (1988) test whenever the DGP is characterised by negative serial correlation after one differentiation, which seems to be the case for many of the time series considered here.
15. This case occurs whenever s_t and i_t follow different deterministic trends: if this happens the Feldstein–Horioka equation (5.1) is misspecified as it should include a time trend.
16. As usual, the possibility of systematic statistical discrepancies cannot be ruled out.
17. The limitation on the number of countries studied in Chapter 6 is imposed by the availability of estimates on human capital stocks in 1960.
18. See Gundlach and Sinn (1992, p. 621); Mamingi (1993); Montiel (1993).

6 Determinants of Net Capital Flows in Developing Countries

1. Uzawa (1965) argued that 'human capital' is only partially approximated by education and it includes other items such as health and some kinds of infrastructures and public goods.
2. See Gundlach (1994), OECD (1998); the topic of the returns to investment in education is extensively treated in Psacharopoulos (1994), among others.
3. A drawback of Romer's (1990) regressions is that he uses data on the literacy ratio – admittedly of poor quality – as a proxy for the level of human capital.
4. Klenow (1998) provides an empirical comparison among alternative endogenous growth models based on US industry data.
5. Alternatively we also tried total GDP as a scale indicator; the two variables are strongly correlated.
6. Levine and Zervos (1993) argue that this should always be the correct economic interpretation of cross-section regressions.
7. Similar results are found using GDP as a scale variable.
8. See Edwards (1993, 1998a) for a thorough evaluation of the degree of trade openness and of its contribution to economic growth in DCs.
9. All other developing economies in the sample belong to Latin America.
10. The initial value of *per capita* income is already included in the regression. The interaction term (the saving rate times initial *per capita* income) is not statistically significant.

11. We neglect the contribution of the elderly population that is likely to be quantitatively less relevant, and more controversial, in DCs (see Bloom and Williamson, 1997, p. 16).

7 Capital Movements, Economic Growth and Investment in Developing Countries

1. In the case of De Gregorio (1992) one is led to think that he refers to FDI; in the case of Cohen (1994) the reader is led to identify 'foreign finance' with the accumulation of foreign debt.
2. See Reynolds (1983, p. 962).
3. However, Durlauf and Quah (1998, p. 45) criticise this robustness criterion.
4. Other right-hand-side variables such as the size of the government, the average inflation rate, measures of terms of trade variability and economic distortions, do not enter significantly into the regressions.
5. As in Chapter 6 we proxy the dependency rate with the share of young over total population, excluding the elderly share on which the evidence produced by Bloom and Williamson (1997) is weak.
6. Once one controls for the initial dependency rate and its change over time, the expected sign of the coefficient of the rate of growth of population is positive according to Bloom and Williamson (1997).
7. Moreover, multicollinearity problems may arise in this case.
8. Of course, one could argue that thirteen years are not enough to test for demographic effects; note, however, that Bloom and Williamson (1997) stress the transitional, not the steady-state features of their approach.
9. Boone (1996) also performs robustness tests.
10. This is consistent with 'demographic'-growth models if the decline in average dependency rates in Asia during the 1970s led to higher rates of investment (and saving).
11. See Section 8.3 for a study of foreign debt sustainability in Central and Eastern Europe.
12. The correlation coefficients between the change in investment and consumption rates, on the one side, and capital inflows, on the other, are all about 0.15 in 1983–8.
13. Note, however, that government consumption is not accounted for in the coordination-failure framework of Section 4.3.

8 External Finance and Foreign Debt: A Study of the Transition Economies of Central and Eastern Europe

1. However, note that in 1995 net capital inflows in Hungary and the Czech Republic are reported to have reached about 15 per cent of GDP.
2. Another reason to accumulate foreign exchange reserves is the need to meet large scheduled repayments of external debt (see Calvo, Sahay and Vegh, 1995, p. 17).

3. In early 1997, rumours of a new moratorium on foreign debt obligations by Bulgaria intensified.
4. 'Dollarisation' (that is, currency substitution) has been one of the early consequences of the removal of foreign-exchange restrictions in transition economies; however, there is evidence that the degree of dollarisation has fallen where successful stabilisation policies have been implemented (Sahay and Vegh, 1995).
5. See EBRD (1996); Temprano (1996).
6. The surge in capital inflows posed a number of macroeconomic and financial monitoring problems for the authorities in transition countries: see, among others, Begg (1996); Calvo, Sahay and Vegh (1995); Ize (1996); Siklos (1996).
7. In principle, FDI are not involved when creditworthiness is at stake. However, direct investment is highly responsive to the reform climate and to privatisations in transition economies. See Chuhan, Claessens and Mamingi (1993) on a distinction between the determinants of debt vis-à-vis non-debt capital inflows in Asia and Latin America.
8. We tried to capture the change in external conditions in a very rough way (with a time trend) but with no significant results.
9. This can also be true of other kinds of bilateral or multilateral assistance for which, however, it is more difficult to distinguish between concessional and non-concessional flows.
10. Debelle and Faruqee (1996, pp. 18–21) find that the fiscal surplus has a considerable (positive) impact on the current account.
11. Other types of non-debt inflows (equity) have been rather marginal in CEECs until 1995, and are neglected here.
12. Of course, this argument does not apply to foreign currency-denominated debt, which represents the largest share of foreign debt in CEECs.
13. The experience of the Czech Republic in 1997 could provide an example of this pattern. Another possibility is that an appreciation (depreciation) of the real exchange rate leads to a lower (higher) *real* cost of servicing the external debt if this is denominated in foreign currency.
14. Throughout this chapter, we use data on net foreign debt stocks (gross debt *less* foreign exchange reserves).
15. A complete list of empirical variables, their definitions and sources is in the Appendix (pp. 177–8).
16. See Nerlove and Balestra (1992). Notice also that no lagged dependent variable is present on the right-hand side of our regressions, so that a potential source of inconsistency of the fixed-effects OLS estimator is absent (Debelle and Faruqee, 1996, p. 11).
17. It should be mentioned that, given the still unsatisfactory quality of the statistics on transition economies, measurement errors may affect the estimates.
18. Following Begg (1996) we have tested whether the rate of change of the *real* exchange rate matters for net foreign borrowing in CEECs. We find the parameter never significant at the 10 per cent level.
19. It is true that fiscal discipline might be relaxed in the presence of large financial inflows; that a currency appreciation following a surge in capital inflows could negatively affect exports; and that net borrowing con-

Notes and References

tributes to the rise of foreign debt, but these reverse causation effects tend to act with a lag and not between contemporaneous variables.

20. See Aizenman (1991). Milesi-Ferretti and Razin (1996a) argue that a high share of FDI improves the sustainability of current account deficits in developing countries.

21. We are abstracting from the severe limitations in the current evaluations of fiscal imbalance in transition economies (see Begg, 1996, p. 79; Buiter, 1996, pp. 29–39).

22. The growth rates are computed from export data expressed in current US dollars (see the Appendix on p. 178); in the case of Slovakia and the Baltic Republics, the growth rates are computed over 1993 through 1995.

23. Provided a fixed share of exports (P) is devoted to interest payments over an infinite horizon, and that these payments keep the debt–export ratio constant, one can write:

$$P = (r\ \text{Debt})/\text{Exports} = (r - z)(\text{Debt}/\text{Exports})$$

or:

$$\text{growth-adjusted}(\text{Debt}/\text{Export}) = (1 - z/r)(\text{Debt}/\text{Exports})$$

24. The data in Table 8.4, which are *not* adjusted for growth, show that even taking into account new net borrowing and partial cancellation or rescheduling of existing foreign debts (ruled out in our exercise), the actual *ranking* of net debt–export ratios *in 1995* is not very different from that predicted by column (3) in Table 8.5.

Bibliography

Abramovitz, M. (1986) 'Catching up, forging ahead and falling behind', *Journal of Economic History*, 46, 385–406.
Aizenman, J. (1991) 'Trade dependency, bargaining and external debt', *Journal of International Economics*, 31, 101–20.
Arestis, P. and P. Demetriades (1997) 'Financial development and economic growth: assessing the evidence', *The Economic Journal*, 107, 783–99.
Astorga, P. and V. Fitzgerald (1997) 'The standard of living in Latin America during the twentieth century', *Development Studies Working Paper*, 117 (Turin: Centro Studi Luca d'Agliano).
Azariadis, C. (1993) *Intertemporal Macroeconomics* (Oxford: Basil Blackwell).
Azariadis, C. and A. Drazen (1990) 'Threshold externalities in economic development', *Quarterly Journal of Economics*, 105, 501–26.
Backus, D., P. Kehoe and T. Kehoe (1992) 'In search of scale effects in trade and growth', *Journal of Economic Theory*, 58, 377–409.
Bagnai, A. and S. Manzocchi (1996) 'Unit-root-tests of capital mobility in the LDC's', *Weltwirtschaftliches Archiv*, 132, 544–57.
Balasubramanyam, V.N., M. Salisu and D. Sapsford (1996) 'Foreign direct investment and growth in EP and IS countries', *The Economic Journal*, 106, 95–105.
Barro, R. (1991) 'Economic growth in a cross-section of countries', *Quarterly Journal of Economics*, 106, 407–43.
Barro, R. and J. Lee (1993) 'International comparisons of educational attainments', *Journal of Monetary Economics*, 32, 363–94.
Barro, R. and J. Lee (1994) 'Sources of economic growth', *Carnegie–Rochester Conference Series on Public Policy*, 40, 1–46.
Barro, R., G. Mankiw and X. Sala-i-Martin (1995) 'Capital mobility in neoclassical models of growth', *American Economic Review*, 85, 103–15.
Barro, R. and X. Sala-i-Martin (1992) 'Convergence', *Journal of Political Economy*, 100, 223–51.
Barro, R. and X. Sala-i-Martin (1995) *Economic Growth* (New York: McGraw-Hill).
Baumol, W. (1986) 'Productivity growth, convergence and welfare: what the long-run data show', *American Economic Review*, 76, 1072–85.
Begg, D.K.H. (1996) 'Monetary policy in Central and Eastern Europe: lessons after half a decade of transition', *IMF Working Paper*, 96/108 (Washington, DC: International Monetary Fund).
Benhabib, J. and M. Spiegel (1994) 'The role of human capital in economic development: evidence from aggregate cross-country data', *Journal of Monetary Economics*, 34, 143–73.
Blanchard, O. and S. Fischer (1989) *Lectures on Macroeconomics* (Cambridge, MA: MIT Press).
Bloom, D. and J. Williamson (1997) 'Demographic transitions and economic miracles in emerging Asia', *NBER Working Paper*, 6268 (Cambridge, MA: National Bureau of Economic Research).

Bibliography

Boone, P. (1996) 'Politics and the effectiveness of foreign aid', *European Economic Review*, 40, 289–329.
Boote, A.R. (1992), 'Assessing Eastern Europe's Capital Needs', *IMF Working paper*, 92/12 (Washington: International Monetary Fund).
Borensztein, E. and P. Montiel (1991) 'Savings, investment and growth in Eastern Europe', *IMF Working Paper*, 91/61 (Washington, DC: International Monetary Fund).
Borensztein, E., J. De Gregorio and J. Lee (1998) 'How does foreign direct investment affect economic growth?', *Journal of International Economics*, 45, 137–72.
Buiter, W.H. (1996) 'Aspects of fiscal performance in some transition economies under fund-supported programmes', *CEPR Discussion Paper*, 1535 (London: Centre for Economic Policy Research).
Calvo, G., L. Leiderman and C. Reinhart (1993) 'Capital inflows to Latin America: the role of external factors', *IMF Staff Papers*, 40, 108–51.
Calvo, G. and E. Mendoza (1996) 'Mexico balance-of-payments crisis: a chronicle of a death foretold', *Journal of International Economics*, 41, 235–64.
Calvo, G., R. Sahay and C. Vegh (1995) 'Capital flows in Central and Eastern Europe: evidence and policy options', *IMF Working Paper*, 95/57 (Washington, DC: International Monetary Fund).
Campbell, J.Y. and P. Perron (1991) 'Pitfalls and opportunities: what macroeconomists should know about unit roots', *NBER Macroeconomics Annual*, 6, 141–200.
Caselli, F., G. Esquivel and F. Lefort (1996) 'Reopening the convergence debate: a new look at cross-country growth empirics', *Journal of Economic Growth*, 1, 363–89.
Chenery, H., S. Robinson and M. Syrquin (eds) (1986) *Industrialization and Growth* (Oxford: Oxford University Press for The World Bank).
Chenery, H. and M. Syrquin (1986) 'Typical patterns of transformation', in H. Chenery, S. Robinson and M. Syrquin (eds), *Industrialization and Growth* (Oxford: Oxford University Press for The World Bank), 38–84.
Cho, D. (1990a) 'Industrialization and growth: a heterogeneous agent model', University of Wisconsin, mimeo.
Cho, D. (1990b) 'Long-run trends of national growth: cross-country and time-series evidence', University of Wisconsin, mimeo.
Chuhan, P., S. Claessens and N. Mamingi (1993) 'Equity and bond flows to Latin America and Asia: the role of external and domestic factors', *World Bank Policy Research Working Paper*, 1160 (Washington, DC: The World Bank).
Claessens, S., M. Dooley and A. Warner (1995) 'Portfolio flows: hot or cold?', *The World Bank Economic Review*, 9, 153–74.
Cohen, D. (1985) 'How to evaluate the solvency of an indebted nation', *Economic Policy*, November, 140–67.
Cohen, D. (1991a) *Private Lending to Sovereign States: A Theoretical Autopsy* (Cambridge, MA: MIT Press).
Cohen, D. (1991b) 'The solvency of Eastern Europe', *European Economy*, Special Edition, 2, 263–303.
Cohen, D. (1993) 'Low investment and large LDC debt in the 1980s', *American Economic Review*, 83, 437–49.

Cohen, D. (1994) 'Foreign finance and economic growth: an empirical analysis', in L. Leiderman and A. Razin (eds), *Capital Mobility: The Impact on Consumption, Investment and Growth* (Cambridge: Cambridge University Press), 217–34.

Cohen, D. (1997) 'Growth and external debt: a new perspective on the African and Latin American tragedies', *CEPR Discussion Paper*, 1753 (London: Centre for Economic Policy Research).

Cohen, D. and J. Sachs (1986) 'Growth and external debt under risk of debt repudiation', *European Economic Review*, 30, 529–60.

Collins, S. and D. Rodrik (1991) 'Eastern Europe and the Soviet Union in the world economy', *Institute for International Economics Studies*, 32 (Washington, DC: Institute for International Economics).

Cooper, R. and A. John (1988) 'Coordinating coordination failures in Keynesian models', *Quarterly Journal of Economics*, 103, 441–63.

Corbo, V. and L. Hernandez (1996) 'Macroeconomic adjustment to capital inflows: lessons from recent Latin American and Asian experience', *The World Bank Research Observer*, 11, 61–85.

Coricelli, F. (1995) 'Finance and growth in economies in transition', *European Economic Review*, 40, 645–53.

Debelle, G. and H. Faruqee (1996) 'What determines the current account? A cross-section and panel approach', *IMF Working paper*, 96/58 (Washington, DC: International Monetary Fund).

De Cecco, M. (1974) *Money and Empire* (London: Basil Blackwell).

De Cecco, M. (1985) 'Il problema dei debiti internazionali nel periodo tra le due guerre mondiali', *BNL Moneta e Credito*, 36, 31–52.

De Gregorio, J. (1992) 'Economic growth in Latin America', *Journal of Development Economics*, 39, 59–84.

De Gregorio, J. (1993) 'Credit markets and stagnation in an endogenous growth model', *IMF Working Paper*, PPAA/93/13 (Washington, DC: International Monetary Fund).

De Gregorio, J. and P. Guidotti (1995) 'Financial development and economic growth', *World Development*, 23, 433–48.

De Haan, J. and C. Siermann (1994) 'Saving, investment and capital mobility: a comment on Leachman', *Open Economies Review*, 5, 5–17.

De Long, B. and L. Summers (1991) 'Equipment investment and economic growth', *Quarterly Journal of Economics*, 106, 445–502.

De Long, B. and L. Summers (1993) 'How strongly do developing countries benefit from equipment investment?', *Journal of Monetary Economics*, 32, 395–415.

De Melo, M., C. Denizer and A. Gelb (1995) 'From plan to market: patterns of transition' (Washington, DC: The World Bank), mimeo.

Diaz-Alejandro, C. (1983) 'Some aspects of the 1982–83 Brazilian payments crisis', *Brookings Papers on Economic Activity*, 2, 515–42.

Dickey, D. and W. Fuller (1981) 'Likelihood ratio statistics for autoregressive time series with a unit root', *Econometrica*, 49, 1057–72.

Dolado, J.J., T. Jenkinson and S. Sosvilla-Rivero (1990) 'Cointegration and unit roots', *Journal of Economic Surveys*, 4, 249–73.

Dooley, M., E. Fernandez-Arias and K. Kletzer (1996) 'Is the debt crisis history? Recent private capital inflows in developing countries', *The World Bank Economic Review*, 10, 27–50.

Dooley, M., J. Frankel and D. Mathieson (1987) 'International capital mobility: what do saving–investment correlations tell us?', *IMF Staff Papers*, 34, 503–30.

Dornbusch, R. (1976) 'Expectations and exchange-rate dynamics', *Journal of Political Economy*, 84, 1160–76.

Dowrick, S. (1992) 'Technological catch up and diverging incomes: patterns of economic growth 1960–88', *The Economic Journal*, 102, 600–10.

Dowrick, S. and N. Gemmel (1991) 'Industrialization, catching-up and economic growth: a comparative study across the world's capitalist economies', *The Economic Journal*, 101, 263–75.

Durlauf, S. and D. Quah (1998) 'The new empirics of economic growth', *NBER Working Paper*, 6422 (Cambridge, MA: National Bureau of Economic Research).

Easterly, W. and R. Levine (1997) 'Africa's growth tragedy' (Washington, DC: The World Bank), mimeo.

Eaton, J. (1993) 'Sovereign debt: a primer', *The World Bank Economic Review*, 7, 132–72.

Edison, H., P. Luangaram and M. Miller (1998) 'Asset bubbles, domino effects and "lifeboats": elements of the East Asian crisis', *CEPR Discussion Paper*, 1866 (London: Centre for Economic Policy Research).

Edwards, S. (1993) 'Openness, trade liberalization and growth in developing economies', *Journal of Economic Literature*, 31, 1358–93.

Edwards, S. (1998a) 'Openness, productivity and growth: what do we really know?', *The Economic Journal*, 108, 383–98.

Edwards, S. (1998b) 'Capital flows to Latin America: a stop-go story?', *NBER Working Paper*, 6441 (Cambridge, MA: National Bureau of Economic Research).

Eichengreen, B. (1990) 'Trends and cycles in foreign lending', University of California at Berkeley, mimeo.

Eichengreen, B. (1991) 'Historical research on international lending and debt', *Journal of Economic Perspectives*, 5, 149–69.

Elliott, G. and A. Fatás (1996) 'International business cycles and the dynamics of the current account', *European Economic Review*, 40, 361–88.

Engle, R.F. and C.W.J. Granger (1987) 'Cointegration and error correction: representation, estimation and testing', *Econometrica*, 55, 251–76.

European Bank for Reconstruction and Development (EBRD) (1996) *Transition Report 1996* (London: European Bank for Reconstruction and Development).

Evans, P. (1997) 'How fast do economies converge?', *The Review of Economics and Statistics*, 79, 219–25.

Evans, P. and G. Karras (1996) 'Convergence revisited', *Journal of Monetary Economics*, 37, 249–65.

Feder, G. (1986) 'Growth in semi-industrial countries: a statistical analysis', in H. Chenery, S. Robinson and M. Syrquin (eds), *Industrialization and Growth*, (Oxford: Oxford University Press for The World Bank), 263–82.

Feldstein, M. and C. Horioka (1980) 'Domestic saving and international capital flows', *The Economic Journal*, 90, 314–29.

Fernandez-Ansola, J. and T. Laursen (1995) 'Historical experience with bond financing to developing countries', *IMF Working Paper*, 95/27 (Washington, DC: International Monetary Fund).

Fernandez-Arias, E. (1996) 'The new wave in private capital inflows: push or pull?', *Journal of Development Economics*, 48, 389–418.
Fernandez-Arias, E. and P. Montiel (1996) 'The surge in capital inflows to developing countries: an analytical overview', *The World Bank Economic Review*, 10, 52–77.
Feyzioglu, T., V. Swaroop and M. Zhu (1998) 'A panel data analysis of the fungibility of foreign aid', *The World Bank Economic Review*, 12, 29–58.
Fischer, S. (1993) 'The role of macroeconomic factors in growth', *Journal of Monetary Economics*, 32, 485–512.
Frankel, J. (1989) 'Quantifying capital mobility in the 1980s', University of California at Berkeley, mimeo.
Frankel, J. (1992) 'International capital mobility: a review', *American Economic Review*, 82, 197–202.
Fry, M. (1997) 'In favour of financial liberalisation', *The Economic Journal*, 107, 754–70.
Fuller, W. (1976) *Introduction to Statistical Time Series* (New York: John Wiley).
Genberg, H. and A. Swoboda (1992) 'Saving, investment and the current account', *Scandinavian Journal of Economics*, 94, 347–66.
Ghosh, A. (1995) 'International capital mobility amongst the major industrialised countries: too little or too much?', *The Economic Journal*, 105, 107–28.
Ghosh, A. and J. Ostry (1993) 'Do capital flows reflect economic fundamentals in developing countries?', *IMF Working Paper*, 93/94 (Washington, DC: International Monetary Fund).
Ghosh, A. and J. Ostry (1994) 'Export instability and the external balance in developing countries', *IMF Staff Papers*, 41, 214–35.
Goldstein, M. and M. Mussa (1993) 'The integration of world capital markets', *IMF Working Paper*, 93/95 (Washington, DC: International Monetary Fund).
Golub, S. (1990) 'International capital mobility: net versus gross stocks and flows', *Journal of International Money and Finance*, 9, 424–39.
Granger, C. and P. Newbold (1974) 'Spurious regressions in econometrics', *Journal of Econometrics*, 26, 1045–66.
Gray, C.W. (1996) 'In search of owners: privatization and corporate governance in transition economies', *The World Bank Research Observer*, 11, 179–97.
Greene, W.H. (1993) *Econometric Analysis* (Englewood Cliffs, NJ: Prentice Hall).
Grilli, V. and G.M. Milesi-Ferretti (1995) 'Economic effects and structural determinants of capital controls', *IMF Staff Papers*, 42, 517–51.
Grilli, E. and M. Wang (1990) 'Internationally traded good prices, world money, and economic activity: 1900–83', *Journal of International Money and Finance*, 9, 159–81.
Gundlach, E. (1994) 'Accounting for the stock of human capital: selected evidence and potential implications', *Weltwirtschaftliches Archiv*, 130, 350–73.
Gundlach, E. and S. Sinn (1992) 'Unit-root-tests of the current account balance: implications for international capital mobility', *Applied Economics*, 24, 617–25.
Haque, N. and P.J. Montiel (1991) 'Capital mobility in developing countries: some empirical tests', *World Development*, 19, 1391–8.

Bibliography

Higgins, M. and J. Williamson (1996) 'Asian demography and foreign capital dependence', *NBER Working Paper*, 5560 (Cambridge, MA: National Bureau of Economic Research).

Hoekman, B. and S. Djankov (1996) 'Intra-industry trade, FDI and the reorientation of East European exports', *CEPR Discussion Paper*, 1377 (London: Centre for Economic Policy Studies).

International Financial Corporation (IFC) (1996) 'Investment funds in emerging markets', *Lesson of Experience Series*, 2 (Washington, DC: International Financial Corporation).

International Monetary Fund (IMF) (1994) *World Economic Outlook* (Washington, DC: International Monetary Fund) (October).

International Monetary Fund (IMF) (1995) *Official Financing for Developing Countries* (Washington, DC: International Monetary Fund).

International Monetary Fund (IMF) (1996) 'Reinvigorating growth in developing countries: lessons from adjustment policies in eight economies', *IMF Occasional Paper*, 139 (Washington, DC: International Monetary Fund).

International Monetary Fund (IMF) (1997) *World Economic Outlook* (Washington, DC: International Monetary Fund) (May).

Islam, N. (1995) 'Growth empirics: a panel data approach', *Quarterly Journal of Economics*, 110, 1127–70.

Ize, A. (1996) 'Capital flows in the Baltic countries, Russia, and other countries of the Former Soviet Union: monetary and prudential issues', *IMF Working Paper*, 96/22 (Washington, DC: International Monetary Fund).

Jansen, W.J. (1996) 'The Feldstein–Horioka test of international capital mobility: is it feasible?', *IMF Working Paper*, 96/100 (Washington, DC: International Monetary Fund).

Jones, C. (1995a) 'Time series tests of endogenous growth models', *Quarterly Journal of Economics*, 110, 495–525.

Jones, C. (1995b) 'R&D-based models of economic growth', *Journal of Political Economy*, 103, 759–84.

Kaminsky, G. and A. Pereira (1996) 'The debt crisis: lessons of the 1980s for the 1990s', *Journal of Development Economics*, 50, 1–24.

Kindleberger, C. (1973) *The World in Depression* (Berkeley: University of California Press).

King, R. and R. Levine (1994) 'Capital fundamentalism, economic development and economic growth', *Carnegie–Rochester Conference Series on Public Policy*, 40, 259–92.

Klenow, P. (1998) 'Ideas versus human capital: industry evidence on growth models', *Journal of Monetary Economics*, 42, 3–23.

Kletzer, K. and J. Roldos (1996) 'The role of credit markets in a transition economy with incomplete public information', *IMF Working Paper*, 96/18 (Washington, DC: International Monetary Fund).

Knight, M., N. Loayza and D. Villanueva (1993) 'Testing the neoclassical theory of growth: a panel data approach', *IMF Staff Papers*, 40, 512–41.

Kogut, B. (1994) 'Direct investment and corporate governance in transition economies', paper presented at the World Bank–Central European University conference on Corporate Governance in Central Europe and Russia (Washington, DC) (15–16 December).

Krugman, P. (1988) 'Financing vs. forgiving a debt overhang', *Journal of Development Economics*, 29, 253–68.
Krugman, P. (1991) 'History versus expectations', *Quarterly Journal of Economics*, 106, 651–67.
Kuznets, S. (1966) *Modern Economic Growth. Rate, Structure and Spread* (New Haven and London: Yale University Press).
Lansbury, M., N. Pain and K. Smidkova (1996) 'FDI in Central Europe since 1990: an econometric study', *National Institute Economic Review* (May), 104–14.
Leachman, L.L. (1991) 'Saving, investment, and capital mobility among OECD countries', *Open Economies Review*, 2, 137–63.
Lee, J. (1994) 'Capital goods imports and long run growth', *NBER Working Paper*, 4725 (Cambridge, MA: National Bureau of Economic Research).
Leiderman, L. and A. Razin (1994) 'Introduction', in L. Leiderman and A. Razin (eds), *Capital Mobility: The Impact on Consumption, Investment and Growth* (Cambridge: Cambridge University Press), 1–9.
Leiderman, L. and A. Razin (eds) (1994) *Capital Mobility: The Impact on Consumption, Investment and Growth* (Cambridge: Cambridge University Press).
Levine, R. (1996) 'Stock market liquidity and economic growth: theory and evidence', paper presented at the VIII Villa Mondragone International Economic Seminar (Rome) (July).
Levine, R. and D. Renelt (1992) 'A sensitivity analysis of cross-country growth regressions', *American Economic Review*, 82, 942–63.
Levine, R. and S. Zervos (1993) 'What have we learned about policy and growth from cross-country regressions?', *American Economic Review*, 83, 426–30.
Ljungqvist, L. (1993) 'Economic underdevelopment: the case of a missing market for human capital', *Journal of Development Economics*, 40, 219–39.
Lucas, R. (1988) 'On the mechanics of economic development', *Journal of Monetary Economics*, 22, 2–42.
Lucas, R. (1990) 'Why doesn't capital flow from rich to poor countries?', *American Economic Review*, 80, 92–6.
Maddison, A. (1987) 'Growth and slowdown in advanced capitalist economies: techniques of quantitative assessment', *Journal of Economic Literature*, 25, 649–98.
Maddison, A. (1989) *The World Economy in the Twentieth Century* (Paris: OECD Development Centre).
Mamingi, N. (1993) 'Savings–investment correlations and capital mobility in developing countries', *World Bank Policy Research Working Paper*, 1211 (Washington, DC: The World Bank).
Mankiw, G., D. Romer and D. Weil (1992) 'A contribution to the empirics of economic growth', *Quarterly Journal of Economics*, 107, 407–37.
Manzocchi, S. (1997) 'External finance and foreign debt in Central and Eastern European countries', *IMF Working Paper*, 97/134 (Washington, DC: International Monetary Fund).
Manzocchi, S. and P. Martin (1997) 'Modèle de croissance neoclassique et flux de capitaux', *Economie Internationale*, 72, 7–24.
Marichal, C. (1989) *A Century of Debt Crises in Latin America* (Princeton: Princeton University Press).

Bibliography 193

Mathieson, D. and L. Rojas-Suarez (1993) 'Liberalization of the capital account: experiences and issues', *IMF Occasional Paper*, 103 (Washington, DC: International Monetary Fund).

Matsuyama, K. (1991) 'Increasing returns, industrialization and indeterminacy of equilibrium', *Quarterly Journal of Economics*, 106, 616–50.

Matsuyama, K. (1992) 'Agricultural productivity, comparative advantage and economic growth', *Journal of Economic Theory*, 58, 317–34.

McKinnon, R. and H. Pill (1997) 'Credible economic liberalizations and overborrowing', *American Economic Review*, 87, 189–93.

Meyer, K.E. (1995) 'FDI in the early years of economic transition: a survey', *Economics of Transition*, 3, 301–20.

Milesi-Ferretti, G.M. and A. Razin (1996a) 'Persistent current account deficits: a warning signal?', *International Journal of Finance and Economics*, 1, 161–82.

Milesi-Ferretti, G.M. and A. Razin (1996b) 'Current account sustainability: selected East Asian and Latin American experiences', *NBER Working Paper*, 5791 (Cambridge, MA: National Bureau of Economic Research).

Miller, S. (1988) 'Are saving and investment cointegrated?', *Economics Letters*, 27, 31–43.

Minsky, H. (1982) *Can 'It' Happen Again? Essays on Instability and Finance* (New York: M.E. Sharpe).

Montiel, P. (1993) 'Capital mobility in developing countries', *World Bank Policy Research Working Paper*, 1103 (Washington, DC: The World Bank).

Mosley, P., J. Huson and S. Horrell (1987) 'Aid, the public sector and the market in less developed countries', *The Economic Journal*, 97, 616–41.

Naqui, S.N.H. (1995) 'The nature of economic development', *World Development*, 23, 543–56.

Nerlove, M. and P. Balestra (1992) 'Formulation and estimation of econometric models for panel data', in L. Mathias and P. Sevestre (eds), *The Econometrics of Panel Data* (Dordrecht: Kluwer Academic Press), 3–18.

Niehans, J. (1994) 'Elusive capital flows', *Journal of International and Comparative Economics*, 3, 21–34.

North, D. (1994) 'Economic performance through time', *American Economic Review*, 84, 359–68.

Obstfeld, M. (1993) 'International capital mobility in the 1990s', *NBER Working Paper*, 4534 (Cambridge, MA: National Bureau of Economic Research).

Obstfeld, M. (1994) 'Are industrial-country consumption risks globally diversified?', in L. Leiderman and A. Razin (eds) (1994) *Capital Mobility: The Impact on Consumption, Investment and Growth* (Cambridge: Cambridge University Press), 13–44.

Obstfeld, M. and K. Rogoff (1996) *Foundations of International Macroeconomics* (Cambridge, MA: MIT Press).

Obstfeld, M. and A. Taylor (1997) 'The Great Depression as a watershed: international capital mobility over the long-run', *NBER Working Paper*, 5960 (Cambridge, MA: National Bureau of Economic Research).

OECD (1998) *Human Capital Investment. An International Comparison* (Paris: OECD Centre for Educational Research and Innovation).

Phillips, P.C.B. and P. Perron (1988) 'Testing for a unit root in time series regression', *Biometrika*, 75, 335–46.

Pritchett, L. (1997) 'Divergence, big time', *Journal of Economic Perspectives*, 11, 3–17.
Psacharopoulos, G. (1994) 'Returns to investment in education: a global update', *World Development*, 22, 1325–43.
Rapaczynski, A. (1996) 'The roles of the state and the market in establishing property rights', *Journal of Economic Perspectives*, 10, 87–103.
Rebelo, S. (1991) 'Long-run policy analysis and long-run growth', *Journal of Political Economy*, 99, 500–21.
Rebelo, S. (1992) 'Growth in open economies', *Carnegie–Rochester Conference Series on Public Policy*, 36, 5–46.
Renaud, B. (1997) 'The 1985 to 1994 real estate cycle: an overview', *Journal of Real Estate Literature*, 5, 13–44.
Reynolds, L.G. (1983) 'The spread of economic growth to the Third World: 1850–1980', *Journal of Economic Literature*, 21, 941–80.
Reynolds, L.G. (1986) *Economic Growth in the Third World* (New Haven: Yale University Press).
Rodriguez-Clare, A. (1996) 'Multinationals, linkages and economic development', *American Economic Review*, 86, 852–73.
Rodrik, D. (1996a) 'Understanding economic policy reform', *Journal of Economic Literature*, 34, 9–41.
Rodrik, D. (1996b) 'Coordination failures and government policy: a model with applications to East Asia and Eastern Europe', *Journal of International Economics*, 40, 1–22.
Rojas-Suarez, L. and S. Weisbrod (1995) 'Financial fragilities in Latin America: the 1980s and the 1990s', *IMF Occasional Paper*, 132 (Washington, DC: International Monetary Fund).
Romer, P. (1986) 'Increasing returns and long run growth', *Journal of Political Economy*, 94, 1002–37.
Romer, P. (1989) 'Capital accumulation in the theory of long-run growth', in R. Barro (ed.), *Modern Business Cycle Theory* (Cambridge, MA: Harvard University Press), 51–95.
Romer, P. (1990) 'Human capital and growth: theory and evidence', *Carnegie–Rochester Conference Series on Public Policy*, 32, 251–86.
Romer, P. (1993) 'Idea gaps and object gaps in economic development', *Journal of Monetary Economics*, 32, 543–73.
Rosenstein Rodan, P. (1943) 'Problems of industrialization in Eastern and South-Eastern Europe', reprinted in A. Agarwala and S. Singh (eds), *The Economics of Underdevelopment* (Oxford: Oxford University Press, 1958), 245–55.
Sachs, J. (1985) 'External debts and macroeconomic performance in Latin America and East Asia', *Brooking Papers on Economic Activity*, 2, 525–74.
Sachs, J., A. Tornell and A.Velasco (1996) 'Financial crises in emerging markets: the lessons from 1995', *NBER Working Paper*, 5576 (Cambridge, MA: National Bureau of Economic Research).
Sahay, R. and C. Vegh (1995) 'Dollarization in transition economies: evidence and policy implications', *IMF Working Paper*, 95/96 (Washington, DC: International Monetary Fund).
Sarel, M. (1996) 'Growth in East Asia', *IMF Economic Issues*, 1 (Washington, DC: International Monetary Fund).

Savvides, A. (1991) 'LDC creditworthiness and foreign capital inflows: 1980–86', *Journal of Development Economics*, 34, 309–27.
Sawada, Y. (1994) 'Are the heavily indebted countries solvent? Tests of the intertemporal borrowing constraints', *Journal of Development Economics*, 45, 325–37.
Scitovsky, T. (1954) 'Two concepts of external economies', reprinted in A. Agarwala and S.Singh (eds), *The Economics Of Underdevelopment* (Oxford: Oxford University Press, 1958), 295–308.
Siklos, P. (1996) 'Capital flows in a transitional economy and the sterilization dilemma: the Hungarian case', *IMF Working Paper*, 96/86 (Washington, DC: International Monetary Fund).
Singh, A. (1997) 'Financial liberalisation, stockmarkets and economic development', *Economic Journal*, 107, 771–82.
Sinn, S. (1992) 'Saving–investment correlations and capital mobility: on the evidence from annual data', *The Economic Journal*, 102, 1162–70.
Solomon, R. (1982) *The International Monetary System 1945–1981* (New York: Harper & Row).
Solow, R. (1956) 'A contribution to the theory of economic growth', *Quarterly Journal of Economics*, 70, 65–94.
Spiegel, M. (1995) 'Threshold effects in international lending', *Journal of Development Economics*, 46, 341–56.
Summers, R. and A. Heston (1991) 'The Penn World Table (Mark 5)', *Quarterly Journal of Economics*, 106, 327–68.
Taylor, A. (1997) 'Argentina and the world capital market', *NBER Working Paper*, 6302 (Cambridge, MA: National Bureau of Economic Research).
Taylor, A. and J. Williamson (1994) 'Capital flows to the New World as an intergenerational transfer', *Journal of Political Economy*, 102, 348–71.
Taylor, M. and L. Sarno (1997) 'Capital flows to developing countries: long- and short-term determinants', *The World Bank Economic Review*, 11, 451–70.
Temple, J. and H.-J. Voth (1998) 'Human capital, equipment investment and industrialization', *European Economic Review*, 42, 1343–62.
Temprano, H. (1996) 'The improvement in the external position of CEECs', *European Economy, Supplement A*, 2, 1–15.
Tesar, L. (1991) 'Savings, investment, and international capital flows', *Journal of International Economics*, 31, 55–78.
Tew, B. (1982) *The Evolution of the International Monetary System 1945–1981* (London: Hutchinson University Library).
United Nations (1991) *Transnational Banks and the International Debt Crisis* (New York: UN Center on Transnational Corporations).
UN Economic Commission for Europe (1996) *Economic Survey of Europe in 1995–1996* (Geneva: United Nations Economic Commission for Europe).
Uzawa, H. (1965) 'Optimum technical change in an aggregative model of economic growth', *International Economic Review*, 6, 18–31.
Vamvakidis, A. and R. Wacziarg (1998) 'Developing countries and the Feldstein–Horioja puzzle', *IMF Working Paper*, 98/2 (Washington, DC: International Monetary Fund).
Veganzones, M.A. and C. Winograd (1997) *Argentina in the 20th Century* (Paris: OECD Development Centre).

Vos, R. (1988) 'Savings, investment and foreign capital flows', *The Journal of Economic Development*, 24, 310–34.

Wang, Z.Q. and N. Swain (1994) 'The determinants of FDI in transforming economies: empirical evidence from Hungary and China', *Weltwirtschaftliches Archiv*, 131, 359–82.

Werner, A. (1992) 'Did the debt crisis cause the investment crisis?', *Quarterly Journal of Economics*, 107, 1161–86.

White, H. (1980) 'A heteroscedasticity-consistent covariance matrix estimator and a direct test for heteroscedasticity', *Econometrica*, 50, 817–38.

Wong, Y.D. (1990) 'What do saving–investment correlation tell us about capital mobility?', *Journal of International Money and Finance*, 9, 55–78.

World Bank (1993) *The East Asian Miracle: Economic Growth and Public Policy* (Washington, DC: The World Bank).

Young, A. (1994) 'Lessons form the East Asian NICS: a contrarian view', *European Economic Review*, 38, 964–73.

Young, A. (1995) 'Growth without scale effects', *NBER Working Paper*, 5211 (Cambridge, MA: National Bureau of Economic Research).

Index

aid, 12, 93–5, 100, 103, 136, 147
arbitrage condition, 37, 39, 46, 49, 58, 82
   see also interest-parity condition
asset–price bubble, 13

bank, 20, 26, 27, 153, 155, 157, 175
bank loans, 21, 24, 159
   syndicated, 19, 20, 28
bonds, 14, 18, 24, 27–8, 175
   see also securities
Brady Plan, 21
borrower, 4, 15, 20, 26, 27, 162

capital-flow cycle, 11–15, 16, 25, 60, 97, 110, 121, 125, 134
capital flows, 15, 17, 44, 48, 70, 105, 127, 158, 160
   consequences, 5, 7, 54–76, 133–51
   determinants, 5, 7, 33–53, 105–28, 141
capital-market integration, 29, 58, 65, 82, 84, 100, 119, 155
   see also capital mobility; financial integration
capital mobility, 6, 52, 54, 64, 79, 100, 128
   measures, 84–94
   partial, 5, 7, 34, 39, 42–7, 56, 105, 127
   perfect, 7, 37, 49, 58, 80, 100
   restricted, 6, 44, 53, 60–1
capital requirement, 3, 46–50, 120, 160
Central and Eastern European countries, 88, 154, 155–77
cointegration, 87, 93, 103
consumption, 6, 8, 27, 29, 54, 56, 73, 82, 89, 134
   excessive, 9

government, 136, 147–51
   private, 136, 147–9
convergence, 35, 38, 54, 70, 125
   absolute, 48, 55, 62, 63
   conditional, 39, 40, 45, 48, 55, 62, 127, 140, 144
   speed of, 55–60, 62, 74–6, 89, 133
coordination failure, 64, 68–9, 71, 73
   model, 55, 62–74
creditworthiness, 8, 159, 160–2, 168, 171, 172, 177
cross section, 7, 85–7, 90, 107, 110, 119–51
currency crisis, 3
currency devaluation, 14
current account, 19, 47, 50–1, 66, 69, 94, 96–9

data-generating process, 96, 97
debt overhang, 3, 136–7
debt rescheduling, 3, 14, 20, 157, 161, 169, 177
default, 18, 20, 28, 29, 61, 88, 113, 125
demographic transition, 34, 51, 121, 123
demographic variables, 34, 48, 123, 125
demography, 48–51, 123, 141
dependency rate, 53, 123, 127, 128, 142, 144
diminishing returns, 37, 42, 57
   law of, 38, 44

economic growth, 5, 16, 26, 29, 40, 105, 135–47
   rate, 6, 20, 37, 41, 55, 108, 133, 162, 164–71
   theory of, 5, 33–76, 135
economic policy, 9, 15, 16, 27, 29, 36
   see also fiscal policy; monetary policy

197

education, 30, 42, 107
  secondary, 111, 120, 121, 123, 131
educational attainment, 56, 110, 131
emerging markets, 26
endogeneity, 53, 93, 94, 105, 120, 141
endogenous-growth model, 33, 40–3, 52, 108, 119
equities, 14, 21, 23, 24, 28
European Payments Union, 19
expectations, 15, 164
export, 14, 19, 20, 25, 29, 88, 132, 136, 154
  growth, 8, 13, 25, 164–71, 174, 175, 177
external borrowing, 30, 154
  see also foreign borrowing
external economies of scale, 64, 65, 72
  see also externalities
externalities, 64, 72

Feldstein–Horioka approach, 85–7, 88, 90
financial autarky, 66, 69–72, 83, 87
financial centre, 16–8, 88
financial crisis, 15, 17, 27, 172
financial instruments, 24, 27–9
financial integration, 66, 69–74, 80
financial liberalisation, 3, 11, 13, 25–6, 135
fiscal policy, 82, 171
foreign borrowing, 62–74, 162, 163–71
foreign capital, 3, 9, 54, 60, 72, 73, 135–47, 154
  net, 6, 14, 133
foreign debt, 6, 29, 47, 60, 72, 111, 134, 155
  crisis, 3, 7, 14, 16, 125, 127, 134, 136, 144
  net, 158–75
  sustainability, 8, 12, 29–30, 149, 171–7
foreign direct investment, 19, 21, 23, 28, 156, 168
foreign exchange reserves, 4, 156, 158, 172

gold standard, 17, 27
grants, 19, 21

gross domestic product, 13, 17, 48, 52
gross national product, 47, 48
growth accounting, 38, 39, 107, 135, 140, 141

health-care, 30, 107, 110, 131
human capital, 5, 7, 25, 28, 38–45, 56, 60, 106–8, 119–27

income, 35, 48, 54, 55, 72
  per capita, 7, 37, 40, 41, 44, 52, 109, 111–31, 142–4
interest-parity condition, 6, 37, 39, 46, 85, 89
  covered, 85, 86, 89
  real, 85, 86, 89
  uncovered, 85
interest rate, 12, 26, 37, 41, 43, 69, 89, 172
international financial institutions, 4, 13, 134
international financial system, 11, 18–9
international investor, 13, 14, 26, 133, 155
investment, 6, 13, 20, 48, 58, 84, 97, 100, 137, 147–52
  rate, 8, 41, 101, 108, 121, 136, 160

lender, 27, 134, 159
  see also international investor
linearisation, 59, 74–6
liquidity, 6, 14, 27, 28, 134, 153, 155, 168
  shortage, 4

marginal product of capital, 38, 39, 43, 44, 50–3, 58, 106–19
monetary policy, 14, 18, 20, 82
moral hazard, 13–4

Nash equilibrium, 68, 71
neoclassical growth model, 33, 47, 56, 58, 119, 133, 147
  augmented, 5, 7, 38–40, 42, 75–6, 105, 107, 128, 137

Index

official borrower, 90, 100, 113, 119, 132
official development assistance, 19
official lending, 21, 23, 169
oil-exporting country, 19
order of integration, 95, 96, 101
overborrowing, 8, 9, 14, 30
overlapping-generations model, 5, 34, 48–51, 71, 83, 105, 134

panel data, 107, 139, 140, 154, 161–71
payoff matrix, 68, 71
physical capital, 5, 28, 38, 39, 45, 56, 106, 120
production function, 35, 41, 42, 57, 63
productivity, 55, 63, 66, 67, 73, 133, 160
political instability, 7, 113–32, 141
Ponzi game, 20, 27
population, 35, 45, 48, 52, 109, 119, 129, 142
  growth rate, 41, 120–8
portfolio flows, 21, 159
private lending, 23

representative–agent model, 5, 105
Ricardian equivalence, 163, 171
risk premium, 37, 113

saving, 5, 29, 47, 48, 84, 97, 100, 133, 154, 163
  rate, 25, 46, 48–50, 62, 101, 120–5

saving–investment correlation, 6, 82, 85, 89
scale effects, 7, 41, 44, 52, 106, 110, 114
school enrolment rate, 107, 132, 142
sectoral change, 65–6, 67, 71, 83
securities, 16, 17
Solow model, 33, 36–7, 38, 56–8, 74, 119, 125, 138
solvency, 6, 14, 27, 66, 72, 134, 149, 164, 171
speculation, 29
steady state, 5, 36–40, 41, 46, 51, 54, 61, 74–6, 119

technical progress, 38, 40, 160
technology, 35, 41, 42, 141
  transfer, 36
terms of trade, 12, 17, 29, 66, 83, 132
time series, 86, 87, 88, 93, 107, 162
total factor productivity, 38, 63
trade, 82, 110, 132, 153, 156, 175
  liberalisation, 25
  openness, 8, 29, 113, 119, 128, 132, 141
transition economies, 8, 24, 25, 29, 88, 153–77
transition process, 153, 154–61

unit root, 94, 96, 97, 103
utility, 64, 90
  discounted, 66–9, 71

welfare, 26, 27, 29, 153, 155, 161